SHEMP!

SHEMP!

The Biography of The Three Stooges' Shemp Howard, The Face of Film Comedy

Burt Kearns
Foreword by Drew Friedman

Essex, Connecticut

APPLAUSE

THEATRE & CINEMA BOOKS

An imprint of Globe Pequot, the trade division of
The Rowman & Littlefield Publishing Group, Inc.
4501 Forbes Blvd., Ste. 200
Lanham, MD 20706
www.rowman.com

Distributed by NATIONAL BOOK NETWORK

Library of Congress Cataloging-in-Publication Data

Names: Kearns, Burt, author. | Howard, Shemp, 1895-1955.
Title: Shemp! : the biography of the Three Stooges' Shemp Howard, the face of film comedy / Burt Kearns ; foreword by Drew Friedman.
Description: Essex, Connecticut : Applause, 2024. | Includes bibliographical references and index.
Identifiers: LCCN 2024010395 (print) | LCCN 2024010396 (ebook) | ISBN 9781493074211 (cloth) | ISBN 9781493074228 (epub)
Subjects: LCSH: Comedians—United States—Biography. | Three Stooges (Comedy team)
Classification: LCC PN2287.H73125 K43 2024 (print) | LCC PN2287.H73125 (ebook) | DDC 791.4302/8092 [B]—dc23/eng/20240329
LC record available at https://lccn.loc.gov/2024010395
LC ebook record available at https://lccn.loc.gov/2024010396

∞™ The paper used in this publication meets the minimum requirements of American National Standard for Information Sciences—Permanence of Paper for Printed Library Materials, ANSI/NISO Z39.48-1992.

For Alison, Sam, and Sally Jade.
And in memory of Shecky Greene.

Shemp Howard by Drew Friedman

Contents

Foreword by Drew Friedman:
Shemp Howard, a Stooge for All Seasons ix

Prologue: The Lumps and Bumps on Our Eyes xiii

Chapter 1: Schmool 1

Chapter 2: Moe, Moe, Moe 4

Chapter 3: Blackface 12

Chapter 4: All Wet 19

Chapter 5: Ted Talks 27

Chapter 6: The Stooge 36

Chapter 7: So Fine 47

Chapter 8: Like a Rolling Stone 55

Chapter 9: The Elephant in the Room 59

Chapter 10: *Soup to Nuts* 68

Chapter 11: Stooges versus Stooges 77

Chapter 12: Return of the Racketeers 84

Chapter 13: The Sex Symbol 91

Chapter 14: "Get Outta My Way!" 100

Chapter: 15: Knobby 111

Chapter 16: The Stage 1 Café 117

Chapter 17: Universal Soldier 133

Chapter 18: The Ugliest Man in Hollywood 147

Chapter 19: Toluca Lake 154
Chapter 20: On Hold at Columbia 164
Chapter 21: The Curly Conspiracy 173
Chapter 22: Return of the Stooge 181
Chapter 23: Shempophobia 196
Chapter 24: Stage and Screen . . . and Stage 206
Chapter 25: The Death of Shemp 220
Chapter 26: Who Killed Shemp? 228
Chapter 27: Shemp Lives! 233

Shemp Howard Filmography 239
Selected Bibliography 245
Acknowledgments 249
Index 251

Foreword

Shemp Howard, a Stooge for All Seasons

Drew Friedman

I have drawn Shemp Howard's face a number of times over the years for books, comics, and prints and even for a cover of the defunct sex rag *Screw*. I've always championed the beauty in ugliness, and there's no kisser I enjoy capturing more than Shemp's, either in all its crazed, wild-eyed glory, or more dignified and refined. I'm not the only artist intrigued with Shemp's glorious mug. None other than Three Stooges fan R. Crumb has also rendered Shemp's visage, dubbing him a "Great Man of the 20th Century" and a "Great American Hero" while also wondering, "What was Shemp's secret?" Shemp has been celebrated on T-shirts ("Legalize Shemp!"), in internet groups, within the Stoogeum (their "Hall of Shemp"), in DVD collections and Stooge books, and, finally, in this long-overdue Shemp biography you hold in your mitts.

I'm a lifelong Three Stooges fan, probably from the moment I first discovered them on TV in the early 1960s via WPIX's Officer Joe Bolton. To me, they were Loony Tunes but with human beings. I've probably watched most of their shorts hundreds of times, and *still* they manage to make me laugh. I love all *six* Stooges, including the two Joes—Besser and the much-maligned DeRita. No one could compare to Curly or Shemp as the *third Stooge*—those were impossibly big and funny shoes to fill. Joe Besser fit the bill, at least physically, when he was (reluctantly) recruited to join the aging Moe and Larry after Shemp's passing. Under the circumstances, limited film budgets, and lesser scripts, Besser gave his prissy, hilarious best as the third Stooge. The veteran burlesque comic Joe DeRita, the final third Stooge, performed his own particular schtick as Curly Joe, with subtle gestures and quips that were easy to miss if you were not paying attention.

No other comedic actor (including Ted Healy) displayed such abject anger, annoyance, or exasperation, at times with little or no provocation, as Moe Howard. To be a Stooge under Moe was to suffer gratuitous slapstick abuse on a relentless basis. Larry Fine was the thinking man's

Stooge, the (usually) innocent Stooge in the middle. As my friend, TV comedy producer Eddie Gorodetsky, has pointed out, Larry is the audience's surrogate. Curly, however, was beyond funny. He was so comedically brilliant that he was not even identifiably human, almost a being from another galaxy. Curly was a high-pitched, sputtering, barking, squealing, dancing, spinning, deranged man-child—which brings me to the original third Stooge: Moe and Curly's older brother, Shemp.

What is it about Shemp? Let me try to explain.

The name *Shemp* evolved from Samuel to Sam to Shem (his Lithuanian grandmother's pronunciation), and, finally, Shemp. It's a beautiful, unique name / word / sound / squawk that fits and becomes him and only him. Charles Dickens was a master of creating names that perfectly delineated his characters: Fagin, Scrooge, Barkus, Heap, Gummage . . . I have no doubt he would have approved of Shemp.

Shemp *looked* like a real guy—maybe the lively relative you would see at large family gatherings (weddings, seders, bar mitzvahs), drinking, dancing, flirting, having *too* much fun, and inevitably making a fool of himself until his poor wife had to drag him out. While Moe, Larry, and Curly *looked* like comedians—broad caricatures of human archetypes—Shemp was more accessible, a garrulous fellow you might see working in a crummy restaurant, shoe store, or cigar store. Shemp *did* have an expressive, rubbery comic face, but with his greasy parted hair; baggy-eyed, pockmarked face; short, stocky build; and wobbly gait, he came across as an oldfangled New York neighborhood character who had somehow wandered onto a Hollywood movie set.

Shemp was once dubbed "the ugliest man in Hollywood," a title I heard he enjoyed. True, perhaps, but he could be dapper and charming and seemed quite comfortable in his skin. Shemp also had range as an actor, explaining why he was an in-demand character actor for years. Watch his smart, low-key, and essential performance as Joe Guelpe, bartender / proprietor of the Black Pussy Cafe, in *The Bank Dick*.

I've championed Shemp for years, and I'm proud to say that I've won over several staunch Curly fanatics to Shemp's side, including former *Late Night with David Letterman* head writer Merrill Markoe, who wrote, "To appreciate Drew Friedman is to appreciate Shemp, maybe even a little too much. Though I grew up endlessly watching The Three Stooges, I'm embarrassed to admit I shrugged off Shemp in favor of Curly. In my opinion, Curly improved the quality of life on planet Earth with his pantheon of new noises and the magnificence of the one-arm floor spin. That's at least how I felt until I became friends with Drew, whose tireless championing of the Shemp oeuvre caused me to not only realize that Shemp HAD an oeuvre, but to view the Stooge replacement landscape from a new vantage point."

Lastly, I simply do not understand why the name Shemp hasn't entered into the vernacular and become a popular baby name like Noah, Elijah, or Emma. My wife, Kathy, and I are happily child free, but if we *did* have a child, boy or girl, they would have been named Shemp. Alas, there are other Moes, Larrys, Curlys, and Joes, but there is only one Shemp. I'm thrilled that we now have this definitive biography by the renowned show business biographer Burt Kearns, celebrating the life of that "Great Man of the 20th Century" and that "Great American Hero," Shemp Howard.

Drew Friedman's most recent book of illustrations, Schtick Figures, *featuring TWO portraits of Shemp, was published by Fantagraphics Books.*

Prologue

The Lumps and Bumps on Our Eyes

April 6, 1950: Moe Howard, Shemp Howard, and Larry Fine, known collectively as the Three Stooges, are in Baltimore, Maryland, to open a one-week stand at the Hippodrome Theatre on North Eutaw Street, the first stop on their latest stage tour. During rehearsals, the trio participates in a telephone interview with Brent Gunts of WBAL-AM radio:

BRENT GUNTS: *Hello, Moe?*
MOE: Yeah.
This is Brent Gunts at WBAL.
MOE: How are ya? Nice talkin' to ya.
Well, fine, we're delighted to have you here in Baltimore.
MOE: Why don't you put a little sun on?
Ah, well I'm sorry that we hadn't got a little sun on. We're trying to get it out for Easter, and that's what we're saving it for.
MOE: (*calls out*) Larry! Say hello to a nice guy in Baltimore. (*back on phone*) Here's Larry.
(*hands phone to Larry*)
Larry, Okay!
LARRY: Hello!
Hello, Larry?
LARRY: Yeah, how are ya?
You didn't hit Moe while you were talking to me, did you?
LARRY: He does the hitting.
Oh, he does the hitting.
LARRY: Much to my discomfort.
Oh, you get hit.
LARRY: Yes, I'm the "he who gets."
Yeah, well, how are you bearing up under it all?
LARRY: Well, you only have to look at my face to see it.

MOE (*in background*): Shemp! Say hello to a nice guy!
(Larry hands phone to Shemp)

SHEMP: Oh, oh.
Hello?
SHEMP: Hello.
Who is this?
SHEMP: This is Shemp. Who is this?
This is Brent Gunts at WBAL. How are you?
SHEMP: Ohhh. How are ya? How are ya, Brent?
What's the matter? You having trouble down there with your . . .
SHEMP: Well, I just—I was lying down. They woke me up.
What did they do? Step on you?
SHEMP: No, I got a belt in the mouth. I'm up. I'm up.
Ahhh . . . I bet you're gonna be knocking 'em around on the stage, aren't you?
SHEMP: Yes, we sure are. Not—not I, but Moe is gonna do the knockin'.
Is he gonna knock you, too?
SHEMP: Well, yes.
You know, I think we oughta take Moe in hand sooner or later.
SHEMP: Well, we've tried that for years, but nuttin' helps.
Well, tell me, strictly off the record and off the stage, does Moe still crack the whip?
SHEMP: Oh, he sure does.
It's not an act, then, huh?
SHEMP: Oh no, no, no, if you saw the lumps and bumps on our eyes, you'd know it.

One

Schmool

It seems only right that it would have been "Shemp" from the very beginning: "Shemp" from the moment of that final push, when he emerged, covered in vernix caseosa, the white creamy biofilm not unlike the Brylcreem that would later drip from his center-parted hair down his sweaty, rumpled, freckled, pockmarked mug; "Shemp" when he was dangled by his ankles by the midwife, given a slap across his bare bottom, and let out a *w-a-a-a-a!* that brought smiles to all within earshot.

It seems only right that when he was placed in the arms of his mother, Jennie Horwitz, the exhausted yet smiling woman would gaze on her perfect little blue-eyed baby boy and whisper, *"Mayn kleyn eyngl Shemp."* That perfect little face, unlined and pink. *"Mayn sheyn beibi Shemp."*

But he was not Shemp—not yet. The child born in New York City on March 11, 1895, was Schmool. *Schmool.* Schmool's not bad, but it's no Shemp. Schmool, actually Schmuel, was the child's given name, pronounced *Shmoo-el,* from the Hebrew "Shem" (name) and "El" (God), meaning "God has heard" or "name of God." Schmuel was a good, strong, masculine name, fitting for a boy who would grow to be a tall, handsome man. A Schmuel—often as Shmuel or Samuel—appears in the Bible (Numbers 34:20) as a son of Ammihud, one of the officials assigned to divide Canaan among the tribes of Israel. The more familiar, Americanized version of the name is in the books of Samuel: Samuel, the prophet, seer, and military leader who led the transition of ancient Israel from the time of the judges to the kingship. He was the judge who anointed David as king.

The child was given the name Schmuel in honor of his mother's grandfather. Both parents were Jewish immigrants from Lithuania—Litvak Jews who spoke the Litvish dialect of Yiddish—and before they were husband and wife, before they ever met, they were already connected closely enough as second cousins. Solomon Nathan Gorwitz's birth date has been listed as November 4, 1872, in Kaunas, Lithuania, then the capital of the Kaunus governorate of the Russian Empire. Jenne Mary Goldsmith, records show, was born on April 4, 1870. They were married in 1888 and two years later fled the country, running not only from the approaching boots of Russian soldiers but also from the hatred of some of their neighbors, the ones who carried out the riots and pogroms targeting Jews throughout the empire. Thousands of Litvak were pulling up stakes and sailing away to sanctuary and new lives in places like South Africa and, in the case of Solomon and Jennie Gorwitz, America. The couple made their way across Lithuania and Poland to Germany and the port city of Hamburg, where they boarded a ship for a rough two-week trip across the Atlantic Ocean. Once they arrived in New York Harbor for processing at the Castle Garden immigration center in Lower Manhattan, "Gorwitz" became "Horwitz"—and not because of the stereotypical scenario of mistaken pronunciations, misspellings on immigration papers, or impatient government officials. In the Cyrillic characters of the Russian alphabet, the letter "G" does duty for the letter "H." "Gorwitz" was "Horwitz," however you spell it.

Solomon and Jennie did not come to America unprepared. Jennie's oldest brother, Julius, had already settled in New York, so the couple was able to go from Castle Garden to a room in his apartment on 22nd Street and Third Avenue. They would move on to more than one apartment in Manhattan before ultimately—the only question is exactly when—settling across the East River in Brooklyn. Solomon was a religious man. He found work as a fabric cutter. Jennie, only a schtickle over five feet (if that), was more the go-getter. In years to come, though she still hadn't yet mastered the language of English, she would get involved in the real estate business, buying and selling, and be the architect of the Horwitz family's move to better neighborhoods. For now, in these early years in New York, she was the architect of the family itself.

The couple's firstborn son, Isidore, was delivered on April 15, 1891. Benjamin Jacob followed on February 13, 1893. Jennie may not have been recognized as a pioneer in late nineteenth-century family planning, but she did continue to push out the babies like clockwork in two-year intervals. Schmuel Horwitz arrived on March 11, 1895. A fourth child was born on schedule. A girl would have been nice. A girl was preferred, even prayed for, but a boy came into view on June 19, 1897. He would be named Moses Harry. Jennie would allow his jet-black hair to grow lush and curly—like a girl's—and to the boy's chagrin, he would in his early years be mistaken for a female. This would have an effect on his childhood, something that Moses would learn to fight his way through. In his later years, he would be the one dishing out the punishment—if not for revenge, then at least for laughs.

After delivering Moses, the fourth child, Jennie gave her womb a breather and skipped the next biennial birthing date. She, in fact, waited six years and until the new century before grabbing Solomon and making one last attempt at producing a daughter. Their fifth child was born on October 22, 1903: the fifth son. He was named Jerome Lester Horwitz. Jennie and the others called him "Babe" (as some would find ironic in later years, this child did not have curly hair). Everyone called Isidore "Irving"; Jacob, naturally, was "Jack." Moses was "Moe" from the start. Like Jack, Moe was an easy enough contraction and nickname.

And Schmool? "Schmuel" was Americanized to "Samuel" and shortened to "Sam," and in later years, "Sam" led to, as Moe recalled their mother calling out for his older brother, "Shem! Shemps! Shemp! *Shemp!*"

Shem? *Shemp?* Solomon Horwitz, a quiet man, looked quizzically at his wife. "Jennie," he said. "Vos iz es mit dem 'Shemp'? Zeyn nomen iz Shmuel."

"Yo. Shemp."

"Shemp? Schmuel! *Sam!* Samelleh!"

"Yo, dos iz vos ikh gezagt! *Shemp!*"

Who was to argue? With her thick accent, Jennie could manage to pronounce her son's name only as "Shem." "Shem" became "Shemp." And as authoritative as Solomon might be, it was Jennie who ruled the family.

Solomon shrugged. "Eh. Shemp. Shempelleh."

Shemp it would be. In the end, there would be only one. There would be other Moes. Babe? He was not even the most famous Babe of the early twentieth century. And looking forward, when Babe became "Curly," there would be others. The "Curly" moniker would be bestowed on women and hung on men—those with luxuriant locks and also, in the manner in which an obese man would be called "Tiny," the bald. Larry? Please. There are Larrys being born at this very moment.

But Shemp? *Shemp.* Shemp stands alone.

Two

Moe, Moe, Moe

Shemp, the unique, one-of-a-kind Shemp, would grow up and go on to a successful career in show business and be immortalized as part of what is perhaps the most successful and influential comedy team in modern history. He would, however, be considered the trio's "fourth wheel" because his brother Moe, the comedian Larry Fine, and Horwitz baby Jerome would gain fame first, as Moe, Larry, and Curly: the Three Stooges. As most know the story, Shemp joined the Stooges late, replacing his youngest brother when he became too sick to carry on. Shemp would never receive the acclaim given Curly or the authority of Moe, who controlled the group financially and psychologically and was the prime dealer of the slapstick violence that characterized Three Stooges comedy. But without Shemp, there would be no Three Stooges. He was the original star. He had special talents the others did not. Shemp was there at the beginning.

So we return to the beginning.

Where was Shemp born? Many books and online entries would say he was born in Bensonhurst, in the family home, a child of Brooklyn; that is, until one of his grandchildren came up with what appears to be a copy of a birth certificate, 12184, issued by the State of New York, registering the birth of a white male named Samuel *Hurvitz* on "11 of March 1895." The father is listed as Solomon Hurvitz, age twenty-three, and the mother as Jennie Hurvitz, age twenty-six, both born in Russia. With the exception of the spelling of "Horwitz" (formerly "Gorwitz") as "Hurvitz," the statistics basically line up with the records as we know them. But the residence of the family, as well as that of midwife Olga Dann, is listed as being on the Lower East Side of Manhattan. The Hurvitzes are said to reside at 39 Henry Street and Olga Dann at 59 Rivington Street, a little less than eight blocks away. This does make sense; the neighborhood was not only the center of Jewish immigrant life in New York City near the turn of the twentieth century but also known as "the capital of Jewish America," the starting point for hundreds of thousands of Jews who had fled Eastern Europe. The immigrants crowded into tenement buildings, and they established synagogues, mutual aid societies, and businesses. Just over the bridge from Brooklyn, the Lower East Side is not far from Bensonhurst, but Sol and Jennie Horwitz had already been in America for five years. According to Stooge historian Steve Lally, who uncovered the supporting documents, the four eldest Horwitz brothers were born in Manhattan (and Shemp and Moe were delivered by the same midwife). Only Jerome, the youngest, was born in Brooklyn.

Census records for the United States, dated June 1, 1900, state that the Horwitz family—Solomon, Jennie, Isador, Jacob, Samuel, and Moses—resided in a tenement apartment building at 57 East Fourth Street in Manhattan. In the census five years later, their residence was recorded as 28 Bay 23rd Street in Bath Beach, Brooklyn. So it can be determined that by the first years of the new century, the Horwitz family had finally settled in Brooklyn, which, in Stooges mythology, was their home from the start. Bath Beach was on the southwest edge of Brooklyn, with Gravesend Bay on one side and the neighborhood of Bensonhurst, which would come to be identified with the Horwitz brothers, to the north. Bath Beach, in fact, was known as "Bensonhurst-by-the-Sea." Originally developed as a resort, it even had its own amusement park. Around the time that Solomon and Jennie arrived in America, the area was farmland; it was now being built up, filling up with Jewish and Italian families and soon to be incorporated into New York City's Thirtieth Ward. As the family tells it, Jennie's work in real estate was lucrative enough that the Horwitzes were able to move into a house with a yard in a nicer neighborhood, blocks away at 209 Bay 23rd Street.

Confusion over Shemp's birthplace and other specifics of his youth are multiplied because much of the family history had been passed down by his younger brother Moe. Shemp was the brother closest in age to Moe, and it was Moe, through his writings and many interviews in the decades after Shemp's death, who gave the world his own, not always accurate, version of the family history. Most crucially, he painted a picture of Shemp Horwitz's early childhood years that would cast a shadow over every incident, decision, and example of human frailty displayed by Shemp throughout his life. The Shemp described by his younger brother Moe was a mischievous child but also a whining, wailing worrywart and scaredy-cat who potentially had much of the talent of his younger brother but none of the vision, confidence, or brains needed to move forward to greatness. In his autobiography *Moe Howard and the Three Stooges* (left unfinished on his death in 1975, completed by his daughter Joan Howard Maurer, and published two years later), Moe portrays himself as the precocious show business mastermind, laser-focused on a career in entertainment from an early age. And why not? It was, after all, Moe's book, his story.

COUNTY OF NEW YORK. CITY OF NEW YORK.

STATE OF NEW YORK.

CERTIFICATE AND RECORD OF BIRTH No. of Certificate. 12184

OF Samuel Hurritz

Name.	Samuel Hurritz
Sex.	male
Color.	White
Date of Birth.	11 of march 1895
Place of Birth.	39 Henry st
Father's Name.	Salomon Hurritz
Residence.	39 Henry st
Birthplace.	Russia
Age.	23
Occupation.	merchant
Mother's Name.	Jennie Hurritz
Mother's Name before Marriage.	Hurritz
Residence	39 Henry st
Birthplace.	Russia
Age.	26
Number of previous Children.	2
How many now living (in all).	3
Date of Record.	march 20 1895

Name of Child, Samuel Hurritz

Name and address of person making this report. Signature, Olga Dann midwife

Residence, 59 Rivington st

DATE OF REPORT, 21 of march 1895

An Internet search may tell you that Shemp and his brothers were all born in Brooklyn, but a birth certificate reveals that Shemp first arrived in Manhattan. NYC Department of Records & Information Services

It was Shemp at age four, according to that scripture, who boosted Moe up onto a penny picture machine on Cropsey Street in Ulmer Park, Brooklyn, and held his little brother in place so he could peer into the viewfinder and watch the flip cards simulate motion. And then a fire engine, pulled by a horse, bell clanging, approached. Shemp turned away to watch the firemen clatter by, leaving little Moe hanging until he fell, smashing his face on the corner of the footrest and breaking his nose in an explosion of blood. As their father scooped up the child and ran to a nearby doctor, "Shemp followed close behind, yelping so loud you would have thought he was the one who was hurt."

That incident was related on the second page of Moe's autobiography. By the following page, Shemp was five, "at his mischievous worst," stuffing objects into and stopping up toilets and teasing Moe because of his long, curly hair. According to Moe, older brothers Jacob and Isador—now "Jack and Irving"—were "model children." Shemp, on the other hand, "was an impossible crybaby, a stocking and pants destroyer," and "a general creator of disturbances" who would fake illness to avoid his chores.

But was he? Joan Howard Maurer, in her book *Curly*, a biography of her uncle that was published eight years after Moe's memoir, wrote that "Shemp was a stubborn child. If he fell or hurt himself or did something wrong and was punished, he would never cry, just tighten his lips, clench his teeth, and rarely utter a sound."

Shemp was six years old when he entered school in 1901. While older brother Irving was an average student and Jack "took his studies in stride," Shemp, according to Moe, "barely squeezed his way through" his first few years. When Shemp and Moe attended P.S. 163 in Bath Beach, Shemp's mother and older brothers attempted to help him with his schoolwork, but the boy was unable to focus. Demonstrating a most probable case of attention deficit disorder as well as a typical youthful restlessness, young Shemp would fool around in class, crack distracting jokes, and do whatever he could to break up the monotony. "During his school days Shemp would make up for his childhood silence by becoming the most mischievous and gregarious kid in the neighborhood," Joan wrote in *Curly*. "Neither athletically inclined or a good student, Shemp's favorite pastime throughout grammar school was making comical faces at his fellow students and his teachers and drawing funny pictures. He was constantly clowning and would do anything and everything for a laugh." Already, he was the class clown—the class comedian.

When Shemp graduated from elementary school, according to *Curly*, the principal handed him a diploma and announced, "Students, ladies and gentlemen, this young man did not graduate . . . his mother did." Did he really say that? It doesn't really matter. That was the picture of Shemp Howard that was being painted from an early age: the dummy, the not-too-bright kid who was funny just being himself, the Shemp whom audiences would get to know on-screen. And the main artist behind this portrait was just getting started.

According to Moe, Shemp was twelve when he began "emerging from his whimpering stage." He was freckle-faced, funny, and sly and becoming more and more popular—with the girls as well as the boys. Perhaps that made Moe jealous. Moe wanted everyone to know that he, unlike his older brother Shemp, had no trouble with school and was in fact able to absorb and memorize so much information in class each day that he never even needed to take home schoolbooks to aid in his homework. But by the time Shemp graduated from P.S. 163 and looked toward high school, Moe's schoolwork and attendance had dropped off. He was looking to educate himself in a different way. He had made the decision to dedicate his life to acting. It was 1908.

Moe Horwitz was eleven years old.

While Shemp was the first Horwitz kid to play comedian before an audience (in class), Moe was the first member of the Horwitz family to seriously consider a career in show business. He pursued that career with a passion. When he wasn't dodging truant officers or making an occasional appearance in the classroom, Moe could be found in the ten-cent upper balconies of Brooklyn melodrama theaters, watching plays, following specific actors, and memorizing their lines. (Brooklyn had many theaters and vaudeville houses; Payton's Theatre in Williamsburg and the Gotham on Fulton Street offered ten-cent seats at matinees for dramatic plays, including *The Devil, A Lady of Quality,* and *Master and Man.* Moe listed the Montauk, the Grand Opera House, and the Crescent, which charged a quarter for the seats closest to heaven.)

The next step, of course, was getting work as a performer. One might assume that Moe would consider starting with small roles in local amateur or community productions or even sneak into a crowd scene in one of the local theaters where he had spent so much time studying. The boy had his eye on a bigger, grander prize—and a far more expansive audience. Moe Horwitz was going straight into motion pictures.

In May 1909, when Moe, still shy of twelve, made his foray into filmland, he didn't need to leave home and make his way across the country to Los Angeles, California. Hollywood—*Hollywood* as it would come to be known as a destination and metonym—was a few years away from assembly. It would be another two years before the Nestor Motion Picture Company opened the first permanent movie studio in Hollywood in the Blondeau Tavern building at the corner of Hollywood Boulevard and Gower Street—and Nestor was the West Coast production unit of the Centaur Film Company, based in Bayonne, New Jersey. New Jersey was where the American film industry got under way in the late 1880s, when Thomas Edison and his team first perfected the Kinetograph motion picture camera and Kinetoscope peep show viewing device. Edison's Black Maria in Edison, New Jersey, was the world's first movie studio and produced moving images until 1901, when the facilities were moved to Manhattan and a glass-enclosed rooftop studio on East 21st Street.

Young Moe Horwitz didn't even have to travel that far from home in Bath Beach. It was a half-hour train ride on the Brighton line to the village of Greenfield on the edge of Flatbush in Brooklyn. He could see the landmark long before he arrived at the Avenue M and Neck Road stop: the smokestack, more than four stories high, the tallest structure in the area, emblazoned with the name, spelled out in vertically inlaid brick:

V
I
T
A
G
R
A
P
H
Co.

The American Vitagraph Company was the busiest and most prolific of all the motion picture companies, one of the first to produce and exhibit animated shorts and silent movies that led to America's first "movie stars"—actors who were not already well known for their stage work and became famous for their film roles. Vitagraph had been founded in 1893 as a competitor to Edison, with offices in and an open-air studio on the roof of the Morton Building on Nassau Street in Manhattan. As technology, the market, and goals expanded, Vitagraph had recently begun construction of a studio, lot, and laboratory on the edge of civilization in Brooklyn.

"The property was bounded north and south by Locust Avenue and Elm Avenue, on the west was East 15th Street, and east was the right-of-way of the Brighton Beach rapid transit line, soon to be joined by the Manhattan Beach branch of the Long Island Railroad, which may have had a definite influence on the choice of the Flatbush site," Irvin Leigh Matus wrote on the New York City history website *Urbanography*. The site's proximity to the rail lines allowed actors and crew to travel directly from the Manhattan studio, an arrangement that worked well as the company continued to film interior scenes on Nassau Street and the exteriors—including the parting of the Red Sea for *The Life of Moses*—in Brooklyn.

For a hooky-playing eleven-year-old, Moe had come up with a fairly sophisticated scheme for getting beyond the studio gates and into pictures. He approached a guard and offered his services as an errand boy, and when he began making deliveries for various actors, he refused to accept any money in return. The scheme began to pay off, especially when he got the attention of Maurice Costello, a handsome Italian American actor and silent movie star best described as "Rudolph Valentino *before* Rudolph Valentino." As Moe told it, Costello was amused by the kid who wouldn't take tips and introduced him to a director, leading to the errand boy's being cast in his first film. The ten-minute comedy short *We Must Do Our Best* was released in 1909, directed by Van Dyke Brooke, and starred child actor Kenneth Casey (who would be best remembered for writing the lyrics to the song "Sweet Georgia Brown" in 1925). The Internet Movie Database (IMDb) entry for the picture lists Moe Howard "as Harry Moses Horwitz" in the role of "Bully." The site notes, however, that Moe's appearance cannot be confirmed because "Vitagraph records no longer exist" and the film is considered to be "lost." (A fire in the Morton Building on July 2, 1910, began in the Vitagraph storeroom and was said to have destroyed most of its negatives, dating back to 1896).

"The only known written record of his appearance is Howard's own autobiography, based on his personal recollections, which may or may not be accurate." Moe seemed pretty certain. He also recollected playing other juvenile parts with other prominent Vitagraph actors, including John Bunny, Flora Finch, Earle Williams, Herbert Rawlinson, and Walter Johnstone. Those films, too, are "lost."

Yes, this is Shemp's story, and it would be Shemp who would wind up a star at Vitagraph, a documented and important figure in the studio's history, but it is necessary to continue following Moe Horwitz's trajectory in order to attempt to trace that of his older brother. Moe is the one who wrote the family history. He's the one who insisted that it was his connections that got everything started.

So fast-forward to July 1909, two months after Moe's debut on the Vitagraph lot: "the Saturday of the July Fourth weekend," which makes it July 3. Moe has been twelve years old for two weeks now, and he's with a couple of pals on the beach in Brooklyn, in his bathing suit, performing and drawing a crowd as he strums a ukulele and warbles "Oh, You Beautiful Doll" (unlikely, according to author and historian Bill Cassara, since the song wasn't published until 1911—and Hawaiian culture and ukuleles weren't introduced to the mainland until the Panama–Pacific International Exposition in San Francisco in 1915). Other beachgoers are joining in when a tall young man comes forward, singing a bit louder than the others, and better than Moe. He's another twelve-year-old, though eight months older and a few inches taller than Moe, who won't ever reach a height beyond five feet three inches. The kid introduces himself: Charles

Ernest Lee Nash, a rich kid, a transplant from Texas who tells Moe he's living with his folks on posh Riverside Drive in Manhattan and spending the summer with the family at the exclusive Wawanda Cottages near the beach. The Texas part was true, but the Nash kid wasn't so much a rich kid as a kid whose mother had come into some money. He was born Ernest Lea Nash in Texas. His father was "Black Charley" Nash, a gambler whose morphine addiction killed him at age forty-one in 1907. The boy and his sister had recently been reunited with their mother, Eugenie, who had split from Black Charley years earlier to pursue a stage career in New York. They were all living on West 36th Street in Manhattan. Eugenie, who was calling herself Mary Nash, was working vaudeville and made enough money to send her son to the De La Salle Institute, a Catholic school in Manhattan.

"Call me Lee," the kid says to Moe, and they become fast friends, this real-life *Mutt & Jeff*: the tall, Scotch-Irish, supposedly rich kid and the short Lithuanian Jew who was not so rich. Moe told Lee about his show business aspirations. Lee said he had more practical dreams. When he grew up, he was going back to Texas to make a lot of money as a businessman. Lee's focus would change. So would his name. He would become Ted Healy, the most successful performer in vaudeville. "I thought of Ted Healy as a brother," Moe wrote. That would make the eventual betrayal sting all the more, but for what it was worth, Ted Healy would be a major factor in the eventual success of Moe and his actual brothers Shemp and Jerome.

Three

Blackface

By 1911, both Shemp and Moe Horwitz had given high school a try, and for both brothers, it didn't stick. The official history says that Shemp had entered and soon exited New Utrecht High School in Bensonhurst, which is unlikely since the school didn't open until 1915. Moe had lasted all of two months at Erasmus Hall High School in Flatbush before he dropped out. The boys' parents were not pleased. Jennie and Solomon insisted that their sons learn a trade, so the Horwitz brothers enrolled at the Baron de Hirsch Trade School on East 64th Street in Manhattan. The school had been founded by Baron Maurice de Hirsch, a Jewish German philanthropist whose Jewish Colonization Association had helped thousands of Eastern European Jews emigrate to the United States (and Argentina) in the late eighteenth century. The trade school was established to train Jewish immigrants in professions such as carpentry, painting, plumbing, printing, mechanics, and electricity. Moe studied to be an electrician. Shemp took up plumbing. Both learned the basics; neither one completed the courses. Shemp supposedly threw in the towel after burning his hand while soldering a pipe. (He would at least be able to put his skills to use, with El Brendel, in his 1944 comedy short *Pick a Peck of Plumbers* and, five years later, as one of the Three Stooges in *Vagabond Loafers*.)

In 1912, Lee Nash had forsaken the business world and was following his pal Moe into show business. Moe recalled that the two of them, along with a couple of other guys from the neighborhood, were hired to perform as part of a popular vaudeville act. The Diving Belles were a group of women who would dive into and then perform in a tank filled with seven feet of water. Moe, Lee, and the boys would masquerade as women in aquatic drag: each in a long swimsuit with crumpled newspapers stuffed into the chest area. On October 21, 1913, six Belles were ready to begin their routine at the 86th Street Theatre in Manhattan when something happened that made the newspapers all across the country. It was a matinee. A comedian was onstage getting laughs while half a dozen Diving Belles were behind the curtain, getting into position on their springboards thirty feet above the water. They were preparing to dive in, one by one, as soon as the curtain opened. Gladys Kelly was at one end of the row of six, balancing herself, when she slipped, stumbled, and plummeted. On the way down, she smacked her head on the side of the tank and bounced another ten feet before slamming to the hard floor. Her skull was fractured, her neck was broken, and she died from the injuries. She was twenty-one years old. The news reports didn't mention that there were boys among the Belles. We have only Moe's word. He said that the incident led the young men to quit the act.

Meanwhile, after washing out of trade school, Moe and Shemp worked together at various odd jobs. They set up pins at a local bowling alley, tried out as newspaper boys delivering the *Brooklyn Daily Eagle*, and did some performing around the neighborhood. Moe said that around this time, he was surprised to see that Shemp was a real hit at parties, playing ukulele, singing, and making people laugh. For the first time, the Horwitz brothers performed as a team, singing in a quartet at Sullivan's Tavern. Babe Tuttle sang bass, Willie O'Connor was the Irish tenor, Moe sang baritone, and Shemp—yes, Shemp—sang lead. The group harmonized on popular songs like "Dear Old Girl," "By the Light of the Silvery Moon," and the recently published "Oh, You Beautiful Doll." As the story goes, Moe and Shemp sang every night till nine or ten—until Solomon found out and made them stop. At this early stage, despite Moe's moxie, it doesn't take a read between lines to recognize that Shemp was the focus, if not the star, when it came to performing. Older and taller than Moe, Shemp displayed an outgoing personality and talent. And while Moe had aspirations of becoming a serious dramatic actor, Shemp had a certain charisma and an innate flair for comedy. He wanted to make people laugh, and when he and Moe performed on an amateur night at a theater in Bath Beach, he showed that he could. "Everyone got a big kick out of them and the shows they put on," their friend Charlotte Shurman recalled. "I remember Shemp. He was a riot, simply a riot. And it came so naturally."

Moe's reaction to Shemp's sudden surge in popularity might be reflected in two memories from 1913 that he chose to immortalize in his book. Moe, working at age sixteen, had saved $50 toward the purchase of his first automobile. The old Pope-Hartford runabout had a price tag of $90, so Moe convinced Shemp to put up $40 on the promise of half ownership and driving lessons. The car was every young man's dream, the only flaw being a lack of brake lining, which necessitated application of the brakes far in advance of stopping. When Shemp's driving lesson took place on a Sunday morning, the braking issue was taken into consideration. Moe taught Shemp how to start the car and coached him along as they took to the city streets. Moe wrote that Shemp drove without incident until he approached a business district. In the middle of the street, a block away, was a girl on roller skates. Shemp began to panic when he saw her in his path; he screamed and yelled to Moe, asking what to do. Moe told Shemp he'd let him know when to squeeze the horn and hit the brakes. On Moe's signal, Shemp reached over to squeeze the bulb horn but, in doing so, took both hands off the wheel. The car veered out of control, "went through the front window of a barber shop and stopped when it hit the barber chair."

According to Moe, "Shemp never drove a car from that day until the day he died in 1955." The story fits into his depiction of Shemp as the hapless, fearful, crybaby older brother. But is it even true? In an interesting, even bizarre, twist, Shemp's daughter-in-law Geri Howard Greenbaum told a very similar tale from a much later time period.

Greenbaum and her daughters Jill Howard Marcus and Sandie Howard-Isaac were taking questions from viewers during a livestream session on the *Shemp Howard Goils Group* Facebook page on November 28, 2019. Asked, "What kind of car did Shemp drive?" Greenbaum replied, "I believe it was a Ford . . . but it was only for a short time that he was driving, because he did run into an accident. He was driving with his son, Mort [born in 1927], and they were driving down the road and talking, and all of a sudden he went into a barber shop window! And as he went into the barber shop window, all the mugs fell down on the car and they all broke. He went right through the glass window and . . . Mort said, 'That's the last time I am ever driving with you. I will never drive with you again.' And that was the last time that Shemp drove a car. He never drove after that."

Moe also related the story of a summer night in 1913 when he, Shemp, and two buddies walked with their dates along the beach near Bensonhurst. The young men had taken the girls to see a show at a theater and, strolling across the sand, were very close to convincing the young ladies to go skinny-dipping with them. The females were almost at the point of disrobing when Shemp whispered to Moe that he had developed a terrible cramp, needed to relieve himself, and scuttled off toward the boardwalk to do so. Moe wrote that Shemp ducked under the boardwalk and disappeared into the darkness for forty-five minutes. The nude swim was forgotten, and the boys formed a search party. They found Shemp under the boardwalk, Moe claimed, flat on his face, knocked out cold, "his behind covered with sand and dung and a lump on his head as big as a tennis ball." After the boys dragged him into the water and cleaned him off, Shemp explained how he had arrived in that condition. He said he had stopped at what appeared to be a log in the sand, dropped his pants, evacuated his bowels, and then reached out for something with which to wipe his behind. He saw what he believed to be white paper, grabbed, it and realized it was a handkerchief—being held in another person's hand! That "log" was actually a couple: young lovers seeking privacy under the boardwalk. Again in a panic, Shemp yanked up his pants, leapt up to run away—and forgot to duck. He smacked his head against the hard wood of the boardwalk above and knocked himself out, to be found by his friends face down in the sand, pants pulled down and covered in excrement.

Just another story in which Shemp is humiliated, courtesy of his brother Moe.

Shemp the showman was enthused by the reactions he received from audiences and was anxious to take his partnership with Moe to the next level. He told Moe that a friend had offered to write an act for the Horwitz brothers that could get them onto vaudeville bills. It was a blackface act, blackface being the show business practice in which a performer, in most cases a White performer, used burnt cork to blacken their skin, covering their face in a way that gave the appearance of large, exaggerated lips, in a caricature of a Black person. Often combining the look with raggedy clothes and a woolly-head wig, the demeaning depiction dated back at least to the minstrel shows of the mid-nineteenth century, in which White actors portrayed Black people as lazy, ignorant, oversexed buffoons. The practice was as racist and abhorrent then as it would be today, but in the early twentieth century, it was simply an entertainment tradition that rarely raised an eyebrow. Even Black performers used blackface in the vaudeville era. (Although the practice was shamed out by the mid-twentieth century, Black actors like Mantan Moreland and Dudley Dickerson continued to profit with the stereotypical portrayals onstage and on-screen, including in films featuring Shemp and in Three Stooges shorts.)

Moe claimed that he couldn't get excited about the script for the blackface act. Although he wrote that he and Shemp were getting "chummy" around this time, Moe may have been less eager to share the family spotlight. In early 1914, he found a way out. He was reading through *The Billboard*, the trade paper he read religiously, when he came across an ad seeking a young male actor of average height to perform with a company on a showboat docked in Jackson, Mississippi. Moe was nowhere near "average" height—when full grown, he would just about reach five feet three and a half inches with a cowlick (Shemp was taller, at least five feet six inches)—so when he replied by mail, he enclosed a photo of a handsome, taller neighbor. Moe soon received word that he had been hired and was provided with train tickets to Jackson. When Moe gave Shemp the news, Shemp panicked, Moe wrote. He was worried about their parents' reaction, the blackface act, and his own future—and afraid that Moe would wind up on a southern chain gang. Crying, with an arm around his kid brother, Shemp said, "I wish to God I had your noive."

Moe said that he borrowed $10 and on March 12, 1914, boarded a southbound train. He arrived in Jackson the day before St. Patrick's Day and the next day boarded the showboat *Sunflower*. Not being the average-sized actor whom Captain Billy Bryant had expected, Moe spent a couple of weeks doing odd jobs for his boss before he was cast in *Human Hearts*, a play he was familiar with thanks to all the afternoons he'd spent in theaters. Written by Hal Reid and originally titled *Logan's Luck* when it opened at the People's Theatre on the Bowery in 1895, *Human Hearts* was one of the most popular plays of the era. It had been staged numerous times in Brooklyn in 1909 and 1910 and at theaters including Phillips' Lyceum, Payton's Bijou, and the Gotham—all offering ten-cent cheap seats at matinees.

Moe spent two summers with the *Sunflower* company, performing in many plays and shows and honing his talents and polishing his credentials as a dramatic actor. Stooges biographers have offered various versions of Moe's and Shemp's activities in the five years or so after Moe returned to Brooklyn. Moe was a lifeguard at Coney Island. Shemp ran a novelty shop and worked as a plumber's apprentice—that may have been when he burned himself soldering pipe fittings and gave up the trade. It is clear that the brothers began to work up that vaudeville act that Shemp had put his hopes into before Moe took off.

It is known—and there are photographs to back it up—that the Horwitz family turned to farming in the summer of 1916. Mother Jennie's real estate dealings had paid off well enough that she was able to trade some property in Bensonhurst for a farm in Chatham, New York, about 140 miles north of Brooklyn. Moe said that he helped plant in the spring and harvest in the fall (with some help from baby brother Jerome, whom everyone called "Babe"). Shemp "hated farm work," preferring to "goof off," Joan Howard Maurer wrote in *Curly*, adding,

> He never tired of running around the Horwitz spread in the maddest looking outfit, which consisted of bright red-flannel underwear, an old Continental Army coat and an early American military hat. Each day would find him playing his favorite practical joke. He would don his kooky costume, strike a comical pose in the middle of the cornfield and wait for the neighboring farmers to pass by and stare in amazement at what they thought was one strange-looking scarecrow.

Moe said that he and Shemp worked vaudeville houses in the time between farmwork. Moe had learned a few things during his time in the Deep South, like how the name "Horwitz" wouldn't fly with some audiences. So just as "Moses" became "Moe" (and sometimes "Harry") and "Schmuel" became "Sam," so did "Horwitz" become "Howard," and the Horwitz brothers became the team of Howard and Howard.

Now, it happened that there was already a "Howard and Howard" in show business, and they also were a pair of Jewish brothers who had Americanized their surnames for popular acceptance. As Eugene and Willie Howard, Isadore and Wilhelm Levkovitz were established vaudeville and Broadway stars, known for singing-talking routines like *The Hebrew Messenger Boy and the Thespian*. And while Black, Irish, Italian, and German stereotypes had long been entertainment mainstays, these Howard brothers were among the first Jewish performers to portray caricatures of Jews on the American stage:

> EUGENE: Why, I've had my nose to the grindstone fifteen years.
> WILLIE: You should have seen it before he started.

No worries. The new Howard and Howard would not play up their Jewish roots. Moe and Shemp were reviving the blackface act, which they named *Howard and Howard: A Study in Black*. Songs and routines in hand, they peddled themselves to what seemed like every agent in town. After many turndowns, the boys were at a point of desperation, ready to pack in the burnt cork, when they finally found someone to take them on as clients. Moe wrote that "a jovial Black man" at the Sheedy Vaudeville Agency booked the ersatz Howard and Howard at the Mystic Theatre at Third Avenue and 53rd Street in Bay Ridge, Brooklyn. Moe remembered the place as holding 300 people, with an audience entrance behind the stage (the Mystic was closed in late 1916; plans to replace it with a grand, 1,500-seat vaudeville theater, designed by architect Thomas Lamb, were never realized). Howard and Howard were placed in the closing spot of a weekend vaudeville lineup. With six shows on Friday, nine on Saturday, and eight on Sunday, the brothers were bound to find a big audience, and they did. Unfortunately, they found the audience leaving the theater in the middle of their act.

Moe recalled that the two Jewish teens in blackface ambled out onstage to the tune of "Darktown Strutters' Ball" (there's the fog of memory again—the song wasn't published until 1917) and went into a routine that included lines like "All they do is give you beans. Beans for breakfast, beans for lunch, and beans for dinner. Why, they even send you to war with a bean shooter!" When their own material didn't get a response beyond crickets and coughs, the duo switched gears and resorted to a tactic that fledgling entertainers have used since the beginning: they stole—or at least borrowed—from the best. It was soon clear that this "Study in Black" was actually a study of Black vaudeville stars, in this case, the popular comedy team of Arthur G. Moss and Edward Frye.

Influenced by the earlier work of Black minstrel show and vaudeville pioneers Bert Williams and George Walker, Moss and Frye were billed as "A Couple of Blackbirds" and tagged by the trades as "colored conversationalists." Their act was known for fast-paced, original dialogue and routines in which Frye confounded Moss with rapid-fire head-scratchers like "How high is up?," "How long is a piece of string?," and "S'posin I came along and gave you a handful of nickels. How many nickels would you have?"

"What size is a gray suit? Do you think it's as warm in the summer as it is in the country? If you went to the railroad station and bought a ticket for three dollars, where are you going?" Moe wrote that even the tried-and-true material failed to keep most of the audience from walking out during their twelve-minute spot. He later learned that Howard and Howard's placement on the bill was not one of honor. Vaudeville headliners were often placed in the penultimate position. The last act on the bill was known as the "cleanup act," the one deemed the weakest, to be called out onstage when the theater manager needed to clear out the audience before the next show.

The Horwitz–Howard brothers got over the disappointment and turned *Study in Black* into something successful and, in 1917, somehow managed to be booked simultaneously on the Loew and RKO vaudeville circuits. For rival vaudeville companies to book the same act was unheard of. Moe claimed that they got around the ban by performing in blackface for RKO—and in whiteface for Loew. Any success was short lived. In April 1917, President Woodrow Wilson declared war on the imperial German government. Moe wrote in his autobiography that "our blackface act was broken up briefly by World War I," when Shemp was drafted into the U.S. Army and "went to war" but was discharged after a few months because "he was a bed wetter."

Four

All Wet

If they'd put him in the navy
they might not have noticed he was a bed wetter.

New York State records show that Shemp Howard registered for the draft on June 5, 1917. He was listed as being of medium height and slender build with blue eyes and red hair and a "rupture on left side" (as a claim for exemption). He listed his legal residence as a post office box in Chatham, Columbia County, New York, and his occupation as "farmer." The Horwitz family farm was located in Chatham, and Stooges historian Steve Lally says mother Jennie Horwitz instructed her four eldest boys to list the farm address as their home "since growing food was essential war work" and made it less likely they would be conscripted into the U.S. Army. It did not make them exempt. Despite his rupture, Shemp was selected for service as part of the October Automatic Replacement Draft of 1918, which had been instituted to replace the mounting number of American casualties in Europe.

Shemp was inducted into the U.S. Army in Columbia County on October 25, 1918, and assigned to the Camp Wheeler army base near Macon, Georgia. He held the rank of private in Company C. Seventeen days after his induction, however, the armistice was signed, and fighting ended. Private Shemp Howard was discharged, honorably, on November 29, 1918. No wounds or other medical issues were listed. "The story from Moe . . . was that Shemp was discharged because they found out he was a bed-wetter," Lally said. "There's no indication of that on this record. To me, it's evident that he and his fellow late-war draftees just weren't needed."

Moe's memory and confusion of dates and even facts can be forgiven. What is perhaps not so easy to condone at this point is Moe's characterization of his older—and admittedly funnier—brother. His decision to include in his book and Three Stooges legacy the detail that Shemp suffered from nocturnal enuresis is the type of revelation that was bound to get attention and in fact has far outlived both of them. Shemp's bravery

Horwitz, Samuel (Surname) (Christian name) 5,070,358 (Army serial number) 632 *White *~~Colored~~. 1

Residence: PO Box 685 (Street and house number) Chatham (Town or city) Columbia (County) NEW YORK (State)

[redacted] *Inducted at Columbia Co NY on Oct 25 1918

Place of birth: New York NY Age or date of birth: Mch 18,1895

Organizations served in, with dates of assignments and transfers:
Nov Aut Repl Draft Camp Wheeler Ga to disch

Grades, with date of appointment:
Pvt

Engagements:

Wounds or other injuries received in action: None.

Served overseas from † No to †, from † to †

Honorably discharged on demobilization Nov 27/18, 19

In view of occupation he was, on date of discharge, reported 0 per cent disabled.

Remarks:

Form No. 724-1, A. G. O. Nov. 22, 1919. *Strike out words not applicable. † Dates of departure from and arrival in the U. S.

Although brother Moe claimed Shemp was discharged from the U.S. Army during World War I because he was "a bed wetter," records show that he received an honorable—not medical—discharge weeks after the armistice was signed. New York State Archives

and, despite the brevity of his service, status as a World War I veteran have been forgotten, while "bedwetter" has become part of his biography. What's also notable is that Moe's tidbit of personal (and possibly false) information was not written in a sympathetic tone but was passed off as a joke: *"If they'd put him in the navy they might not have noticed."* The line, on page 28 of more than 200 pages, was not the first negative portrayal or humiliating incident that Moe conjured about his brother.

In the summer of 1919, Moe and Shemp wound up performing with the Marguerite Bryant Players in Jeannette, Pennsylvania, about thirty miles southeast of Pittsburgh. The Bryant acting company put on plays at its playhouse in the Oakford Park amusement park as well as theaters in the Pittsburgh area. Moe is sometimes credited as working solo at this time, but there are photos of Shemp with Moe and others in the Bryant troupe, including a picture of the brothers in blackface.

Shemp is also listed in the IMDb as a cast member in a mysterious baseball-themed film short in which Moe is said to have been featured during his time in Oakford Park. The two-reel film was called *Spring Fever* and starred baseball great Honus Wagner.

In 1919, there was no more beloved local sports hero in the Pittsburgh region (or possibly in all of Pennsylvania) than Johannes Peter "Honus" Wagner, "the Flying Dutchman" of baseball's National League. Considered to be not only the best shortstop but also one of the greatest players in Major League Baseball history, Wagner played twenty-one seasons, most of them with the Pittsburgh Pirates. He led the team to four National League pennants and, in 1909, its first World Series title. Two years after his retirement in 1917, Wagner was said to be one of the first baseball players to star in a commercial film. In *Spring Fever,* Wagner teaches batting skills to a young boy, played by Moses Horwitz. By some accounts, the two-reel short was filmed in an open field in Bakerstown, Pennsylvania. The problem is that no one has ever managed to find the film to determine when and where it was shot, whether it was released under a different title, or whether it ever existed at all.

Evidence of the existence of *Spring Fever* came to light in 2004, when Robert Edward Auctions sold a set of five movie lobby cards advertising "Hans Wagner in *Spring Fever*." One card calls *Spring Fever* "a two reel comedy." Another says it was "produced by Filmgraphs Inc." Each card features one large photograph. Three cards show Hans Wagner (as Honus Wagner was sometimes referred to) fishing. Two cards depict a group of wood nymphs. The labels were not part of the original cards but photographic overlays.

Wagner biographer Arthur Hittner suggested that the cards may have had nothing to do with Moe Howard but promoted the *Hans Wagner Comedies,* "a rather bizarre series of vignettes which were shown at Alfred McClelland's Greater Pittsburgh Film Exchange. Promotional stills . . . range from the sublime to the ridiculous." Hittner pointed out a sixth card that "features the Pirate shortstop in full uniform, fishing beside a gentle waterfall." The stills of the "bevy of scantily-clad wood nymphs [are] suggestive, perhaps, of the joys of hunting."

Later in life, Moe Howard said that he had appeared in a dozen two-reel shorts with Wagner. The claim was repeated and embellished in Three Stooges biographies, but Major League Baseball historian John Thorn wrote that Moe's daughter Joan Howard Maurer, who coauthored two of the books that make the claim, said that the information "did not come from her, and she was not aware of anything in her father's papers that may have sourced the information."

Hittner's biography and the book *Total Baseball* suggest that Wagner could have made the batting film with Moe Horwitz in 1909 for Vitagraph Studios. That timing makes more sense, as it was the period in which Moe claims he was appearing in juvenile roles in Vitagraph shorts—when he was a juvenile. By 1919, at age twenty-three, he was no longer the "young boy" learning how to bat. With no records of the film being produced by Vitagraph, no sign of the film itself, and Moe's track record of accuracy, the claim that he and the baseball great made a dozen two-reelers and that Shemp appeared in one of them may fall into the category of myth.

In January 1920, Moe and Shemp were living with their parents and younger brother in Bath Beach, Brooklyn, at 39 Bay 29th Street. In the 1920 census, Solomon is listed as working in "men's furnishings, leather." Jennie is a real estate broker. Moe, listed as Harry M. Horwitz, lists his occupation as an agent in the real estate industry. Only Shemp Howard is listed as working in the "theatrical industry." Occupation: actor.

And then Moe's old friend Lee Nash was back in the picture. He was "Ted Healy" now. Nash had followed his mother into vaudeville and made a name for himself with his own blackface act. By the end of 1922, he had scrubbed himself pink and was performing with his new wife, Betty Brown (born Braun), in a song, dance, and comedy act that included their dog. "He went in one branch of show business and I went in another," Moe recalled, saying that he met up with his childhood pal when Healy appeared in a vaudeville show at the Prospect Theatre, a grand, 2,500-seat palace (with a projection booth behind the balcony so that films could be part of the shows) in Park Slope, Brooklyn. "I happened to go back and say hello to him," Moe said on the *Mike Douglas Show* in 1973. "He was with his wife . . . I was going in the stage door and he was coming out and he said, 'Moe, you're just the guy I wanna see. My acrobat left me'—he was doing the toe-to-toe catch. He says, 'My acrobat left me. Can you help me out till I get a new one? You can still do the backflip, cantcha?' I says, 'The backflip? Where?' We used to do it on the sand on the beach, but I said, 'Under the stage, there's concrete!' He says, 'Help me out for a week.'"

"Well, the week," Moe said, "lasted eleven years."

Moe repeated time and again that the reunion with Healy took place in 1922. But Bill Cassara, author of *Nobody's Stooge: Ted Healy*, the definitive Healy biography, in consultation with Gary Lassin of "The Stoogeum" (the Three Stooges museum in Ambler, Pennsylvania), sorted through documented dates and appearances and placed the actual meeting at some time between June and August 1923.

Indeed, a study of Brooklyn newspapers shows that in the first half of 1923, Moe Horwitz was in Brooklyn, working in amateur community theater in Bensonhurst. On April 15, a night that Ted and Betty Healy were playing a vaudeville bill in Connecticut, Moe Horwitz was directing and starring in a play presented by the Dramatic Society of the Young Folks' League of Congregation Sons of Israel. *Potash and Perlmutter* (an ethnic Jewish comedy that ran for 441 performances on Broadway in 1913) was staged in the auditorium of the Community Club at Cropsey and 20th avenues. The role of Potash was played by David LeShack, president of the Dramatic Society. Moe portrayed Perlmutter. Proceeds from the performance went toward the upkeep of the congregation's Talmud Torah. The show was presented again on May 27 at the Montauk Theatre on Fulton Street, a benefit for the Jewish community house in Bensonhurst.

So it was the summer of 1923 when Ted Healy may have asked his old friend Moe Horwitz to take the place of an acrobat in his vaudeville act. Moe wrote that he agreed without hesitation and found out quickly why the acrobat took a powder from this particular routine. The backflip gag was part of a bit called "Fire and Ice." The acrobat would lie down in a box. Healy would pour water into the box, soaking the acrobat, who would jump up and out, executing a backflip and landing on the hard stage. The acrobat, borrowed from another act on the bill, was tired of getting soaked and socked by Healy. Moe was willing to take the abuse and claimed to have come up with a better tag to the gag: he would jump up, grab the waistband of Healy's pants, and pull them clear off. Healy thought it was hilarious. Moe became part of the show, introduced into the act as a "stooge."

In this case, the "stooge"—although the role wasn't going by that label yet—was a member of the team, often planted in the audience (as some magicians and stage hypnotists do today) to pop up and interrupt the proceedings in an intrusion that turns into a routine. Healy would be in the middle of a song or sketch when the "stooge" would butt in—a heckle from the crowd or a message from a supposed stagehand—and repartee and slapstick would follow. Healy's version was known as a "roughhouse act." Items were thrown, vegetables flew, and there was yelling and, in this case, slapping. That was Ted Healy's big and, as it turns out, lasting contribution to the form. Healy would ask a question, the "stooge" would answer, and Healy would respond with a hard smack across the face. *Slap!* The slaps were open-handed, real slaps—hard slaps, cheek stingers, bell ringers, headache-ers—slaps that could be heard in the last row and slaps that were always a little harder than expected, especially when Healy had a wisp of whisky on his breath, which, as years progressed, he would, too often. These were the slaps that Moe Howard made immortal in decades of Three Stooges shorts—only Moe's whacks on camera, like his pokes and bops, would be amplified with sound effects. Here, the sound effects were real. Tall, balding, veiny-nosed Ted Healy appeared even taller onstage when alongside little Moe, who was all grown up to maybe 140 pounds and five feet three inches, with his hair combed forward and trimmed in a bowl cut that would become his signature. Moe, remembering looking up to big Ted Healy, estimated his old friend and new boss to be well over six feet tall. Healy was five feet ten and a half inches. "He smacked the hell out of us," Moe said.

And then his brother Shemp got into the act.

"I used to come from the audience and work with Healy," Moe said. "I'd give him a note of reference and a recommendation and just praised myself to the sky, told him I sang like [the popular operatic soprano Amelita] Galli-Curci. And he says, 'Galli-Curci's a woman.' And I would say [nance-like], 'Oh, I know that.' And finally I heard my brother Shemp laugh in the audience so I whispered to Ted. I said, 'Ted, Shemp's out there.' So he stepped to the footlights and says, 'I'd like to have another young man come up here, preferably from Brooklyn.' And sure enough, Shemp came up."

Shemp was eating a pear, and he happened to have a pair of galoshes in his pocket "because no matter any city he went they had a pair of rubbers stashed away in the checkroom, case it rained when he was there." Shemp arrived onstage, took a bite of the pear, and offered it to Healy.

"Have a bite."

"I don't want a bite."

Shemp tried to force him. He pushed the dripping pear toward Healy's face. Healy pushed back, smashing the pear into Shemp's kisser. There was laughter from the Brooklyn crowd. There was a roughhouse ruckus. The bit continued. Maybe Healy gave Shemp his first slap in the face. Maybe he slapped a little too hard, hard enough for the slap to be heard in the back of the house, hard enough to sting. The show was on. "The pear wound up in one of their faces. It became Ted, Moe, and Shemp."

Then again, there are those who were close to Shemp who claim that he was the first to work with Ted Healy. "Moe established this narrative and Shemp didn't," says Cassara. Healy's biographer is a former police investigator and one of the few who have managed to cut through much of the mangled, muddled Stooges oral history that has become accepted as fact. "There's nothing to follow Shemp on his professional career, other than what's written in the newspapers. And no one ever interviewed Shemp, so we have Moe's version and then not too much representation from Shemp, other than what he told his wife. And his wife informed his offspring how they wanted it. So Moe said he was the first Healy stooge; Shemp's family said, 'No, Shemp was Healy's first stooge.' And it's inconclusive. So you could debate that till Timbuktu, but I don't think we're going to ever find documentation."

So who came first? Did the brothers join Ted Healy's act the same night? Are there any verifiable facts in Moe's autobiography at all? In another published account, Healy had taken out an ad in a theatrical weekly, seeking replacements for his team of acrobats, a trio of Germans who had given their notice. In this version, Shemp, Moe, and younger brother Jerry showed up, and Healy offered them forty weeks of work. Jennie Horwitz, however, refused to let her youngest son (he was nineteen) go on the road, so it was down to Moe and Shemp. Neither was an acrobat, and they fell into the role of "stooges," getting knocked around and learning on the job how to roll with the punches and slaps. In any case, it did turn out to be Ted, Shemp, and Moe—no, make that Ted, Shemp, and *Harry*. Moe was billed as "Harry Howard" at the time. But again, it's Moe who wrote it down and repeated the story again and again.

Another interesting yarn comes from older brother Jack Howard. He said that their mother Jennie was dead set against allowing any of her sons to enter the low-down vaudeville game and that Ted Healy met with her to plead his case. When his charm offensive didn't work, he simply paid her off. "Jennie," Healy said, "I'll give you one hundred dollars for your synagogue building fund if you let the boys come with me." According to Jack Howard, "She thought about the good that the money would do, and agreed, reluctantly"—a nice story, even though Moe was twenty-six at the time and Shemp twenty-eight.

As Moe tells it, for a time, it was Ted Healy and two stooges to slap around. A third stooge, not to be one of the Three Stooges, was added about a year later. "Ted took his brother-in-law in as a third man because his wife had asked him to give him a job of some kind. He was very inexperienced and so inexperienced it became funny only to us. So that traveled along for about four months and Ted couldn't stand that any longer. So it was Shemp and I until early 1925, when we picked up Larry.

"We were off a couple of days from Shubert's show *A Night in Spain,*" Moe told Mike Douglas. "Now we're at the Marigold Gardens watching the show and here comes this little fella in tails and a high hat and a violin. He starts playing a violin . . . not good . . . and doing a Russian dance at the same time playing the violin, so Healy looked at me and said, 'Are you thinkin' what I'm thinkin'?' I said, 'Yeah, let's talk to him.' We watched the rest of the show, we went back in the dressing room. He had a robe on. He had wet his hair. And while we're talking to him, his hair started to crawl up in knots. It was drying out. So Healy looked at him and said, 'Hey, your single out there. Not too hot. You want to join with the other two boys and become three?' He says, 'I'd love it.' He says, 'I'll give you ninety bucks a week—and ten dollars more to throw that fiddle away.' And he threw it away and it became three in 1925. With Ted. Now we went all the way down the line with Larry, Shemp, and I.

"In nineteen hundred and thirty-two, Shemp got the opportunity to play the character Knobby in the Joe Palooka pictures on the coast. He didn't want to go. He said, 'What're you gonna do for another guy?' I said, 'Shemp, go. It's a great opportunity for you. We'll get the kid brother Curly.'"

And that, according to Moe Howard, was how it went down, a quick progression from that meeting with his boyhood friend Lee Nash at the stage door of the Prospect Theatre in Brooklyn. "'Help me out for a week.' Well, the week lasted eleven years."

Except it didn't go down like that—not at all.

It wasn't a solid eleven-year run, not for Moe and not for anyone. Ted Healy didn't hire his brother-in-law Sam "Moody" Braun in 1924. Moe was not present to witness Louis Feinberg's (aka Larry Fine's) drying hair begin to sprout out on either side of his balding dome like some fast-motion Chia Pet. The momentous meeting with Larry Fine didn't take place at the Marigold Gardens nightclub on North Halstead Street in Chicago. It didn't take place in 1925, Moe wasn't there when the meeting *did* take place, and Shemp didn't leave the act in 1932 to play Knobby Walsh in a Joe Palooka short! For years, Moe's stories of Moe, Larry, Shemp, and Curly had been repeated, condensed, and reprinted until Bill Cassara, with the help of expert Stoogeologist Gary Lassin, came along and began to untangle the mess, comb out the kinks, and straighten things out.

And it all begins with Shemp, who, a correct reading of history will confirm, was the star from the start.

Five

Ted Talks

And, by the way, it wasn't always "Ted Healy and His Stooges," either. "Ted Healy was primarily a singer," his biographer Bill Cassara says. "People have a hard time with that, but Ted was a professional singer and at one point when he was in vaudeville, he would open up to the audience and say, 'Whatever someone requests, I can sing that song.' So music was big in his life. He established himself as a solo artist in blackface, like a lot of them did, and because his idol was Al Jolson. It's kind of hard to separate yourself from the pack with that kind of gig back then, but he did! His breakthrough came in 1922 in a variety show called *Cuddle Up*. He got rave reviews in that." By the spring, Healy had quit *Cuddle Up* and was working solo, billed alternatively as a "comedy monologist," "singing and talking comedian," and sometimes simply, "comedian." In June, working the Lyric Theatre in Indianapolis, he shared the bill with a piano, singing, and dancing act called Brown, Syrell, and Dreyer. Dave Dreyer played piano. Betty Brown and Louis Syrell were dancers who, according to *Variety*, "offer a splendid contrast with their blonde and brunette bobs." Healy found himself instantly attracted to the brunette Betty, possibly because she also offered, as described in *Variety*, "a bare-legged Oriental (Cleopatra) dance that discloses her as an adept contortionist, with splits and back kicks of the advanced type included." Healy and Betty married on June 5.

So, after making a name for himself as a solo performer, Ted became an even greater success with his high-kicking bride in a song, dance, and comedy act. Billed under various names like "The Vaudevillians" or "The Flapper and The Philosopher," the act gave Healy a good chance to show off his personality and comedic abilities, especially when he would mix it up with other acts on the bill, like the aforementioned acrobats. In 1923, Healy made sure he would be able to butt in on other acts by adding a segment to his own act called "Syncopated Toes." Isabelle Churchill, Florence House, and Matt Mooney were graceful hoofers featured in a "dance fantasy" routine that the audience assumed to be a separate act—until the Healys joined in. Each portion of Healy's display was praised by the

Nashville *Tennessean* when the show played the downtown Princess Theatre in November, supporting the headliners, Dan Fitch's Minstrels and their presentation of "The Land of Old Black Joe":

> Ted Healy, inimitable, injecting drolleries and personality into his own act and the one following it . . . won a high place in the affections of local theater attendants. He sings, talks, dangles by his wrist from the wings and does a number of other things that amuse. . . . In "The Flapper and The Philosopher," he is supported by Betty Healy, who dances well and looks the role. . . . "Syncopated Toes" . . . is a clever exhibition both of eccentric dancing and athletic skills.

Ted also had his knockaround assistants on the team, but notice that the work of the "stooges," Harry and Shemp Howard, are not mentioned in the ads or the reviews. The brothers would appear in a bit or two, maybe interrupt Healy, get slapped around, and fade back like anonymous breakaway props. When Healy and company played the Palace Theatre in Peoria, Illinois, in December, the program listed a "Harvey Howard" under Isabelle Churchill and Florence House in "Syncopated Toes," but the first time the pair may have gotten any notice in print appeared on April 16, 1924.

"Ted Healy carries the comedy burden which consists of quick entrances on dances for ad lib clowning and dance travesties," read the review in *Variety*. "There are two funny bits, one where two boobish looking saps apply for a job with a comedy letter. They assist Healy to mount a ladder to attempt work on the rings then get into an argument after the ladder is removed and leave him hanging in mid-air. This is repeated for big laughs. Another laugh-getter was a magic travesty with Healy placing one of the boobs in a box, then emptying his revolver into it."

We can only assume that the "boobish-looking saps" and the "boobs" were Harry and Shemp. The routine in which the "saps apply for a job with a comedy letter" shows up in the 1930 film *Soup to Nuts* in a scene in which characters played by Healy, Shemp, Moe (billed as "Harry Howard"), and Larry Fine perform their stage routine at a Fireman's Ball:

> SHEMP (*hands Healy a folded sheet of paper*): Here it is, right here, from company A.
> HEALY (*unfolding the paper*): What's this?
> SHEMP: That's the reference of recommendation.
> HEALY: May I read it?
> SHEMP: Yes.
> HEALY: Well, I see. (*reading*) "Dear Ted. May I introduce three charming boys. These boys are exceptionally clever. Hoping to

hear from you again, I remain faithfully yours, signed, yours truly." (*to Shemp*) Who wrote this?
SHEMP: I did.
And Healy gives Shemp a good, hard shove to the right shoulder, knocking him back a step.

The term "boobish looking saps" was mild compared to their description in the *Indianapolis Star* when the show played later that year downtown at B. F. Keith's Theatre, the former Grand Opera House. There, the reviewer noted that Ted and Betty Healy "were assisted by several dancers and grotesque characters." Shemp and Moe were not dancers. What was evident from both mentions was that although the Howards may have stood out, they were not considered the stars or even the costars of the show or the act. That was made barkingly clear in a review published in their hometown *Brooklyn Daily Eagle* on June 17, 1924. Performing at Keith's Orpheum on Fulton Street, it was one thing for the brothers to be overshadowed by the women in "Syncopated Toes"—and it was, as the reviewer noted, a "pleasant surprise" when Ted and Betty popped up in the second act with Churchill and House, "a pretty pair of dancers in a

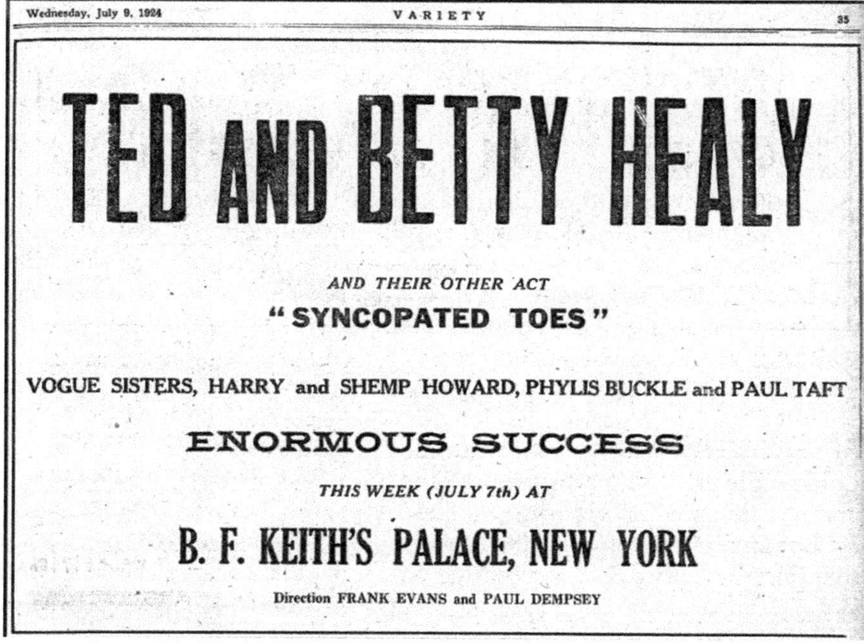
Wednesday, July 9, 1924 VARIETY 35

TED AND BETTY HEALY

AND THEIR OTHER ACT

"SYNCOPATED TOES"

VOGUE SISTERS, HARRY and SHEMP HOWARD, PHYLIS BUCKLE and PAUL TAFT

ENORMOUS SUCCESS

THIS WEEK (JULY 7th) AT

B. F. KEITH'S PALACE, NEW YORK

Direction FRANK EVANS and PAUL DEMPSEY

Shemp and "Harry" finally saw their stooging recognized in July 1924, when their boss, Ted Healy, gave them credit in a Variety *ad. Courtesy of the Media History Digital Library* very pretty terpsichorean number." It was quite another for Shemp and Moe to play second fiddle in comedy to Ted and Pete—Pete being Ted Healy's dog, a German shepherd trained to do the opposite of whatever Healy commanded. "Healy and his police dog are seen in bits of foolishment. Ted claims his mutt is a brother of Strongheart, the famous movie dog and so he calls him 'Weak Liver.' The dog walked off in a huff."

Shemp and Moe got thrown a bone and some recognition a few weeks later when the act unpacked in Manhattan to "play the Palace." Keith's Palace Theatre at the corner of Broadway and 47th Street was the greatest vaudeville theater in the country, the 1,740-seat flagship of the B. F. Keith Organization. Every vaudeville performer dreamed of playing the Palace, and when they did, they had "made it." A half-page display ad ran on page 35 of *Variety*, wishing "enormous success" to Ted and Betty Healy, "their other act" (Syncopated Toes), and (in smaller typeface) the Vogue Sisters, Harry and Shemp Howard, Phyllis Buckle, and Paul Taft. The brothers were supporting players for sure, but they had their names in print if not in lights.

This is where Moe's timeline and neat history of the Stooges' ascent gets thrown off once again. On March 15, 1925, four days after his thirtieth birthday, Shemp Howard got married. He tied the knot with Gertrude Frank, a girl from the neighborhood who had celebrated her twentieth birthday the day after Shemp's. Everyone knew Gertrude as "Babe," which caused a bit of confusion with Shemp's youngest brother, Jerome "Babe" Horwitz. After Gertrude entered the family, Jerome gave up the nickname and began to be referred to as "Curly." According to Shemp's granddaughter Sandie Howard-Isaac, Shemp's bride had "started out in vaudeville; she was part of a popular song and dance act known as the Gertrude Frank Girls. We're not sure why, but Babe found talking about the past to be a painful experience." Perhaps that's a reason why, after the wedding, Shemp took a break from Ted Healy and company.

Twelve weeks later, on June 7, twenty-eight-year-old Moe followed Shemp's lead and married his longtime gal pal. Helen Schonberger was twenty-five. She wasn't in show business, but her cousin Erich Weisz was doing quite well as a performer, known the world over as the escape artist and illusionist Harry Houdini. At Helen's urging, Moe also left the Healy act not long after stomping the napkin-wrapped glass. In part because of that timing, neither Shemp nor Moe was along for the ride when Ted and Betty Healy and their dog made the leap from vaudeville to Broadway in July 1925. To be honest, it wasn't that great a leap. The couple was signed on to the third edition of the *Earl Carroll Vanities*, a theatrical revue that fell somewhere between a big-budget musical production and a burlesque skin show. Earl Carroll, the producer, director, and impresario, had cooked up the first version of the *Vanities* in 1923 as a more provocative and sexier version of the *Ziegfeld Follies*. Florenz Ziegfeld's shows had flourished on Broadway since 1907 with shows inspired by the Folies Bergère in Paris: lineups of popular performers accompanied by dozens of beautiful chorus girls parading in elaborate costumes. With sprawling casts that often included more than 100 showgirls ("The Loveliest Girls in America"), Carroll's *Vanities* was deliberately risqué enough to run up against the censors—creating scandals that Carroll used to his advantage, generating publicity and greater ticket sales.

The latest *Vanities* show opened on July 6 at the Earl Carroll Theatre on Seventh Avenue near 50th Street. It was a wild scene from the beginning, with the front of the theater transformed into a nightclub. First-nighters walked in to see that the first few rows had been replaced with tables, "waiters" were serving ginger ale to the ringside seaters, and chorine "hostesses" were guiding patrons to their seats, wandering the lobby, and dancing with men from the audience. The emcee held up the show by introducing dignitaries and celebrities in the audience. He even invited some—including New York's popular governor Al Smith and the governors of Florida, Nebraska, and Oklahoma—to take their bows on the stage. The show began an hour late, and there were still twenty-two of forty scheduled scenes to go when the reviewer for the *Daily News* bolted after the first act to make his 11:00 p.m. deadline. Ted and Betty Healy danced and performed in sketches, and *Variety* pointed out that Ted Healy "is on frequently in the first part" and "gets laughs with his talk and should, since the gags are nearly all surefire after testing." (Coincidentally, Ziegfeld's *Summer Follies of 1925* opened the same night at his theater on 54th Street, starring *Follies* regular Will Rogers with his chewing gum, rope tricks, and topical jokes and headliner W. C. Fields.)

The reviews for *Vanities* were fair at best. *Variety*'s Don Carle Gillette complained that this latest version contained "not one strong entertainment feature" and that Ted Healy, "a capital comedian," was "sadly handicapped by poor lines, when any." Even "a couple of 'nance' specialties, which Carroll probably inserted in the hope that the authorities would object to them and thus bring publicity to the show . . . looks to be a bloomer"—"bloomer" meaning "a serious or stupid mistake." Yet, despite the stinky pans, Ted Healy came out smelling just fine and was soon receiving offers from vaudeville producers that almost doubled what he was getting to keep the Earl Carroll turkey from getting its head chopped off.

By November, about eight weeks before *Vanities* pooped out on December 27, Healy had wriggled himself and Betty out of *Vanities* and was hoofing, singing, and providing "fun in the Healy manner," headlining a vaudeville bill two shows per day at the Flatbush Theatre in Brooklyn. Then it was on to the Orpheum circuit, with their police dog, cat, and "a couple of half-wit appearing gents, who have graduated from 'Shoe College, just a little higher than Oxford,'" as the *Omaha Daily News* pointed out when the Healys topped the bill at the city's Orpheum in January 1926. The couple trudged across the Midwest and into the great white North, hitting St. Louis, Kansas City, Minneapolis, Winnipeg, and Calgary. Then it was down the West Coast—Seattle, Sacramento, Oakland, and San Francisco—working their way to the Orpheum on Broadway in downtown Los Angeles on March 22 (on a bill that included the tenor John Steel and Moss & Frye).

A potentially much larger audience and greater acclaim was promised the following week, when the act moved around the corner from the Orpheum to the Hillstreet Theatre. Awaiting backstage after one of the shows was an offer for Ted Healy to make the jump to the movies that were now playing for the crowds in between vaudeville performances—or was it the other way around? Healy jumped at the opportunity and signed with Hal Roach Studios to play a supporting role in a silent short starring Helene Chadwick and comic actor James Finlayson: the instantly recognizable Scotsman with the big fake mustache and laugh-out-loud double takes and squints. The film was *Wise Guys Prefer Brunettes*, a hot twist on *Gentleman Prefer Blondes*, Anita Loos's comic novel, published the previous November. Silent comedy veteran F. Richard Hines and Stan Laurel directed—some months before Laurel's official screen teaming with Oliver Hardy. Ted Healy would play the wise guy. Beginning on May 14, he took a three-week break from the Orpheum circuit and went through the motions at the Hal Roach Studios in Culver City, about seven miles southwest of Hollywood. When shooting wrapped, he returned to the road.

The *New York Daily News* reported in July that Ted Healy was back on the vaudeville circuit "in a new act with Betty Healy—Ted recently having returned from making Hollywood pictures." On July 29, he and Betty were turning on the "fun in the Healy manner" at the Keith-Albee Palace in Akron, Ohio. They were top of the vaudeville bill but, in a sign of things to come, second to screenings of the Priscilla Dean silent movie drama *The Danger Girl*.

A new opportunity was soon in sight, however. This one was offered by Jacob ("J. J.") and Lee Shubert, the theatrical producers and theater owners. The Shuberts had a show limping through vaudeville houses around the country that needed a mainline injection of fun in the Healy manner to keep it alive. *The Passing Show* had begun life on Broadway as *The Merry World* after the Shuberts imported London producer Albert De

Courville's British sketch comedy revue and added American singers, production numbers, acts, near-naked chorus girls, and French comedian Emil Boreo, who specialized in making funny faces.

When *The Merry World* opened at the Imperial Theatre in June, the *Daily News*'s Burns Mantle wrote that "the result is good entertainment"—but apparently not good enough. The show underwent some rejigging and reopened at the Shubert Theatre on August 2 as *Passions of 1926*, closed nineteen days later, and resurfaced on August 23 at the Garden Pier Theatre in Atlantic City, New Jersey—this time as *The Passing Show*. The Shuberts owned the title, which had been used for decades for annual editions of Broadway revues. The road tour, which included a sprawling cast and a chorus "which comprises the prize-winning beauties from fifteen different states," was under way.

Ted and Betty Healy joined the show in Cleveland the first week of September at a time the show was sputtering. Emil Boreo took his funny faces and quit in Ohio before the company arrived at the Four Cohans Theatre in Chicago on September 12. The ads promised "the greatest of them all . . . radiant as the morning sun . . . a cyclone of hilarious travesties . . . sparkling melodies by brilliant artists . . . a kaleidoscope of feminine pulchritude. . . gorgeous gowns and dazzling decorations . . . the crowning peak of spectacular splendor." They apparently oversold the show. "It is safe to say that any stock burlesque show has a better first thirty minutes than *The Passing Show* and that is no fault of the people in it," according to *Variety*. "Ted Healy . . . easily the comedy hit of the show . . . alone, then with Betty, did a great deal of kidding and got a laugh at almost every quip." Ted Healy, as emcee and comedic interloper, continued to receive high marks (or at least an "A for effort") in every review that panned the overall production in each city the show shambled into, from the *Cincinnati Enquirer* in October ("Entertainers, no matter how talented, cannot rise above the material") to the Baltimore *Evening Sun* in November ("One of the most insipid, doleful attempts at spectacular revue which have come this way").

Wise Guys Prefer Brunettes began to be screened in vaudeville palaces on October 3, 1926. The short movie did not turn Ted Healy into a movie star. His Hollywood dreams would be put on hold. By December, *The Passing Show* had also passed away, but the Healys' efforts did not go unrecognized by the Shuberts. The organization had another show for them to lead. This one would not be crawling away from Broadway but rather charging toward a grand premiere. Once again, the Shuberts dusted off one of their old trademarks. *A Night in Paris* was a Broadway revue that had opened in January 1926 at the Casino de Paris, a 500-seat space atop the Century Theatre on Central Park West. With some of the better-working parts from *The Passing Show*, a new book by their resident librettist Harold Atteridge, songs by the celebrated team of Jean Schwartz and Al Bryan, colorful costumes, lots of chorus girls, some Iberian touches (such as mantillas, high combs, and castanets, clacked by the impressive Peruvian dancer Helba Huara in her American debut), and singer Tito Coral, they concocted *A Night in Spain*. On December 11, the *Daily News* reported the Healys' involvement "as principals" in the show ("He'll fool around in a revue," read the photo caption), "which expects to open New Year's Eve at the Casino de Paris."

That grand premier atop the Century Theatre did not take place, but the Shuberts had even bigger plans, and *A Night in Spain* would have many nights to work out the kinks. When the show had its first preview on January 11, 1927, it was across the East River at the Majestic Theatre on Fulton Street in Brooklyn. The ad in the *Brooklyn Daily Eagle* trumpeted, "The Greatest Cast of Musical Comedy Stars Ever Assembled," but a greater marketing point was the contingent of leggy dancers. This show featured both the Gertrude Hoffman Girls and the Allan K. Foster Girls (along with the Shubert chorus girls and some Casino de Paris Girls), which, according to the *Brooklyn Daily Eagle*, was "the first time there have been two well-known chorus troupes in one production." The abundance of "girls"—more than sixty of them—and flesh was often just as attractive to a ticket buyer as a cast that included stage stars including the Healys, Georgie Price, Kathryn Ray, Vanessi, Salt and Pepper, Olga Smirnova, and Bert Gardner.

Opening night in Brooklyn was standing room only for a show that was equally overstuffed. Thirty-nine scenes were scheduled, but only thirty-four had managed to be squeezed in by the time the curtain rang down at 12:30 the following morning. "*A Night in Spain* encompasses all of the sensuous, exotic, swaying elements that are indigenous to the soil," raved the reviewer for the *Brooklyn Standard Union*. "It is a Shubert revue and contains all of the loveliness, pulchritude, expensiveness and lavishness associated with the producers. Ted Healy's master of ceremonies and a more entertaining comique never trod the boards in Brooklyn. The Gertrude Hoffman Girls and Foster Girls dance like so many parts of the machine with, however, the fine athletic wholesomeness that prevents the work from being automatic. The Casino de Paris girls make it an international affair."

There was more to this show that made it not only a success but also very significant for Ted Healy—and show business history. Readers making it to the penultimate paragraph of the *Standard Union* review would come to a mention of two performers in the show. The first name they would recognize. Georgie Price was a singer and comic. He was twenty-seven and had been working vaudeville and Broadway shows since he was a kid. With his warbling of the song "Bye Bye Blackbird," he was being compared to stars like Al Jolson and Eddie Cantor. But according to the man from the *Standard Union*, maybe his act was getting a little tired. "Since Georgie Price, the erstwhile vaudevillian, has so big a part in the show, he deserves a special mention. He will probably never make a good burlesquer of Shakespeare but he can sing loudly and vigorously. Someone should sit on him and tell him Al Jolson has a monopoly on the exploitation of the ego. A quiet comedian like Shemp Howard gets more laughs in one minute than Georgie gets in an act."

A quiet comedian like *who?* Yes, *that* Shemp Howard. Shemp was in the cast, working with Ted Healy again, but not as an anonymous "stooge." Already, on his first night, he was making a name for himself.

Shemp was back in the game.

Six

The Stooge

A Night in Spain and Shemp Howard got off to a promising start in 1927. The show's debut at the Majestic Theatre in Brooklyn packed the house and impressed the critics with its gathering of what the *Brooklyn Citizen* called "one of the largest and most talented casts ever seen in a revue," with most of the principals "recruited from the two-a-day"—the first-class, big-time vaudeville circuits that presented matinee and evening performances only. "The production . . . should, with the aid of the pruning knife, and after a few more rehearsals, take its place alongside of the current revue hits at present appearing on Broadway." Shemp, the formerly anonymous player and punching bag in his previous stand with Ted Healy, was now getting noticed—by name. "Shemp was unique," Bill Cassara acknowledges. "He was a comedian, visually, and he moved funny, and he had great reactions. That's what you call a comic stooge. He was there to supplement Ted Healy's show."

In advance of the troupe's arrival in Atlantic City for a week at the Apollo Theatre on the boardwalk, the local *Daily Press* heralded "a bright, snappy entertainment, with exceptional talent, a perfect chorus and elaborately staged . . . entertainment for all, clever comedies, splendid music, good singing, fast dancing and richly mounted, in fact everything that is required to satisfy the desires for solid entertainment."

All that and Shemp Howard, too. Although he was working as Ted Healy's foil, his name was listed in the advertisement along with the other leading members of the "great cast"—in the same size font as Ted and Betty Healy's. Shemp had prime roles and got hearty laughs in most of the sketches, each of which presented ample space for one-liners, double takes, double entendres, slaps, hits, and falls—lots of slaps, hits, and falls. Shemp was featured as various characters in "County Fair and Circus," which was set in Barcelona; in "The Sky Girl," featuring a song by Grace Bowman and some Foster Girls on a trapeze; as a taxicab driver in "Three Questions"; and in "A Spanish Café," with Healy as a detective. The most surefire laugh-getter was "The Photographer," set in a photographer's studio, with Shemp as the proprietor, Healy as his friend, and a pretty girl as a model. The scene goes to blackout just as Healy mistakes the girl's long black skirt for the camera's cloth hood. Up goes the skirt, down goes Ted's head, and out go the lights!

Only a few weeks since its opening, after the show rolled out in Baltimore at the Auditorium theater on January 31, the local paper revealed what was already an open secret: *A Night in Spain* didn't have all that much to do with Spain, at least not most of the time. The reviewer concluded that "it doesn't really matter . . . since it's a revue" and since Ted Healy explained to the audience early on that the show "begins in Valencia and ends in Syracuse." That initial review in the *Baltimore Sun* praised the "excellent comedy, catchy music, some fine voices and a great deal of very good dancing," especially by the South American star Helba Huara. "Castanets in her hands are almost speaking things."

Ted Healy was "the high light and faired-haired boy of the Messers. Shubert's entertainment, whether he is for the moment being a misunderstood husband, an animal trainer, a photographer or a side-show barker."

It was hours later, when the Baltimore *Evening Sun* arrived on doorsteps, that a more uncomfortable open secret was addressed by the critic Gilbert Kanour. A fastidious tastemaker who noted at the top of his review that the curtain rose eighteen minutes later than its advertised 8:13 p.m. start, Kanour showed that the revue's comic emperor "Don Healy," if not wearing no clothes, was at least dressed in hand-me-downs. "The majority of the jokes, practically all of those purveyed by Don Healy, have been culled from *The Passing Show*, here not so long ago," he charged. "Although Don Healy fumed and fussed to send his comic messages home, he was left high and dry by the librettist. Much of the better banter it is suspected is his and his alone."

There was more going on behind the scenes. Along the way, Betty Healy's brother Sam "Moody" Braun had joined the troupe, showing up in minor roles in some sketches. This is probably the time Moe had referenced when he wrote about Ted Healy hiring his brother-in-law, although Moe was not in the picture. Ted and Betty's partnership was not as close as it had been in past years, especially not with four groups of chorus girls walking around nearly naked backstage and in hotels and not beyond the comedy star's grasp. Also within Ted Healy's grasp were tumblers. He was drinking more and working overtime to get those laughs, slapping a little harder to make sure they echoed in the last rows. Shemp Howard was taking it—for now.

The show went on, tuning up and tightening up along the way. The music, the laughs, the legs, and the fact that this Broadway-style revue offered more than a touch of low-down, bluish burlesque were more than enough to keep the crowds coming. Beginning on February 7, there were several weeks at the Chestnut Street Opera House in Philadelphia, where the reviewer for the *Inquirer* commented that the show's strongest feature was "the several battalions of bouncing beauties." Ted Healy, he wrote, appeared in some "mildly amusing" sketches when he wasn't dishing out "mellow humor that has done duty in a variety of offerings."

The show was still drawing crowds and about to enter its final week in Philadelphia when, on Saturday, February 26, Shemp's wife, Babe, gave birth. It was a boy! Shemp's first and only child was named Morton.

Philadelphia was not that far from home, but Shemp would soon have a chance to get even closer to his boy and spend some quality time making funny faces for him. *A Night in Spain* returned "by popular demand" to the Majestic in Brooklyn on March 14, "more joyous and glittering than on its previous showing in Brooklyn a month ago," according to the *Brooklyn Daily Times*. "The performance displayed that surfeit of pretty girls, dazzling costumes and infectious music which has ever been the forte of work from the Shubert hand. With all his old tricks and a few that were new, Ted Healy carried the burden of the comedy in a fully satisfactory manner. . . . Ted Healy has never been in better fettle with his crazy troupe of songsters, his laconically disobedient dog, and his own contagious good humor. He captivated last night's audience, and the producers are to be complimented on allowing him so much time to work his skillful pranks. He is a comedian who stands quite alone when he is standing at all, and his antics enliven this show to a pleasurable degree."

On to the Alvin Theatre in Pittsburgh, with Shemp listed as part of "America's Foremost All-Star Cast." *Variety* had eyes in the audience on April 3. The reviewer was most impressed with comedian Phil Baker, who played an accordion and worked with a jazz group called the Raccooners. Baker also worked with Sid Silvers, a plant in the balcony, getting major laughs from their banter and "Pinochle and Sauerkraut" bit. Silvers was Baker's comedy partner (so a bit more than a "stooge") and his heckling was a hit. (The act was said to be the basis for the 1951 film *The Stooge*, starring Dean Martin and Jerry Lewis.)

Ted Healy "has the heavy work and appears in about every other turn," but (again that complaint) "he offers nothing new and a lot could be

Shemp got attention in 1927, working solo in A Night in Spain *and other shows as, one reviewer put it, "a foil, battering-ram, or what-have-you" for Ted Healy. Courtesy the Shubert Organization*

eliminated." Betty Healy and Shemp were lumped in with the foremost all-star cast members that "just get by. If it were not for the Foster and Hoffman girls and now Phil Baker the show would be lost." The show was extended a week at the Alvin and played a week at the Hanna Theatre in Cleveland, and then it was time to step up.

Next stop: Broadway.

May 3, 1927: Opening night for *A Night in Spain* at the 44th Street Theatre just off Broadway, and Times Square is crawling with sailors. The Atlantic and Pacific fleets of the U.S. Navy have ships docked in New York Harbor, and the "gobs"—seamen—have taken over the city, looking for action. But despite the sixty chorus girls and complaints on the road that *A Night in Spain* is too racy, with too much skin on display, Burns Mantle of the *New York Daily News* warns that "the navy will be disappointed if it expects to find anything nude under the Shubert sun, for all the girls are properly upholstered and even the jokes are discreetly corseted."

Mantle gave short shrift to the show, perhaps because on the very same night, he was reviewing Sophocles' tragedy *Electra* at the Metropolitan Opera House.

The critic returned to the activity at the 44th Street Theatre on May 9. He described *A Night in Spain* as "tuneful, spirited, and gorgeous with color" while noting that "of course only the costumes are Spanish. The jokes are burlesque and the legs are native." Phil Baker with his accordion was, again, the critic's choice: "a wise monologist" who "keeps away from the low stuff and the coarser allusions, and tricks laughs out of puns and the quickness of wit that eludes the mob." Ted Healy, on the other hand, was *da people's cherce,* "evidently capitalizing long years in or fearfully close to burlesque. . . . He, too, is funny; a rough and tumble lad with a good kick in either foot and a natural sense of physical fooling that is as sure of results as a prohibition cocktail. And as pure. Shemp Howard is his perfect foil, suffering most of the falls and the kicks."

It had taken sixteen weeks from that first notice that first night in Brooklyn, but all the kicks and falls and abuse that Shemp Howard had taken from his boss Ted Healy were paying off with some attention in the city where it counted most. "Ted Healy is the same old Ted," wrote the reviewer for the *Brooklyn Daily Eagle,* "good for innumerable laughs any place he appears. Shemp Howard likewise provided much amusement as a foil, battering-ram, or what-have-you for Healy." The home-borough praise was welcome, but no notice was so important as one from the stately and influential *New York Times*. The critic singled out in the opening paragraph "a droll newcomer by the name of Shemp Howard" as among the "fine caballeros and undoubted comics" who "insured in advance a high content of merrymaking." Later, he reiterated, "He whom the program described as Shemp Howard made the most of an exceedingly comic face and a diffident manner."

Gordon M. Leland of *The Billboard* represented the critical appraisal: "Thru a long process of revamping at the behest of disparaging reviewers on the road these past few months, *A Night in Spain* finally arrives on Broadway as one of the best all-round shows of its type ever brought in by the Shuberts. Whatever it may have been originally in the hinterlands, it is now a swift-moving, diversified revue just brimming with talent."

Leland gave high marks to Healy, pointing out that he "carries the biggest burden and carries it well. He is on stage the greater part of the evening and surprised even his closest followers with his versatility, introducing many new accomplishments and even conducting his own orchestra." But it was Leland's mention of two other cast members that would prove to be prophetic. "Betty Healy has next to nothing to do and would be entirely lost if Ted did not call attention to her now and then. . . . Among the other men [is] Shemp Howard, an excellent comedy foil and real comic in his own right."

Also prophetic was the opinion of *New York Times* drama critic J. Brooks Atkinson, who later in the month called Healy

> one of those loud, rough, hustling fools who make the most satisfactory comedians. When he tackles a refractory close-harmony singer murder burns in his eye. When he assaults from the rear, he kicks to kill. When he stuffs two eggs in a bumpkin's mouth, he does not temper the artistic effort with gentleness. Sex does not abash this democratic buffoon; he tackles women around the neck quite as roughly as men. . . . He is dangerous.

The other men in Healy's sketch team included brother-in-law Moody Braun, Lou Warren, and comedy dancer Bobby Pinkus. Shemp, though, was first among Healy's lieutenants—lead "stooge," although that title was yet to be bestowed officially. He received what could be regarded as equal billing before a much larger audience on June 18, when he was not only featured but also photographed along with Ted and Betty Healy in the *Daily News* amusements section. The trio appeared in an early example of the *fumetti*—a comic strip in which sequential photographs rather than cartoons illustrate a joke told through superimposed speech bubbles. The three panels of "Broadway—A Late Discovery," probably taken from the show's "A Spanish Café" sketch, were staged by *Daily News* Broadway columnist and future film producer Mark Hellinger:

PANEL 1: *Ted and Betty sit on either side of a small round table. Ted wears a suit, tie, and vest. Betty, hair in a flapper bob, is in a scanty dance costume, with bare shoulders and very short skirt. She sits on her hands, her bare left leg extended toward center of the frame.*
TED (*hand across his stomach*): I don't think that last dish agreed with me.
BETTY: We'll call the waiter and find out what is wrong.

PANEL 2: *Shemp Howard as a waiter, in a loose-fitting suit coat and with a large napkin over his arm, stands behind the table, between them.*
TED: Say, waiter, do gooseberries have legs?
SHEMP: Oh no, sir.

PANEL 3: *Everyone looks into the camera.*
TED: (*arms folded*): Then I've eaten a caterpillar!

Ted Healy's success in *A Night in Spain* kicked off a Broadway tradition when his caricature was displayed in Sardi's restaurant, the show business hangout at 234 West 44th Street, down the block from the 44th Street Theatre. His would be the first of hundreds of caricatures of Broadway stars that would eventually cover the walls of the joint—a practice that continues to this day. Shemp Howard received a similar honor on July 1, when, described as "one of the principals" in *A Night in Spain,* he had his caricature featured in his hometown *Brooklyn Daily-Eagle*.

A Night in Spain played a combined twenty-seven weeks—more than six months—on Broadway. The show continued to run at the 44th Street Theatre into October. On the tenth of that month, it moved to the Winter Garden, the Shuberts' showplace at Broadway and 50th Street. The show had logged 174 performances before it closed on November 12, 1927. The *Daily News* counted 218 shows and listed *A Night in Spain* among its "Golden Dozen of current attractions in New York theaters that have recorded longest runs"—in fourth place among musical comedies.

And closing night did not mean the close of the show. Once the sets were packed up at the Winter Garden, it was back on the road.

A Night in Spain's post-Broadway national tour opened two nights later in Boston at the Shubert Theatre on Tremont Street. To the reviewer at the *Boston Globe,* "Thirty-two scenes did not seem too many. Somehow the producers appear to have struck a happy balance between bewitching beauty and a glorious comedy. It whirls around for three hours or more and everybody is delighted." Ted Healy was hailed as "a fast-moving fun maker" and Shemp Howard singled out among the performers without whom "the show would not have been as good as it was."

"A Night in Spain"

An Impression of Shemp Howard, One of the Principals in the Lively Revue at the Forty-fourth Street Theater.

In 1927, Ted Healy's caricature was the first to be displayed in the Broadway haunt Sardi's; costar Shemp got similar star treatment in the hometown Brooklyn Daily Eagle. *July 1, 1927,* Brooklyn Daily Eagle*; Local Newspapers on Microfilm Collection, BCMS.0028; Brooklyn Public Library, Center for Brooklyn History*

There was no mention of Betty Healy, and although she is listed among the cast, an item ran a day earlier in the *Detroit Free Press*: "Betty Healy, who functioned chiefly in *A Night in Spain* in a highly decorative capacity, while Ted Healy provided much of the comedy, is going out with an act that includes 20 girls. Ted continues in *A Night in Spain*."

Betty's act did not go out on tour, and she was no longer listed among the cast when *A Night in Spain* moved on to Chicago and opened at the Four Cohans Theatre on November 28.

The *Chicago Tribune* gave the show a passing grade, with Ted Healy again vying with Phil Baker and Sid Silvers for comedic supremacy (one can bet that the one-upmanship had him slapping a little harder in the sketches). "The show is funniest when Mr. Healy serves as conductor of a band—then and when Mr. Baker and Mr. Silvers go to it. It is loveliest in the vision when, quite early, a stage-wide line of barelegged girls dance in unison in costumes of green and fuchsia."

Also mentioned was "a new chap for the come-on parts named Shemp Howard."

It has been written that Betty's absence from *A Night in Spain* was her own decision, that she was the one who chose to sit out the national tour because of her husband's philandering and drinking, vices that had not created an issue or problem for the Shuberts or for audiences. ("Ted didn't perform drunk onstage," Cassara says. "It upsets your timing.")

As the show settled in for a long run in Chicago, Ted and Betty Healy were a team onstage after all. Ted Healy had picked up a side gig. At night, after the final bows at the Four Cohans, he and Betty performed together at the College Inn, a jazz club and restaurant downstairs in the Hotel Sherman. The joint was an easy run from the theater—only half a block away at the corner of Clark and Randolph streets. It was also one of the country's most incendiary hotspots during Prohibition, a time when alcohol wasn't allowed to be sold but somehow managed to flow anyway.

The couple opened on January 2, 1928, billed as "America's greatest cafe entertainers," leading a cast that included the dance team of Surway and Norway and singer-dancer Bee Palmer. Bee had been credited with inventing the "shimmy" in the 1910s and was now billed as "the Bernhardt of song," accompanied by her husband, Al Siegel, on piano and a four-piece Black jazz band. Between shows, Maurice Sherman's twelve-man All Star Orchestra provided "the hottest dance music in town" with some of the best jazz musicians in the business (*White* jazz musicians, as discriminatory practices kept Black musicians from being hired in "White" hotels).

A reviewer from *Variety* checked in at the College Inn on February 1 and saw that the room had "blossomed out with almost a cabaret show" with Ted Healy as emcee. "Considering the Inn gets all the good-time Charlies from in and out of town, it's a revelation to watch Ted keep enthusiasts under control" with his "mixture of gagging, clowning, dancing and table-talk." Betty Healy got a mention for her "crossfire" routine with Ted—lots of fast gag lines back and forth, leading to Betty singing and showing off her dance moves. "Healy has a straight man from 'Spain,' working fast, short and snappy gagging and cashing in on it extensively." The straight man was not identified. He most likely was not Shemp. The man from *Variety* suggested that the show would go over very well in New York.

While Ted Healy was moonlighting at the College Inn, big changes were on the horizon over at the Four Cohans Theatre. At the beginning of March, Phil Baker, Healy's main laugh rival in *A Night in Spain,* quit the show. He claimed illness. *The Billboard* hinted that there was more to the pullout, alleging that "there has been a noticeable falling off of attendance at the Four Cohans." Sensing an emergency, J. J. Shubert arrived in Chicago, sussed out the situation, made a phone call, and called in a few favors. "Come and help me out," he asked an old pal, and Al Jolson responded by boarding the *20th Century Limited* from New York City to save the day. Jolson arrived at Chicago Union Station on Friday, March 11, and was onstage that night. Phil Baker? He was out of the show, according to the Shuberts, "permanently"—which meant at least for the time being.

Jolson was perhaps the biggest star in show business. Already a legend in vaudeville and on Broadway, he had only gained in stature since his film *The Jazz Singer* had begun playing in movie and vaudeville houses in October 1927. The movie unspooled as a silent picture with background music, then exploded into scenes with dialogue and music—six songs performed by Jolson. *The Jazz Singer* wasn't the first "talkie," but its success hastened the end of the silent movie era (and eventually closed the lid on vaudeville). So when Jolson joined *A Night in Spain,* his name alone was enough to attract the crowds. Jolson left the heavy lifting to Ted Healy and the gang, often strolling into the theater after 10:00 p.m. to make an appearance onstage at 10:30, when the show might otherwise have been over, and bringing down the house with his own act.

J. J. Shubert's idea to sign Jolson to a four-week deal was a success all right. "*Spain* was finished when Jolson stepped in," *Variety* reported on March 21. "Jolson, however, has brought back the show to capacity. . . .

Addition of Al Jolson saved this one: Jolson's routine near the end of the show holds 'em until all the other shows are out and capacity houses leaving theatre (around 11:30) an ad in itself. . . . His four weeks' visit will give *Spain* a new record on a seventeen-week stay in this town."

Jolson's arrival in Chicago as the new star of *A Night in Spain* sold out the house, gave new legs to the show, and took some of the heat off Ted Healy. It also led to an invitation that would clear the way for Shemp Howard to quit.

Seven

So Fine

The entire cast was invited. Shemp was there, and so were Al Jolson and Ted Healy one morning after a performance of *A Night in Spain* when everyone headed from the theater to another speakeasy in plain sight. This was the historic occasion in the origin story of the Three Stooges, the moment when a crucial point in the comedic triangle was located, reeled in, and made part of the team. Moe Howard had written and talked about it often. Moe remembered it like it was yesterday. How could Moe Howard forget the look in Ted Healy's eyes when his old pal and boss turned to him and said, "Are you thinkin' what I'm thinkin'?"

Then again, Moe remembered it as 1925 at the Marigold Gardens nightclub on North Halsted Street. It was not. The place was the Rainbo Room, part of Fred Mann's Million Dollar Rainbo Gardens entertainment complex at North Clark Street and Lawrence Avenue. The restaurant lounge and showroom was attached to the Rainbo Fronton, a 1,700-seat indoor sports arena built for the Basque sport of jai alai, a gambler-friendly game in which players or teams hurl a ball against a wall and catch it in wicker baskets until one of them misses. In the foreword to Moe's book *I Stooged to Conquer* (a new edition of his autobiography), his daughter Joan mentions the mix-up between 1925 at the Marigold Gardens and 1928 at the Rainbo Gardens. "My father was right about the difficulty of trying to recall hundreds of events and dates. . . . We'll have to forgive him for an inaccuracy or two."

In this case, Moe can be forgiven for not getting the exact details right but not much else. Because there is one fact that Moe left out of the story of Larry Fine's discovery: the fact that *he wasn't there at all!*

"When you read recollections from stars like Milton Berle or George Burns, they'll get the dates wrong, but they're likely to remember the name of the theater or city where an incident took place," says Jeff

Abraham, the comedy archivist, historian, and author. "Let's not forget that Moe was seventy-five years old when he was writing his autobiography, so you can give him something of a pass. At the same time, was Moe telling the story he wanted to be told? You have to ask if Moe had an agenda and was deliberately conflating incidents for his own purposes and self-aggrandizement. If he was, it was done at the expense of Shemp."

Was Moe going beyond exaggeration or a faulty memory? Did he have an ulterior motive? History can be the judge because the "night in Spain" connection was what brought Ted Healy, Al Jolson, and *Shemp* Howard to the Rainbo on Saturday, March 24, 1928. Moe Howard was not there. He was about 800 miles away and not part of the act. We know the date because it was advertised in the *Chicago Tribune* that day. Rainbo owner Fred Mann was hosting special midnight jai alai ("Say *Hi-Li,*" the ad noted helpfully) matches called "The Al Jolson Handicap." Jolson would make a personal appearance, and the company of *A Night in Spain* would be special guests in the Rainbo Room to celebrate the imminent end of their Chicago run. The Rainbo Room was large enough to fit 2,000 diners and another 1,500 dancers. There was soft, romantic lighting; a revolving stage that kept the entertainment and music going nonstop; and, for a place that was prohibited from serving booze, busboys and waiters providing setups and, somehow, enough whisky and other spirits passed around to keep everybody happy.

It was during the show that the men at the Jolson table first laid eyes on the emcee: twenty-five-year-old Larry Fine (born Louis Feinberg in Philadelphia). He was another little guy, about five feet four inches with his hair slicked down. He was wearing a top hat and tuxedo and tails when he grabbed a violin and bow and went into his signature "Russian dance" routine. Everyone in the place clapped along to the beat as Larry leapt and kicked like a Cossack, all the time sawing away at the fiddle as he got closer to the floor, then bounding to his feet. Once on his feet, he was quick on them, a smart and funny emcee who kept the show moving. It wasn't Moe to whom Ted Healy turned to ask, "Are you thinkin' what I'm thinkin?'" It was Shemp who encouraged his boss to hire Larry Fine.

Shemp made the suggestion because he was quitting Ted Healy's act.

"Shemp had received an offer from another agent to do a double act at a much bigger salary, so he gave Healy his two weeks notice and coincidentally that night they threw a party at the Gardens for the cast of *A Night in Spain,*" Fine was quoted in *One Fine Stooge*, the biography by Steve Cox and Jim Terry. "Healy and Shemp took one look at me and Shemp, who was about to leave, suggested to Healy that he could use me and called me to their table and offered me the show."

That was where and when, as the most accurate and verifiable version of the legend has it, the offer was made: "I'll give you ninety bucks a week—and ten dollars more to throw that fiddle away." Or maybe it was "seventy-five dollars a week and ten to ditch the fiddle." Recollections, as we've seen, vary. In this case, Larry Fine recollected that he thanked Healy very much but informed him that his boss, Fred Mann, wouldn't let him out of his contract. Larry Fine further recalled that, as luck would have it, he arrived at work a few days later to find the Rainbo padlocked by the Internal Revenue Service for serving liquor and that, soon after, "Mr. Mann committed suicide from the shame." As Larry told it, on the Wednesday evening after that offer at the Rainbo, he was in the wings of the Four Cohans Theatre. He was standing alongside Al Jolson himself, watching Healy perform, when, on Healy's signal, the great Jolson shoved Larry onstage and into the scene. Larry, forced to wing it, got into the act. He secured the job.

Sigh. It wasn't until May 3, more than a month later, that a federal judge declared the Rainbo club a public nuisance and ordered it padlocked for one year on the basis of "liquor observation evidence" (there were no claims that liquor was sold, only that patrons were seen pouring for themselves). Fred Mann did indeed commit suicide, placing the muzzle of a .32-caliber pistol to his right temple and pulling the trigger while seated on a bench in Chicago's Lincoln Park. But that was on October 8, 1930. Whether Larry Fine actually was pushed onstage by Al Jolson in March 1928 doesn't totally add up, either, considering that Jolson was known to breeze into the theater shortly before his 10:30 p.m. entrance onstage.

What is confirmed is that Shemp Howard was walking away from Ted Healy to go out with an act of his own. He may have been fed up with the battering he had taken from his boss on a nightly basis (and in matinees on Saturdays), working so hard for comparatively little pay while Ted Healy became a bigger and bigger star and, too often, more of an abusive drunk. More likely, Shemp had racked up favorable notices of his own and, judging by the audience reaction, realized that he had enough talent and charisma to give it a go. He did not, however, leave the show immediately. He stayed on for at least a couple of weeks, perhaps to help Larry Fine learn the routines.

The cast of *A Night in Spain* performed their last two shows in Chicago and said "so long" to Al Jolson on Saturday, April 7. The show opened the following day at the Shubert Theatre in Cincinnati, Ohio. Ted Healy was co-headliner, with popular singer Aileen Stanley (born Maude Elsie Aileen Muggeridge). Betty Healy stayed behind. Shemp Howard's name was listed in the ads for the Cincinnati stand. He apparently was still in the production—"apparently" because William Smith Goldenburg at the *Cincinnati Enquirer* singled out "Shemp Clark" and Sam Braun for lending "their capable support to Ted Healy," who "injects hilarious humor, much of it of the rough-and-tumble variety interspersed between those moments of rare intimacy that he knows so well how to establish with the sympathetic audience. Without Ted Healy, *A Night in Spain* would be dreary amusement. With him, it is perfect or as nearly so as a revue could be."

Shemp was listed in the newspaper ads for the April 16 touchdown at the Alvin Theatre in Pittsburgh. It appears, however, that his two-week notice had been fulfilled and that Larry Fine had moved in. Elmer Rigdon wrote in the *Pittsburgh Press* that "Ted Healy . . . weaves his way throughout the piece wise-cracking in a manner that gets many laughs. . . . Bobby Pinkus, Larry Fine and Sam Braun are absurdly funny in a burlesque singing act."

An equally significant item had popped up a day earlier in the *New York Daily News*: "The newest of the nocturnal revue series the Shuberts are in the habit of presenting on Broadway will be an opus called *A Night in Venice*. This will be done with the *A Night in Spain* troupe including Phil Baker, Sid Silvers and Ted Healy. Rehearsals will start June 15."

The crossover was definitely complete by the time the show reached the Shubert Detroit Opera House on April 30. Shemp Howard's name was still in the press release articles printed in the local newspapers, but in the display ads, his name had been replaced by Larry Fine's. And as the show moved on, Larry held his own and even managed to stand out among the more than 160 performers spread among two acts and thirty-one scenes. After a one-nighter in Des Moines, Iowa, the show rolled into Kansas City, Missouri, for a week at the Shubert Theatre on 10th Street. Of opening night on May 20, the reviewer for the *Kansas City Times* singled out for praise "a little comedian named Larry Fine. He gets kicked all over the place and seems to like it."

Like it or not, that was how it had to be played with Ted Healy. Little Larry was getting big laughs but taking hard hits from Healy, who was drinking but dominating as the masterful lowbrow joke teller and emcee. In Kansas City, Phil Baker had rejoined the show. He was back to his more sophisticated stooge act with his compatriot in the balcony and drawing big laughs with his accordion. Maybe that got Ted slapping harder, but Larry Fine knew there was a goal. And he was closer to it. After a week in Kansas City, the train, pulling a dozen baggage cars and Pullmans, blew into Tulsa, Oklahoma, for Monday night at Convention Hall and then chugged on into Texas for one-night stands in Dallas, Abilene, and, on May 31, El Paso.

Two days after that final Texas stop, the train full of comics, singers, dancers, musicians, acrobats, and chorus girls disembarked at Central

Station in downtown Los Angeles and made their way a mile up Fifth Street to the Biltmore Theatre, at the corner of Grand Avenue.

J. J. Shubert wasn't sure how the jaded crowd would respond when *A Night in Spain* met Los Angeles on June 2. Just in case, he made sure that he was holding an ace up his sleeve. He had Al Jolson in the audience. Everyone in the theater was made aware of Jolson's presence, and the show was literally stopped when Phil Baker introduced the star and convinced him to come onstage. Jolson did twenty minutes, a performance that included, according to the *Los Angeles Evening Express*, singing a ballad "sans makeup," meaning that the audience did not get to see him in blackface. Jolson also let slip "that he was a part owner with the Shuberts of the enterprise"—which probably sweetened the deal that got him to hop that train to Chicago to join the show in April.

J. J. Shubert needn't have worried. The crowd was wildly enthusiastic even after Jolson left the stage, and in the days ahead, *A Night in Spain* did well enough without the opening night treat. *Los Angeles Times* critic Edwin Schallert called the revue "a show of speed, giddiness and frequently very effective broad humor" that "aroused a somewhat fevered response of enthusiasm upon its opening." The usual suspects, including Sid Silvers in the balcony bit, Helba Huara's dancing, the chorus girls' "seminudity," and Ted Healy, were singled out. So, somewhat surprisingly, was a supporting player. "Ted Healy . . . is most consistently victorious, with the help of a very funny-faced and semi-inarticulate type in the person of Larry Fine," Schallert wrote. "There is no end of an uproar when they are doing their serenade act with the 'hey-hey' shouting of Fine gradually leading to the loss of his evening clothes, owing to revengeful treatment by Healy."

It is ironic, stepping in and filling the breach, that Larry Fine was singled out for a number that Shemp Howard may have spent months perfecting. "Hey Hey" was a popular jazz term and, coincidentally, the title of a concurrent vaudeville revue "built around the idea of modern youth and the jazz age" accompanying picture shows on the Paramount/Publix circuit. A version of the "Hey Hey" routine shows up in the 1933 Metro-Goldwyn-Mayer (MGM) short *Plane Nuts*, a filmed version of Ted Healy's vaudeville act, starring Healy and (Moe) Howard, Fine, and (Curly) Howard. All the comedy onstage leads to a rendition of the bouncy number "Dinah."

It's a bit of a free-for-all, with Healy and his stooges singing and dancing—"Dinah, is there anyone finer in the state of Carolina?"— until Larry, at Healy's left, begins to dance wildly while ad-libbing, Jolson style, "I'm from the South, the good old sunny South, and I'm coming home again, mammy! *Hey hey*!" And when Larry says, "Hey hey!," Healy gives him a hard smack across the face and tears off a piece of his clothing. It begins with his tuxedo shirt front—"Hey hey!"—another slap and a sleeve of his jacket—"Hey hey!"—*Smack!*—and more jacket—until Larry's pants fall down and he and the Howards beat a hasty exit stage left. (A similar version, in which Shemp is whacked when he interrupts the song "Nellie" with the jazz exclamation "Hotcha!," shows up in that Fireman's Ball performance in *Soup to Nuts*. Both films show the inherent comedy between the tall Healy and the much shorter assistants—and display the force and impact of Healy's slaps and shoves, which were real and would cause even a film viewer to flinch.)

After three weeks in Los Angeles, *A Night in Spain* moved up the coast and opened on June 24 at the Curran Theatre in San Francisco. By this time, Ted Healy, always the crowd-pleaser, had added a new, foolproof bit to his act: an Al Jolson impersonation.

Meanwhile, Shemp was about 2,800 miles east, on the road with his own act. The author and investigator Bill Cassara found that the act, Shemp Howard & Co., was at the Stroud Theatre in Stroudsburg, Pennsylvania, on June 14, 1928, starring in a revue called *Hokum of 1928*. According to Gary Lassin, they played three nights, but there wasn't much more to Shemp's solo tour. He was back with the Shuberts, Ted Healy, and Larry Fine on September 2, when *A Night in Spain* returned to Chicago for two weeks at the Majestic Theatre.

The first announcement of Shemp Howard's return to *A Night in Spain* was low-key: he was name-checked in a capsule review in the *Chicago Tribune* on September 5 and listed in an ad in the *Cincinnati Enquirer* a week before the show arrived at the Shubert Theatre on September 30. The names of Larry Fine and Bobby Pinkus also were listed among the cast. In the ever-evolving group of Ted Healy assistants, brother-in-law Sam Braun was out.

It would take a second glance at the newspaper ad to notice the names, however. The centerpiece of the display was the picture of a scantily clad chorus girl, one of "70 sweetly seductive senoritas" who were among the reasons for the capacity crowd at the Shubert that Sunday evening (and for criticism from bluenose critics in some cities). The review in the *Enquirer* praised Ted Healy as one who "knows how to keep an audience chuckling. . . . His acrobatic stunts and his eccentric direction of the Serenaders bring one perilously close to convulsions." Shemp Howard and Larry Fine were among the Serenaders in that sketch. Not mentioned by name in the *Enquirer*, they were singled out in the *Kentucky Press*, published in Covington, just across the Ohio River. When reviewer Frank Aston wrote that "Shemp Howard, Larry Fine and Bobby Pinkus are immense in a series of grotesque characterizations," it may have been the first time that Shemp and Larry Fine were reviewed together, as part of a team.

Shemp and the cast opened a week at the Shubert Rialto Theatre in St. Louis on October 7. The critic for the *St. Louis Star* marked the show as "in spots, extremely crude and ribald" yet "extremely fast and tuneful, and above all . . . extremely humorous." Ted Healy "was all over the place, winding up with an impersonation of Al Jolson that was a knockout. He also gave a burlesque of the master of ceremony business . . . in this, he was assisted by Larry Fine, a long-haired gentleman whose expression is good for a laugh or a whole series of laughs."

A week later, the show unpacked in Kansas City—without co-headliner Phil Baker, who, according to the *Kansas City Times*, "'jumped the team' after the Saturday night performance in St. Louis with little warning and less courtesy. He went back to New York and took Sid Silvers, his chattering ally, with him." Baker and Silvers missed out on the Shubert's largest-ever Sunday night crowd. The show was much the same as when it passed through Kansas City in the spring. The *Times* reviewer wrote that "some will think the girls could stand more clothes in more than one instance, and a couple of the 'gags' should be given a large dose of fresh air," but also proclaimed, "This Ted Healy is funny" and "of the rest of the company, Shemp Howard and Larry Fine are funny as 'boob' comedians."

The show made its way through Indianapolis, Buffalo, Columbus, Akron, and the Victory Theatre in Dayton, Ohio, where Joe Keller wrote in the *Herald* that "the refreshing and jovial" Ted Healy "works with an easy manner that makes you think he is having the best time in his life working for you." While working for Healy, "the three merry misfits, Larry Fine, Shemp Howard and Lawrence Andrenni, who are with Healy almost constantly, bolster up the comedy on more than one occasion."

The only really negative reaction came from the *Buffalo Evening News* after the show opened on October 29 at the city's Shubert Teck Theatre on Main Street. The combination of hilarious comedy, stunning dance work, and song was boiled down by the reviewer to "a combination of vulgarities, carnalities and banalities" and "anatomical displays . . . presented with little eye for beauty, grace or dignity" (an observation that was reflected in the display ad for the show that ran on the same page: a cartoon of a near-naked chorus girl with the captions "An eye full for all" and "A leg up on all revues ever produced").

> The humors are largely of the physical culture type, such as the fetching of resounding kicks upon the persons of unexpected young ladies, the tearing of coats, collars and shirts from the low comedian, and the grabbing of him about the nose and pulling and hauling of him about the stage. These playful antics are the indulgences of Ted Healy, the principal buffoon.

Shemp Howard, who would know all too well about being grabbed, pulled, and hauled across the stage by his nose, got another break from the "playful antics" in December. While Ted Healy retreated to his estate in Darien, Connecticut, Shemp could return to Brooklyn with his wife and twenty-one-month-old son. He would be back on the road with Healy soon enough. There would be shows on the vaudeville circuit in January and February and rehearsals for the Shuberts' latest Broadway-bound revue. Just as *The Passing Show* was reassembled into *A Night in Spain*, so would the shiniest pieces of *Spain* be polished and transformed into *A Night in Venice*.

The coming weeks would be a time to recharge and to answer a nagging question: whatever happened to Moe?

Eight

Like a Rolling Stone

Let's jump ahead six months or so to June 18, 1929; hand a couple of pennies to the newsboy; grab the *New York Daily News*; and flip through to the amusements pages. Running across the top of page 34 is another of Broadway columnist Mark Hellinger's photo comic strips. This three-panel fumetti, titled "Broadway—Sounds Reasonable," is "posed by Shemp Howard, Ted Healy, Larry Fine, and Harry Howard" of the hit Broadway revue *A Night in Venice*.

In each panel, Shemp Howard is on the left, and Healy is crouched in the middle. Harry Howard—that's Moe—is far right, with Larry Fine standing behind Moe and Healy. The quartet is dressed for the stage: Healy in a top hat, jacket, and tie and the other three in their flamboyant Venetian carnival costumes. Larry sports a gondolier's boater. Moe is hatless but shows off his trademark bowl cut. Shemp wears a long, cylindrical, brimless stovepipe hat, taller than Healy's:

> PANEL 1: *Shemp looks up at Larry. Larry and Moe look at Shemp.*
> LARRY: Let's play a game, fellows. The guy that makes the funniest face wins a prize.
>
> PANEL 2: *All eyes on Shemp.*
> TED (*giving Shemp the side-eye*): I'm not going to play that game.
> LARRY: Why not?
>
> PANEL 3: *Ted, Larry, and Moe look at Shemp. Shemp stares into the camera, deadpan.*
> TED: Look at the start he has!

Regarding the comic strip more than ninety years later, one notices the details in the first panel. The photo retoucher's work makes it appear that Shemp is wearing eyeliner. The feminine *prettiness* is enhanced by the locks of his long hair flowing from inside his tall hat to below his right ear.

Like a Rolling Stone: When the trio made it to Broadway in A Night in Venice, *Shemp was the star.* © Daily News, *L.P. (New York). Used with permission.*

Combine that with their stage costumes and lids, and the group resembles not so much a vaudeville team as a rock 'n' roll band, specifically the Rolling Stones, in those photo sessions from 1967 and 1968: the era of *Their Satanic Majesties Request*, *Beggars Banquet*, and *Rock and Roll Circus*. One thing is quite clear from the staging of the photos. Moe "Harry" Howard might be Charlie Watts. Larry could be Bill Wyman, the everyman. And Ted Healy? Obviously, he's the front man onstage but in this case as an equal to the star; let's say he's Keith Richards.

But there's no doubt: the tallest hat, that look into the camera lens, that face with its beauty in ugliness. In this group, Shemp is Mick Jagger.

Or was Shemp actually Brian Jones, the founder and original leader of the Rolling Stones until he was edged out of the leadership role and, ultimately, the band by Jagger and Richards? That may offer another reason why Moe seemed eager to denigrate his older brother while laying down his official first-person account of the Three Stooges' evolution, good-naturedly combining some very tangled history into a neat eleven-year, unopened package. "Help me out for a week," begged Ted Healy. "Well, the week lasted eleven years," Moe claimed to Mike Douglas on his television show. "I was smart. I took Healy's place later on."

By Moe's telling, he was always the character he had come to play onscreen in dozens of short film comedies—the boss, the mastermind, the taskmaster, the star of the show—even when he graciously stepped back to let his younger brother Curly take the spotlight. But within that "week that lasted eleven years," there was a major gap from the middle of 1925 until the beginning of 1929. During this period, closing in on three and a half years, Moe was out of the picture.

Shemp, whom Moe painted as the bedwetting, phobic whiner, had spent two of those years working night after night on stages across the country, traveling by train with the cast of *A Night in Spain,* sleeping in strange hotel rooms, arriving on Broadway, getting big laughs, getting singled out, and getting recognition in the *New York Times.* When the show went on the road, he took the hits along with the curtain calls. When he had the confidence to quit the successful revue and strike out on his own, he first helped find and train his replacement. After returning to *A Night in Spain* near the end of its run, he got in sync and comedic rhythm with Larry Fine—all the while perfecting a distinct comic persona.

So where was Moe Howard? Where was the brains of the operation, the star?

He was back in Brooklyn, working for his mother.

Not long after Moe Howard married Helen Schonberger in June 1925, his bride urged him to stay home. Sure, she had show business in the family—who was more "show business" than cousin Erich Weisz, known to the world as Harry Houdini? But Helen didn't want a husband on the road with all the distractions and temptations. So Moe Howard went back to being Moe Horwitz of southwest Brooklyn and went to work for his mother, Jennie, in the real estate business. In the summer of 1926, Helen discovered that she was pregnant, and with a baby on the way and the added responsibilities that would bring, Moe studied for and obtained his real estate license.

That's not to say that Moe didn't keep a hand (or at least a finger or two) in show business—more specifically, the theater, although nothing on the level of professionalism that Shemp was carrying out. On March 9, 1927, a musical comedy called *Stepping Along,* billed as "a musical dream in three episodes," opened at the Stillwell Theatre on 24th Avenue and 86th Street in Bensonhurst. According to the *Brooklyn Daily Times,* the play boasted "a cast composed entirely of Bensonians" and was produced under the auspices of the Young Folks' League of the Bensonhurst Jewish Community House. Members of the Young Folks' League sold tickets. Proceeds would go to the building fund of the Jewish community center under construction at Bay Parkway and 79th Street (the center was completed and opened in November). "Moe Horowitz" and Sam S. Cohen wrote the book, lyrics, and music and were codirectors.

"Seldom does a show begin a half an hour late and despite the handicap come galloping home a winner, to the almost continuous applause of the audience, but *Stepping Along,* a musical dream in three episodes, was a winner from beginning to end. This rollicking comedy . . . played to a jammed house last night, and its patrons said they got more than their money's worth."

The *Daily Times* reviewer wrote that "stars were out in plenty . . . in all there were about sixty" and pointed out a number of the local "stars" in the cast, including Beatrice Hoffman, Ruth Podd, Esther Weinstein, Morris Golden, Milton Medlin and Milton Heffer, and the Epsteins: Hockey, Morty, and Sam. Moe stayed behind the scenes.

According to Moe, he and Helen were renting an apartment on Avenue J near Coney Island Avenue, a couple of miles north of Bensonhurst. There would be another show, *Still Stepping*, later that year, but Moe's greatest production premiered on April 2 with the birth of daughter Joan.

In Stooges lore, 1927 was the year in which Moe went all out in real estate and made $40,000 buying and selling properties. The following year, he took some of that money and, with more funding from investors, including his younger brother Jerome, went into the construction business. He and his team built four houses on a block of 43rd Street in Bath Beach. The project bankrupted him. Moe tried opening a store selling distressed merchandise. That didn't pan out, either.

In December 1928, Moe made a call to Ted Healy. By Moe's account, the timing was fortuitous. He claimed that Healy told him, "You know Moe, I was going to call you in the morning to ask you, Shemp, and Larry to join me in the Shuberts' *A Night in Venice* on Broadway. How about it, Moe?" One would guess that there was a little more bowing and scraping on Moe's part, but around Christmastime, Moe, his wife, and baby daughter made the pilgrimage to Healy's estate in Connecticut. Moe and Healy worked up some routines for the new show, and Healy worked Moe back into the act.

Rehearsals were some weeks off. In the meantime, Moe would join "Ted Healy & Company" on a quick tour of vaudeville houses. This time, it was very clear: Moe would also be playing a supporting role to Shemp.

NINE

The Elephant in the Room

Ted Healy had expenses, such as the upkeep of the palatial estate in Connecticut and of his former stage partner and unhappy wife, Betty, who was floating in and out with divorce certainly in the future (if she didn't kill him first). Healy knew what the problem was. He was a star. He liked to drink, and, sure, he played around with the girls. What did Betty expect when he's backstage or on the road with seventy bare-ass dancing girls floating in and out of his dressing room? Moe wrote that he saw it firsthand when Betty returned to Darien. He claimed to have witnessed Betty enter through the front door while Ted shushed and shoved a showgirl out the back. Of course, Moe made it up and exaggerated, but the kernel of truth was there. Ted Healy's marriage to Betty Braun was as good as kaput, and before the end of the year, the split would be made public.

This last run of *A Night in Spain* had turned Ted Healy into a bona fide star. Healy knew that he had it all. The stage was his living room. He could step into any act and make it funnier. He could roll off an old joke pulled from a dirty burlesque show and make it seem clean, all because he knew how to tell it. And when he worked with these—assistants, this gang, these short little goons—the laughter grew with every slap, shove, and kick.

Now, as he was sliding into another Broadway show, he was perfecting all the elements of his act, and for that, he needed to warm up. And he could use the cabbage.

In January 1929, soon after the holidays, Healy signed with the Radio-Keith-Orpheum circuit for a tour of vaudeville theaters. He would roll out a "greatest hits" version of his bits from *A Night in Spain* and work the rest of the bill as emcee in what was a cut-down, cut-rate version of that revue. Healy opened a week's engagement at the Albee in Cincinnati on January 27, leading a bill that included Florrie Levere doing impressions of stage stars, accompanied by her husband, Lou Handman, on piano; an auburn-haired jazz group called Babe Egan and Her Hollywood Redheads; and

Chinese acrobats Dack Shing & Co. The show played between screenings of the Norma Shearer silent comedy *Lady of Chance*.

Opening night at the Albee was, according to the *Cincinnati Enquirer*, "a nonstop party with Ted Healy as master of revels," Healy being "a comedian with few equals [who] explodes numerous bombs of mirth. He has retained many of the stunts and sketches he performed in the Shubert revue. . . . Two of his hard-boiled playmates with 'Hey-hey' complex assist him."

Note the mention of *two* "hard-boiled playmates" rather than three. While this was an opportunity for Shemp, Moe (billed alternatively as "Moe Howard" and "Harry Howard"), and Larry Fine, the future "Three Stooges," to work together onstage for the first time, the momentous first appearance would have to wait. While the Healy show went on the road, Larry Fine was in Atlantic City, New Jersey, with his wife, Mabel, who was soon to give birth. A daughter, Phyllis Jo Fine, would be born in Atlantic City Hospital on February 9.

Meanwhile, the Ted Healy revue rolled on through Cleveland and Youngstown, Ohio, before arriving at Fox's Academy Theatre on East 14th Street in Manhattan, where *The Billboard* had a reviewer in the audience for the afternoon show on February 18. Sidney Harris wrote a review that was published on February 23 in which he referred to Shemp and Moe Howard as "comedians of a high order." He returned to *The Billboard* on March 2 to focus on Ted Healy and company. "Ted Healy is our idea of a knockout of a comedian. . . . Shemp and Moe Howard and a pretty girl dancer capably assist Healy. Shemp is an excellent comedy foil and a first-grade funster in his own right.

"Effective chatter between Healy and the Howard boys starts the offering off in real laugh-getting style. Shemp scores also in low comedy business with Healy." Harris pointed out Healy's skirt-lifting blackout standby "The Photographer," with Moe standing in as the proprietor; "more clowning with the Howard boys"; and "a rib-tickling session with a canine wrestling with Shemp and the girl."

Two items of note. Once again, it was Shemp Howard, not his younger brother, who was the preeminent Healy assistant and something of a star in his own right. And it is puzzling, in light of the tales of Shemp's unreasonable phobias and fear of canines, that he would be grappling onstage with Ted Healy's German shepherd. If one is to believe Three Stooges lore, the idea of Shemp wrestling a dog makes about as much sense as Shemp wrestling a bear!

We'll get to that soon enough.

In early March, the Shuberts announced that rehearsals were under way in New York for the third of their "continental nights." "Having concerned themselves with evenings in Paris and Spain out of town," they would now set their revue in Venice, Italy. *A Night in Venice* would be headlined by Ted Healy and actress Ann Seymour, who had starred in the Shuberts' *Boom Boom*. A Broadway musical comedy revue with a dash of French farce, *Boom Boom* was closing at the end of the month. The *Venice* book was by Harold Atteridge, music by Lee David and Maury Rubens, and lyrics by J. Keirn Brennan and Moe Jaffe. Lew Morton and Thomas A. Hart would direct, while Busby Berkeley choreographed much of the dancing for a cast that included sixty dancers. As the Shuberts did with *A Night in Spain*, they hired on two distinct dancing troupes. The Chester Hale and Allan K. Foster Girls would prove that the more legs and the more bare flesh, the better. The Shuberts planned to begin previews somewhere out of town sometime in April. The show would land on Broadway whenever it was good and ready—although the previews could be extended if the ticket demand was great enough.

Once again, as emcee, Ted Healy would just be Ted, running rampant through the production, working with his own supporting cast, and stepping into the acts of others. While he would rely on some of his crowd-pleasing evergreen material, Healy also worked to reconfigure his team. Waiting for Larry Fine to get back on board from paternity leave, he had added Fred Sanborn to the company. Sanborn (aka Fred "Pansy" Sanborn) was twenty-nine, a strange little vaudeville musician and comic actor with more than a touch of similarity to Charlie Chaplin's Tramp. He had a funny, swishy walk and performed mostly in pantomime. Rather than a small bushy mustache, he had big bushy eyebrows that bounced and bobbled expressively along his forehead. Sanborn was a virtuoso on the xylophone (another vaudeville specialty that he would show off in *Soup to Nuts*) and would be one of a group of supporting players, along with Shemp Howard, Larry Fine, and Harry Howard, that would be billed as "Ted Healy and His Gang."

"I don't think anyone was counting them as a trio or four," Bill Cassara clarifies. "They were part of the ensemble. In *Soup to Nuts*, Sanborn was an interesting character, the mute, he kind of carried the plot, and he really had the best ending. He was necessary for the stage, but I don't think he intermeshed with Moe, Larry, and Shemp."

Fred Sanborn seemed a little frail for the abuse that Shemp, Larry, and Moe could take and would find his place in and around the action. He would also show off his chops on the xylophone, playing in the orchestra pit during intermissions. But the other three—the brothers Howard and Larry Fine—all matched up pretty well heightwise, all equally rough and funny-looking, and once they found their rhythm did have a quality that could make them a team. Healy began to craft more of his act around encounters with them. He even cut from his act a talent that he was most proud of: his singing. Now Healy would start a song, only to be interrupted by one or all of the idiots. Audiences loved it. Over the course of the *Venice* run, Shemp, Larry, and Harry would become identified as a trio—Ted Healy's Racketeers or Ted Healy's Southern Gentlemen:

HEALY: Tell me, where are you boys from?
SHEMP: We're from the South.
HEALY: Did you ever hear, did you ever hear of Abraham Lincoln?
SHEMP (*extending a hand*): Glad to meet you stranger—
Healy responds with a hard slap.

A Night in Venice—two acts and a couple dozen scenes—opened its first preview on April 2, perilously close to the Great White Way, at the Shubert Theatre in Newark, New Jersey. This would be the first show in which Shemp Howard, Larry Fine, and Moe Howard would work together as a trio. Whatever the critics would ultimately say about the production—and, yes, one could already guess they would say there wasn't much of a book and that the show probably won't have much to do with Venice—there was no arguing that it was big. After Newark, when *Venice* skipped over Manhattan and moved to the Majestic Theatre in downtown Brooklyn on April 8, Arthur Pollock of the *Brooklyn Daily Eagle* called it the biggest production to ever come to the Majestic. "There are four carloads of scenery and properties and 24 large vans are required to cart it. A stage crew of 60 men worked 14 hours to take in the show; a crew of 48 took 12 hours to 'set' it." The cast numbered around 150. Along with the dozens of dancing girls, comedians, acrobats, and other performers were the Stevens Brothers, a duo who included in their act a partner who was not a Stevens but a member of the Ursidae family—"Ursidae," as in ursine, a bear. After a prolonged face-slapping routine, one brother would lead the large bear (later identified by the *Boston Globe* as a grizzly named "Big Boy") out from the wings and hold the animal back by its halter and strap while the other brother and an assistant would wrestle it. Then, as Pollock recounted, Ted Healy would step in.

"Ted Healy drew four paid spectators from the audience, inviting them to wrestle with a bear. The four unsightly fellows spent some fifteen long minutes slapping each other's faces. That was perhaps the highest point in the evening's humor, following which one of the slappers wrestled with the bear and had his clothes ripped off."

Those four "paid spectators," as might be expected, included Healy's gang members. Shemp would be first to approach the bear, which would

Larry Fine, Moe Howard, and Shemp work together for the first time as Ted Healy's Southern Gentlemen after Moe returned from a long hiatus in his mother's business.

grab his ankle and send him sprawling and then, when Shemp jumped up, chase him around the stage. The routine worked so well the first time out that the Healy gang played it every night and twice on matinee days. In each show, Shemp Howard, the "scaredy-cat" with a deathly fear of animals, went one-on-one with a bear. It's one thing to roll around with a dog, something else for even a brave person to rassle with a 400-pound grizzly bear.

Shemp Howard's name was listed among other featured acts in newspaper ads in the days leading to the show's arrival in Philadelphia. Hometown boy Larry Fine and Moe—as "Harry Howard"—were also billboarded, each separately, not as a group. *A Night in Venice* opened at Shubert's Forrest Theatre on April 15. *Variety* had a reviewer on the aisle the following week. Arthur B. Waters called the Shuberts' latest—"referred to as an extravaganza and not revue"—"one of the best of the firm's productions in recent seasons" with "plenty of comedy, and although there is a generous amount of dirt in the comedy, it registers with a bang." Waters added,

> Healy works with a gang, that, for looks, is collectively and individually, homelier than the bunch Joe Cook has around him and just as funny. Shemp Howard reappears with his brother Harry and Larry Fine, and this trio serves as a remarkable foil for Healy's nonsense. They work with him in virtually every number, in his special appearances before the curtain and in the scenes that advance whatever plot there is to the piece. They also appear in a pretentious sketch in the second act, a travesty on "Street Scene." Their parts demand that they take plenty of punishment and also look dumb. They accomplish both.
>
> In addition, there are the Stevens Brothers and their bear. . . . Healy and the Howards work in with this one and it's a riot.

Waters pointed out that the show was very expensive and that "it will have to gross plenty everywhere to profit. That it should do on the comedy angle alone, not forgetting the gorgeousness, the nudity and the risqué lines."

His prediction didn't quite pan out. Despite the friendly reviews and audiences, business was slow (*Variety* blamed it on the theater), so the Shuberts cut their losses. Although the Philadelphia stop had been penciled in for four weeks, the show closed early on May 4. *A Night in Venice* moved on to the Alvin Theatre in Pittsburgh two nights later. The *Pittsburgh Press* offered a preview by quoting additional praise that Arthur B. Waters had written for the *Philadelphia Public Ledger*. Waters also doubled down on his comparison of Shemp and his colleagues, in terms of looks, to the comic assistants working with the versatile vaudeville and Broadway entertainer Joe Cook:

> Mr. Healy has enlisted the services of a strange collection of assistants whose faces surpass those of Joe Cook's corps of helpers for weird and fantastic ugliness.

Both of Waters's reviews support the fact that Shemp Howard, not Moe, was preeminent among the gang, the "boss stooge." Waters's addendum in the *Public Ledger* should also be noted as the first review in which Shemp Howard's delicate features were immortalized in print as "ugly."

After a week in the Midwest, the Shuberts wasted little time before taking their latest revue straight to Broadway. *A Night in Venice* opened on May 21 at the Sam S. Shubert Theatre on West 44th Street. The cast had been trimmed, tweaked, and shifted and the routines edited. Arthur Pollock, critic for the *Brooklyn Daily Eagle*, had been very critical of the show when it pulled into the Majestic in April. Now, he said, "It's good."

"It was back-lot entertainment when it first appeared," Pollock wrote. "It has become a big, vigorous and lively show."

There was, as with past productions, the issue of the plot. Every critic wanted a plot. Story lines and cultural accuracy were never the strong points of the *A Night In* franchise, and *A Night in Venice* upheld the tradition. The show opened at the Roosevelt Field airport on Long Island, made a stop in the city of canals, checked in at a gymnasium aboard an ocean liner, spent time with a bunch of near-naked chorus girls on an ice floe in the North Atlantic, arrived at a golf course, and ultimately wound up with Shemp Howard being knocked about by a trained bear.

Wilfred J. Riley, reviewing the show for *The Billboard*, understood that "*A Night in Venice* is a little bit of everything without being much of anything. It begins and ends as a book show; in between it is a hybrid of revue and vaudeville. Its in-between moments are the most successful." And the most successful of the in-between moments were the ones featuring Ted Healy, who "heads the cast and stands head and shoulders above every other feature of the production.

"The highlight of the show comes in the second act when Healy and his band present their 'nut comedy' specialty with the assistance of Shemp Howard, Harry Howard and Larry Fine." That "nut comedy" routine, during which Shemp interjected a "Hey hey!" or a "Hotcha"! amid the close-harmony singing of "Nellie," also got a mention from esteemed theater critic J. Brooks Atkinson in the *New York Times*: "Healy . . . is leading his jazz band while three of the frowziest numbskulls ever assembled are trying to put over, with the familiar flourishes of the show business, a ballad about that dress that Nellie wore. It is innocuous enough until the most vocal and disreputable of the trio insists upon interjecting, between bars, two thick-witted claps of the hand and two 'Hey, Heys' denoting rising enthusiasm. Then it is that this scuffle begins, shirt fronts are torn, feet stamped on and the singer is savagely tackled around the neck. Although Mr. Healy and his numbskulls have already exhibited this violent skit in a previous Shubert revue, it is still a masterpiece of slapstick comedy, and the best number in the new summer carnival."

Shemp, "the most vocal and disreputable of the trio," was also singled out in *Variety*'s review. "Healy's four plants are funny boys, one (Shemp Howard) more outspoken than the average goof character and himself a comic of apparent ad lib ability."

Rowland Field, in the *Brooklyn Daily Times*, praised Ted Healy for keeping the laughs coming, "thick and fast . . . again accompanied in several of his best scenes by his three ludicrous assistants who always are a joyful help in creating laughter." Of the three, only Shemp Howard was mentioned as one of the principals in the show—along with "the trained bear that wrestles."

If Moe Howard was looking for attention as the first among equals, he made it hard on himself by performing under a different name. As was mentioned earlier, he was identified as both "Moe Howard" and "Harry Howard" in various newspaper display ads. In the playbill for the Broadway run, he was listed on page 19 as Moe Howard, and on page 23, he was Harry Howard, playing the character "Moe." Shemp was listed as "Shemp Howard," his name right below Ted Healy's.

So Moe had his place, Larry had his, and, with Shemp at the helm, the trio solidified. In early June, before that "Rolling Stones" fumetti appeared in the *Daily News*, newspapers around the country ran an item similar to this one:

> The tremendous popularity of Ted Healy and the so-called "gang" which supports him in the Shubert revue, *A Night in Venice*, has brought about their signing of a contract whereby Mr. Healy and his supporters, including Shemp Howard, Harry Howard and Larry Fine, will stick together for a period of not less than three years. While the act may be altered from time to time, the new contract arrangement is principally to keep the same company working together, especially in New York.

No matter that the contract—if it was ever signed—would not hold for three years; the time on Broadway was a break for Shemp, who, more than Moe, had spent so much time on the road with little else to do in his off-hours than play around and gamble. The facilities and treatment backstage at a Broadway theater were superior to what he had experienced on the vaudeville circuit, and the accommodations—well, now, he could head home to his wife and two-year-old son after the show, with fewer distractions on the way.

With his own marriage in shreds, Ted Healy could leave Betty back in Darien and bunk at another of his properties, a house in Sea Gate, the exclusive community at the far western end of Coney Island. The *Brooklyn Daily Eagle* mentioned the "large country home" in a feature on Healy that ran on July 7. "As a personality Ted's done what a great many well-known actors who can afford to do so have known: he has surrounded himself with the gang of friends. Not yes men, but friends. Al Jolson, Phil Baker, Dr. Rockwell, Eddie Cantor—nearly all the Broadway stars—'support' a mob of friends. Ted's 'gang,' however, appears with him on the stage." The *Daily Eagle* added,

> Shemp Howard, for instance, has been his side-kick for more than 22 years. "He knew Ted when—" Howard, in case you haven't seen *A Night in Venice*,

> is that roughneck whom Ted mauls all over the stage because he won't give the right answers. Besides Shemp, there is his brother Harry, who quit the gang temporarily during a period of wealth. Harry is also in the show, and likewise Larry Fine.

It is ironic or sad—or frustrating—that Moe, who had built his show business origin story on a longtime friendship with Ted Healy that began in childhood, would be shunted aside for his timid older brother, a spectator at this point in their success.

"Mr. Healy hardly repeats himself," the *Daily Eagle* feature concluded. "He is always experimenting with new material. The bear act now employed in *A Night in Venice* is absolutely new. Only the other day he asked Shemp Howard about the prospects of working with an elephant."

Incidentally, there exists a photo of Shemp, his brother Moe, Ted Healy, and other members of the cast of *A Night in Venice* in Luna Park, the amusement park on the Coney Island boardwalk, standing around Tillie, a 7,700-pound elephant. Although supposedly phobic and deathly afraid of animals, Shemp is closest to the pachyderm and is the only one besides the animal's trainer with a hand on the beast.

Ten

Soup to Nuts

August 6, 1929, was designated "A Night in Venice Day" at Luna Park. In a clever bit of cross-promotion, park management invited the show's company to spend the afternoon swimming and enjoying the rides and other attractions. Cast members boarded buses outside the Shubert Theatre at noon and made it back from Brooklyn in time for that evening's performance.

The event might have been lost to history had some of the day not been preserved on celluloid. Approximately five minutes of Fox Movietone newsreel footage was "discovered" in the film archives of the University of Southern California in the 1990s. And while Ted Healy was promoted as leading the troupe to the seaside park, it's Shemp Howard and his brother Moe who are featured in the unedited clips. The first segment shows Shemp and Moe standing before a kick line of a dozen chorus girls in slim-fitting tank-top swimsuits and, to the side, a group of men, most dressed like the Howards in tank tops and tight shorts. One wields a ukulele, another a kazoo. Skinny as a rail with long center-parted hair, Shemp is comedy cool and wielding a baton as he looks up toward the camera for his cue and then leads the musicians and singers in a version of the popular Tin Pan Alley tune "My Blackbirds Are Bluebirds Now." Moe, short and sturdy behind his brother, jumps in a second or two late in an attempt to show authority. "All right, you ready? Go!" The music had already begun. Shemp waves the baton and strikes funny poses, spreads his arms wide, and crouches. The girls kick in unison. The kazoo player pantomimes a slide trombone. Everyone sings. "All day long I sing a song, I sing a song 'cause nothing's wrong." Moe scampers behind Shemp, keeping time with his right hand like an orchestra conductor and looking for his moment. He grabs his brother by the arm, turns him around, and slaps him in the face. Shemp reacts comically, dipping to bended knee. When they reach the end of the first verse—"my blackbirds are bluebirds now"—Moe stops the music. "Okay, girls! It's hot enough, I think we go in for a swim and then some eats!" The camera pans with the group as they move to the pool, where a crowd has gathered. Then "Cut!" A close shot, in the water. Moe and Shemp are swimming. Shemp's hair plasters one side of his face. In seven seconds, with strokes that are graceful enough, the Howards swim out of frame.

There's more. Shemp and Moe pose poolside with the chorus girls, on and around the diving board, eating watermelon. When they get their cue, Moe smashes some melon in Shemp's face. Shemp smacks Moe with a long slice. Amid much laughter from the girls, the two men trade watermelon slaps and hits, wrestle, pull hair, and slap each other's faces until one of the girls pushes Moe into the pool. The segment ends when the girls and Moe are about to send Shemp into the water.

According to the official Three Stooges website, it's not known if the footage was ever edited into a newsreel and released to the public. But in an appraisal of Shemp Howard, some of it is invaluable. The opening scene again establishes him as the comedic leader while showing Moe's attempts to assert dominance even in this early stage of his comeback. Most critical are those seven seconds of swim footage. It is enough time to see that Shemp was not panicking, could swim just fine, and was not exhibiting any extreme fear, just as he had not shown phobic fear of animals. The "new" footage, especially those seven seconds, raised the eyebrows—and doubts—of more than one comedy historian who had always read (and sometimes repeated) stories of Shemp's supposed lifelong fear. At this point in his life and career, Shemp may have been an anxious man, but reports of his extreme phobias and fears appear to have been greatly exaggerated.

Ted Healy and his gang returned to Coney Island on September 6 to put on a show for the kids, hundreds of them, at the Half Moon Hotel, the new fourteen-story landmark on the boardwalk. The show was part of an exhibition by the Brooklyn Borough Gas Company, showing off and trying to convince locals of the benefits of gas appliances. Promoting the appearance, the *Brooklyn Daily Times* mentioned that Healy had "for years lived in Bensonhurst and Coney Island, and was currently a well-known resident of Seagate." The item also gave a shout-out to another local hero Healy was bringing along. "Chief among the entertainers will be Healy's 'Nightmare Trio,' headed by Shemp Howard, who is also a resident of Bensonhurst."

A Night in Venice played at the Shubert through the middle of September, then, on September 16, moved seamlessly up 44th Street to the Majestic Theatre. Any doubt about the prominent player in Ted Healy's "Nightmare Trio" was put to rest that month by Mark Hellinger in his

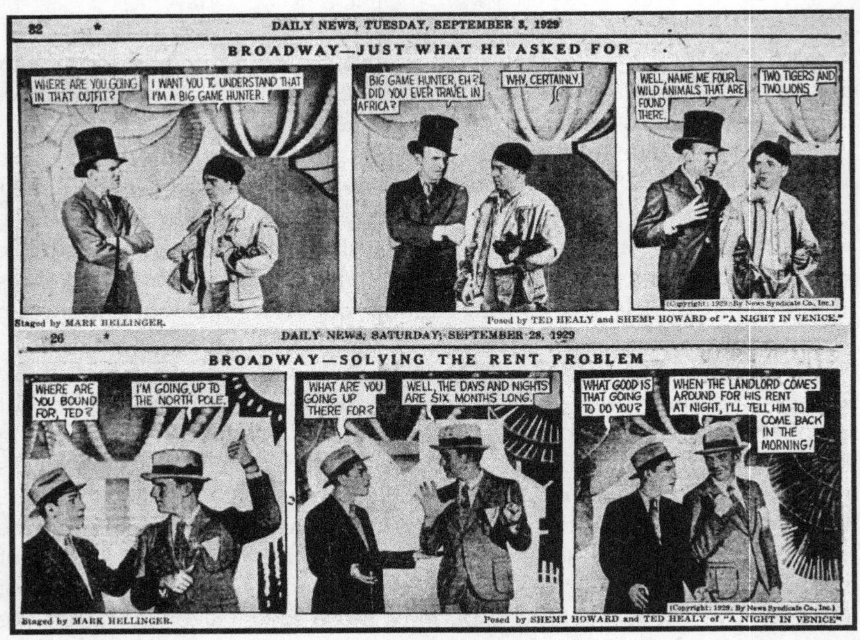

No Moe: By September 1929, readers of the New York Daily News *might have assumed that Ted Healy and Shemp Howard were a two-man team.* © Daily News, *L.P. (New York). Used with permission.*

Broadway photo comic strips in the *Daily News*. The three-panel gag that ran on September 3 was titled "Just What He Asked For" and featured only Shemp and Ted Healy. Healy wears his top hat and suit. Shemp is dressed in his Venetian costume:

PANEL 1
TED: Where are you going in that outfit?
SHEMP: I want you to understand that I'm a big game hunter.

PANEL 2
TED: Big game hunter, eh? Did you ever travel in Africa?
SHEMP: Why, certainly.

PANEL 3
TED: Well, name me four wild animals that are found there.
SHEMP: Two tigers and two lions.

Any suspicions that Larry and Harry were left out inadvertently were put to rest when Hellinger returned to *A Night in Venice* for another fumetti on September 28. "Solving the Rent Problem" again featured only Shemp and Ted Healy. This time, both men were wearing suits, ties, and hats. They could have been a two-man team—and in more ways than one, they were:

PANEL 1
SHEMP: Where are you bound for, Ted?
TED: I'm going up to the North Pole.

PANEL 2
SHEMP: What are you going up there for?
TED: Well, the days and nights are six months long.

PANEL 3
SHEMP: What good is that going to do you?
TED: When the landlord comes around for his rent at night, I'll tell him to come back in the morning!

A Night in Venice, "the extravaganza in two acts," closed on October 19, 1929. It had run for a total of 175 performances on Broadway. Now, as was the tradition with successful Broadway shows, the show went on the road. The first stop was Boston, a two-week stand that opened spectacularly on October 21. The Shubert Theatre echoed with laughter and applause, and the next morning, the *Boston Globe* raved about the extravagant spectacle and "riotous comedy," courtesy of Ted Healy and his gang, "fun-makers, singers, dancers and resourceful specialists whose numbers reach more than five score."

The company was entering its second week in town on Monday, October 28, 1929. That would be Black Monday, the day the Dow Jones Industrial Average declined nearly 13 percent. On Tuesday, the market dropped nearly 12 percent as panicked investors traded some 16 million shares on the New York Stock Exchange. On what would be known as "Black Tuesday," around $14 billion of stock value was lost, and thousands of investors were wiped out. It was the beginning of a stock market crash that ended in November, when share prices on the exchange collapsed. The Roaring Twenties were officially pronounced dead, and the industrialized world swirled into a deep, dark Great Depression.

But for now, for Ted Healy and his Racketeers, the show would go on.

"TED HEALY in the gorgeous extravaganza 'A NIGHT IN VENICE' with ANN SEYMOUR, BETH & BETTY DODGE, 125 Others—And a BEAR!"

With his name above the title, a giant company of performers in support, and a trained bear to boot, Ted Healy took his Racketeers to Philadelphia, Pittsburgh, Newark, and, on November 25, the Grand Opera House in Chicago. This was the beginning of another long stay in the city that would last into the new year. Midway through the month, the company jumped to Chicago's Majestic Theatre, performed a special midnight show on New Year's Eve, and left town a few days into 1930. The show opened at the Shubert Detroit Opera House on January 5 and a week later moved on to Cincinnati.

After the *Venice* road show faded out in February, Ted Healy wasted little time moving directly to the vaudeville circuit. The final week of the month, Healy and his Racketeers, the Stevens Brothers, and Big Boy the bear joined a bill at the Palace on Broadway (and if Moe Howard was looking to take a leadership role among the three foremost Racketeers, he might have started by working under a single name—the *Daily News* preview of the Palace stand identified him as *Joe* Howard).

This time, Healy did not include Pete the dog in the act. Instead, he worked out a new routine with Joe Mendi. Was that a way to ease the pressure on the supposedly animal-fearing Shemp? Not really. Joe Mendi was a chimpanzee. According to the *Daily News* review a few days later, the chimp "spits on the floor in bar-room fashion." Shemp, Larry, and Moe, described as "three scarcely-human-looking disreputables," sang close harmony while Healy "tried to end their agony by having sandbags dropped from the wings" (a routine they would show off in the film *Soup to Nuts*). The team also trotted out some of their golden oldies, like the bit in which Healy winds up on a trapeze and the Racketeers walk away with the ladder, leaving him hanging. The *Daily News* said the show was "a complete riot . . . ridiculously funny." The *New York Times* went further:

> The "racketeers," headed by the natural comic named Shemp Howard, still wrestle that trained bear, still trade those sadistic slaps and still emerge as that terrifying singing trio which is never permitted to finish a number. There are one or two attractive feminine additions to the Healy ranks, but it is the grotesque collection of males that provides the frequent moments of cachinnation.

The review of the show in the March 5, 1930, issue of *Variety* contained a historical reference to the trio as "Shemp Howard, a natural comic himself, and his two partner stooges." That phrase, "his two partner stooges," may be the first time that the three of them—Shemp, Moe, and Larry—were referred to as "stooges." Healy himself would not use the term for a couple of years, and when he did, it would be in vain.

Later in March, with reports that Healy was hauling in $6,000 per week—not bad for any performer heading into the Great Depression—Healy jumped from the RKO to Loew vaudeville circuit and Loew's State Theatre in Times Square. The *Daily News* reported that he arrived "with Shemp Howard, Moe Howard, Larry Fine, the wrestling bear and eight anonymous men whom Healy calls racketeers." Next was a return to Brooklyn and a stand at Loew's Metropolitan. "Part of the crew which Healy brings to the Metropolitan was with him in his recent musical comedy engagements," Charles Hastings wrote in the *Brooklyn Daily Times*:

> They include Shemp Howard and his brother Moe and Larry Fine and the wrestling bear. Healy's act originated in Brooklyn over at what was known as the Wawanda Cottage on Cropsey Ave., Bensonhurst. Shemp and Moe Howard, who have been "pals" with Healy ever since they were "kids," still live at 8200 21st Ave., Bensonhurst. . . . The comedy antics of Healy and his gang just manage to stop this side of murder.

That story was in the Sunday paper on March 30, good news all round. The really important news was an item that ran in the *Daily News* on April 1. Irene Thirer, a newspaperwoman on the movie beat, scooped the big-name Broadway gossips like Walter Winchell and Ed Sullivan with two sentences:

> Ted Healy and his gang will become Fox Movietone performers early in June. The gang includes Shep Howard, Moe Howard, and Larry Fine, who have worked with Healy for many years.

Yes, she identified Shemp as "Shep." After all, Irene Thirer was from the movie, not the stage, beat. She would have time to learn the name. There would be only one Shemp.

Syndicated Hollywood gossip columnist Louella Parsons filled in the details on April 21, 1930: "Rube Goldberg arrived in Hollywood just in time to spend Easter. Rube was signed by Winfield Sheehan to come to the Fox studio and make pictures and bring with him his own particular brand of wit. His first picture is *Soup to Nuts* and, of course, it is comedy. . . . He will probably help design sets, write dialogue and do all sorts of things, for he is one of the talented sort that can do anything. His first big number will star Ted Healy, also recruited from the Broadway musical comedy fold."

Ted Healy had reportedly been approached backstage at the Palace by a scout from Fox Studios. His second shot at Hollywood stardom, Moe's return to the screen, and, if Shemp really was in *Spring Fever* in 1919, his second film in eleven years, promised to be as off-the-wall as anything they had carried out onstage. Rube Goldberg was neither a movie producer nor a screenwriter. He was an inventor and author and best known as a prolific newspaper cartoonist. His most popular comics depicted contraptions that performed very simple tasks in wildly complicated and extremely convoluted ways. The "Rube Goldberg machine" would find its way into *Soup to Nuts*. (An example of a Goldberg invention, sketched out in cartoon form, was the "Simple Mosquito Exterminator," which kills a mosquito by leading the insect down a board "strewn with small chunks of rare steak," which the mosquito munches on before being knocked out by chloroform fumes, coming to, and peering through a telescope at the reflection of a bald head in a mirror, and, thinking it a real human target, dashing "his brains out against the mirror, falling lifeless [into a] can." The three-dimensional board game "Mouse Trap," first released in 1963, is designed in the image of a Rube Goldberg machine.)

The move to motion pictures occurred without much delay. "Frances McCoy has been assigned the leading feminine role in Rube Goldberg's Fox revue, *From Soup to Nuts*, we learned yesterday," Grace Kingsley, motion picture editor for the *Los Angeles Times*, reported on May 15. "Ted Healy, who is to play the male lead, arrived in town yesterday. Today there will arrive three of his famous clowns, Harry Howard, Shemp Howard and Larry Fine. Fred Sanborn, another of the troupe, will be here in a few days."

When the three Racketeers did arrive, if the press agents are to be believed, they brought along "wives, children, servants, and a few relatives who were just along for the trip. Studio greeters met the Healy funsters with a limousine, but one look at the party caused hasty chartering of a bus." The group wasn't there to sightsee. The Fox Film Corporation put the team to work on the lot and also made hasty arrangements to get them onstage. Beginning on May 30, Ted Healy, "billed as the highest salaried comedian on the American vaudeville stage . . . and his merry-making Racketeers" took over the vaudeville portion of the show at Loew's State Theatre, accompanying screenings of the Warner Baxter talking western *The Arizona Kid*. The review in the *Daily News* could be seen as a preview of what was in store on-screen. "His revue, in the Healy manner, is distinctive, three pseudo acrobats furnishing many of the laughs. And there is a Chaplinesque chap with galloping eyebrows that has a confidential way of putting over good comedy, depending largely on a swishing walk and ability to play the xylophone."

After a week at Loew's State, they moved to Grauman's Egyptian Theatre on Hollywood Boulevard in Hollywood. While this was advertised as the gang's last engagement before filming, Healy and the Racketeers also cut it up onstage on July 2 at the all-star Hollywood Midsummer Jubilee at the Hollywood Bowl.

Cameras rolled on *Soup to Nuts* on July 14 on the Fox Studios lot at Western Avenue and Sunset Boulevard in Hollywood. There was also exterior filming in downtown Los Angeles in the Skid Row section east of City Hall.

Young Benjamin Stoloff, very experienced in comedy, had the director's megaphone. The script was indeed written by Rube Goldberg, with uncredited contributions from Lou Breslow, who had received "story" credits on a few shorts and the 1928 film *The Farmer's Daughter* (directed by Norman Taurog, who would go on to a long career and, in 1951, direct Dean Martin and Jerry Lewis in *The Stooge*). The film was an odd duck in any genre—Rube Goldbergesque in its very construction, from A to B.

Soup to Nuts is the story of old Otto Schmidt (Charles Winninger), the owner of a costume shop who lets the place slide into bankruptcy because he spends most of his time inventing Rube Goldberg–type machines. Creditors seize the business and appoint the young Richard Carlson (Stanley Smith) to manage the place. Carlson falls for Schmidt's niece Louise (Lucile Browne), but when she realizes the reason he's there, Louise won't have anything to do with him.

Meanwhile, Ted Healy is "Teddy," a salesman for the shop who hangs out at the fire department with three firemen, played by Shemp Howard, Larry Fine, and Moe—er, *Harry* Howard. Fred Sanborn is a "mute fireman." Teddy bickers with his gal pal Queenie (played by Frances McCoy, "a petite blonde, who," according to Louella Parsons, "has more real 'it' than any other girl in the film colony") and wangles some business for the failing shop by conning the fire department into ordering costumes for the Fireman's Ball. He also concocts a scheme to help Carlson woo Louise. Ted orders identical costumes and masks for Carlson and himself and then escorts Louise to the masquerade ball, where he and Carlson switch places. At the ball, Teddy and the three firemen perform some bits made popular onstage by Ted Healy and his Racketeers. Meanwhile, Louise realizes that she has been tricked by Carlson and runs to her home over the costume shop and locks herself in her room. Carlson follows and inadvertently sets the place on fire. The firemen rush from the ball to the scene, leaving Fred Sanborn to demonstrate his xylophone skills in an empty room. The blaze is extinguished with help from old Schmidt's inventions, and the lovers are reunited in a happy ending.

There are many more shenanigans and gags throughout the picture. Rube Goldberg himself has a cameo as a restaurant patron. Little-person actor Billy Barty, age five, plays an infant. And ubiquitous background and bit player Bobby Barber is seen in his first film role as part of a group of revolutionaries. They come to the shop for uniforms but run away in fear when baby Barty pops a balloon, a sound they mistake for a gunshot. Cheerleading gossip Louella Parsons wrote that "*Soup to Nuts* is expected to be the chief fun maker of the film year."

But according to Bill Cassara in *Nobody's Stooge*, "There seemed to be trouble in the making of *Soup to Nuts*; with delays, rewrites, and egos, filming took five weeks to complete. What started out to be a musical comedy was edited with only two songs making the final version."

As the Fox team got to editing the picture for a release in September, there was one more slight bit of trouble behind the scenes. Shemp, Larry, and Moe had walked out on Ted Healy. They quit, breaking up the act. Howard, Fine, and Howard were on their own.

Eleven

Stooges versus Stooges

August 1930. Suddenly, it had come together. Ted Healy's three stooges were indeed on their own as a team of three stooges. Although they were not yet using the term "stooges" as a calling card, they were no longer answering to and taking abuse from a taller, more attractive and versatile leader but rather leaving the answering and abuse to themselves. They were no longer Racketeers or Southern Gentlemen. They were Howard, Fine, and Howard, a trio not weeks past making their first moving picture with their former boss Ted Healy. So what happened? What made them take such a drastic step when success could be six reels away?

Moe Howard, in his factually suspect autobiography, claimed that after the filming on *Soup to Nuts* wrapped, Fox Studios boss Winfield "Winnie" Sheehan offered the Racketeers—Moe, Shemp, and Larry—a seven-year movie contract but that Ted Healy put the kibosh on the deal. Moe wrote that Ted Healy complained to Sheehan that signing the team was "ruining my act," so the deal was canceled. In the face of that betrayal, Moe claimed that it was his idea that the trio go out on their own—and so they did, as Howard, Fine, and Howard, eventually and occasionally labeled as the "Three Lost Souls."

Bill Cassara doesn't buy it, just as he doesn't buy the scenario that Healy was an abusive, drunken boss. "I've mulled that around a long time, and I can't wrap my head around Moe's version that Fox wanted to sign the Stooges up for their own movies. I find that kind of hard to believe because they weren't names. It certainly wouldn't have been features. This was 1930, the start of the Depression, and movie studios were cutting back, not building on." Cassara's research showed that Fox was no longer producing two-reel comedy shorts and had no plans to start up a shorts department. "They would have to build up a whole backlog of other comedians, other teams, and storylines."

Whether the film experience simply gave the trio the confidence to go solo or, more likely, they were dissatisfied with the money split that Healy had decreed, it was, for now, over. The breakup was bitter—and even more so on Ted Healy's part after the William Morris Agency was so quick to find work for the new comedy team. The agency booked Howard, Fine, and Howard for a week, beginning on August 28, at the Paramount Theatre in downtown Los Angeles. The trio would be part of an elaborate stage show—unusually elaborate at a time when movies were taking precedence—conceived and rehearsed on the Paramount studio lot, packed with comedians, singers, dancers, specialty acts, and lots of chorus girls, choreographed by Busby Berkeley. While that spectacle alone might be enough to draw crowds to the grand theater, the stage show was not even the main attraction, but second-billed to the premiere engagement of *Animal Crackers*, the second film from the very popular Marx Brothers. So, for their debut without their tall, handsome, confident leader, Howard, Fine, and Howard would be advertised as "eccentric comedians" and subjected to a side-by-side comparison to the more sophisticated Marx Brothers. What a contrast that would be.

And so would begin the period when their characters and roles would become even more defined: Shemp, the comedic, wisecracking center, and Larry, the nasally wise guy between Shemp and Harry who would sooner than later become Moe, the angry Healy substitute. All three of the Racketeers had their sneering, wise guy moments in *Soup to Nuts*, but Moe's bellicose persona had really popped out in the *Soup to Nuts* Fireman's Ball performance, when, in the middle of singing "Nellie," he suddenly knocked off Larry's hat. "Pick it up or I'll crack your skull open!" he barked, pulling his fellow assistant into a headlock, delivering an uppercut, and then getting back to the song. What was a sideshow would soon become the main event.

Would the audience recognize Howard, Fine, and Howard as the three Southern Gentlemen or as the Racketeers from Ted Healy's gang? Quite possibly, and in light of another act on the bill, there could be some confusion over whether the act had split up at all. The Paramount lineup also included Ted Leary, described in the *Los Angeles Record* as a "personality comedian who dashes on and off the stage at odd intervals and regales audience and actors alike with wise-cracks." This sounded familiar and quite possibly could be mistaken for a typo.

Whatever the expectations, the Paramount show was a smash, with long lines outside the theater and record-breaking sales at the box office. According to the *Illustrated Daily News*, although the four Marx Brothers had a large following that turned out, the diversified stage show was "considered partly responsible for the record box office receipts." The film and stage show was held over for a second week, beginning on September 4. Then Howard, Fine, and Howard followed up with bookings in San Francisco and up the coast to Portland and Seattle.

Not that Ted Healy didn't try to stop them. He immediately complained to the Vaudeville Managers Association, the cartel of theater chain owners, that Howard, Fine, and Howard were out there performing material they had stolen from him. The trio ultimately responded with a letter from the Shuberts that gave them the right to use any material from *A Night in Venice* and another from Fox Studios that allowed them to use any and all dialogue and business from *Soup to Nuts*. Howard, Fine, and Howard went on the road and stayed there. Ted Healy would file more complaints—although stories that he threatened to blow up at least one theater where the act was booked have been discounted.

Healy had headed back east and by mid-September had a new gang onstage at the Palace on Broadway. And talk about confusion. Some newspaper articles promoting his return listed Shemp Howard, Larry Fine, and Harry Howard as part of that gang. Other articles and ads intimated that the emcee had brought along his three most famous Racketeers, described in the *Daily News* variously as his "gang of ruffians" and "his disreputable gang of assistants." But Healy had replaced them, as if Shemp, Larry, and Moe were interchangeable punching bags who happened to harmonize. The switch was pointed out in the *New York Times* on September 15: "It is to be noted but not with alarm that a new aggregation of the ruffians quaintly called the Healy 'Racketeers' has been enlisted. They are, at the moment, less menacing than Shemp Howard and his associated malefactors, but they are learning fast and before you can drop a sandbag out of the flies they will be thugs of the first order."

The folks who paid for tickets did notice, and when Healy returned for another round at the Palace two weeks later, the newspaper ads announced "TED HEALY" (in large letters) and (in a much smaller font) "His New Racketeers." It wasn't until November, when Healy began yet another Palace stand, that the *Times* sent up a warning flare—and not only because his "new band of 'racketeers' now contains several young women." The critic wrote that Healy "is amusing, in, for him, a rather subdued fashion. Gone is much of the hilarious roughhouse of his former devil-may-care act, although efforts are made to recapture it by reviving one or two of the earlier Healy escapades."

Soup to Nuts began to show up in theaters in mid-September 1930, and reviews rolled out in the weeks to follow. They weren't all bad, but there were few raves. The *Chicago Tribune*'s Mae Tinee called the film "a nonchalant and loose strung farce-comedy" that "goes about its business with deliberation and appears to shrug at its own absurdities." She added,

> You're mildly diverted, albeit experiencing the sensation that not one of the entertainers gives a particular whoop whether or not such is the case. . . . Firemen who never go to fires are spasmodically on the job with hook, ladders—and harmony. These firemen sing. If you can call it that. So does Ted Healy sing.

Variety's reviewer called the film an "abortive comedy" that should have remained on the shelf, "for what the Fox studio turned out in *Soup to Nuts* is a two-reel Keystone of the silent days, padded into over six reels with dialogue." The *Los Angeles Times* was most complimentary, reporting that a screening at the Boulevard Theater "kept the audience amused. In a few spots, it threw the cash customers into uproars." The laughs were attributed to Ted Healy, Shemp Howard, Larry Fine, and Harry Howard:

> Healy's boys, burlesquing a fire department, clowned through the picture to their hearts' content, gave imitations, escorted their fair ladies to a masquerade party on a truck and gave a fine demonstration on how not to fight a fire. It's all in the name of fun, however, and when the boys were on the scene the comedy proceeded at a lightning tempo. . . .After all is said and done it is Healy and his gang who win the honors. His boys are not named, yet furnish most of the appeal.

Conde G. Brewer supplied not only a review in *The Billboard* ("The picture defies classification . . . but . . . produces the desired effect of getting the laughs at the right times") but also advice on how to best promote the film: "The Healy-Goldberg combination is ideal for exploitation, as also

Shemp dominated the trio when he, Moe (as "Harry Howard"), and Larry arrived on-screen with Ted Healy in Soup to Nuts. *Fox Film Corp/Photofest © Fox Film Corp.*

are the gang of stooges, loosely-garmented, dumb-looking and deadpan-mugging nincompoops. . . . Several men answering description of stooges might be hired to parade the streets to attract attention to their outlandish attire and the picture."

And with that, it was quite obvious that the three Racketeers, or firemen, though not listed as such in the credits, were already a team. *Soup to Nuts* also made clear that Shemp Howard was the star of this team. Shemp has the first words in the film. Larry and Harry are spectators to his back-and-forth with Healy in the opening scene as Shemp attempts to get Ted to speak to his gal on the telephone. Shemp mutters his soon-to-be trademark ad-libs throughout the picture and is the one character who gives a twist to the title when in a diner scene he orders "a bowl of soup with some nuts in it." After all the years of stage work, Shemp was fully formed as a comedic screen presence, on par with his much-higher-paid boss.

In November 1930, despite Ted Healy's continued griping, Howard, Fine, and Howard rejoined the Publix circuit in a revue called *Masquerade*. (Fred Sanborn had also split from Healy and gone solo with another Publix unit in the show, *Syncopated Menu*.) According to Larry Fine, in the wake of Ted Healy's complaints and legal threats about the use of material, they had worked up new routines, including one in which they posed as musicians in the orchestra pit. "A riot would break out and mayhem took over as they broke instruments over their heads and a fight erupted among them," Steve Cox and Jim Terry wrote in *One Fine Stooge*. "The hysterical act took off."

As the trio carried on into 1931, working and perfecting their act, Ted Healy was off on another major project. He had been offered the starring role, alongside dancer Ruby Keeler (aka Mrs. Al Jolson), in the Broadway musical *The Gang's All Here*. For this opportunity, he had assembled another gang of Racketeers. Paul "Mousie" Garner, Jack Wolf, Dick Hakins, and Eddie Moran were foremost among them. "The title of the musical was also its theme song, 'Hail, Hail, the Gang's All Here.' It was a song of bravado," Garner wrote in his autobiography. "The Depression was spreading to all levels of society, and people needed to feel that they were all in the same boat even if it was sinking. They were part of a gang."

The gang behind the show was even more impressive. Oscar Hammerstein II and Morrie Ryskind worked on the book. Hammerstein had written the libretto and lyrics for *Showboat* and other musical comedies. Ryskind wrote the musical *Strike Up the Band* and worked with George S. Kaufman on the Marx Brothers' Broadway shows and screenplays. *The*

Gang's All Here went through delays and revisions in Philadelphia and Newark before it opened on Broadway on February 18. The show closed after twenty-three performances. "The truth is, our gang didn't make it," Garner wrote. "The show was a big flop even with Ruby's clever dance numbers and her spirited singing. . . . Some of the trouble stemmed from the fact that people were feeling the pinch of hard times."

Stooges fans might appreciate the historical significance of the show and the names of its characters. According to the program and playbill, Ted Healy portrayed "Doctor Indian Ike Kelly." Eddie Moran was "Professor Cavanaugh." Garner, Wolf, and Hakins were listed as "Stooges." All three of them. Three . . . stooges.

"A stooge was a performer who helped the star," Bill Cassara says. "They used to call Sid Silver a 'stooge in the box' because he was up there yelling out insults and engaging Phil Baker to go back and forth. W. C. Fields would use a stooge when he was juggling. He would bounce the ball off his stooge's head and they would get a lot of laughs. But the first time I saw 'stooges' relating to Ted Healy was in 1931. And that was *after* Moe, Larry and Shemp left to start what they were hoping would be a successful trio, and Healy hired Mousie Garner and Jack Wolf (and Dick Hakins).

"In the late thirties, after the Three Stooges were a big success at Columbia, Ted Healy picked up Mousie Garner, Dick Hakins, and Sammy Wolfe (replacing Jack Wolf), to support him in his stage and radio acts. Stooge fans have come to term them as a 'replacement Stooges.' And that may or may not be true, because in 1931 they were the original Stooges! At least as far as the term 'stooges' was concerned. Mousie Garner was always kind of perturbed about that. He was introduced at one of the Three Stooges conventions as one of 'the replacement Stooges' and he bashed on his piano—'*BLA-A-A-NG!*' I think that irritated him."

On other stages in other theaters, Howard, Fine, and Howard continued to trudge through the vaudeville circuit. By the spring of 1931, they had beefed up their act and also made it more familiar by adding straight man Ted Macke (yes, another Ted) and dancer Ruth Goodwin. Macke was a singer who had worked the circuits the past year or so with a comedian partner, Jack Flynn. Goodwin was eye candy and did a mean tap dance.

Variety caught the revised fifteen minutes—"the stooge act in the last degree"—at the Academy in May. "Three nutty looking fellows with a neat straight comprise this offering of the dizzy school of comedy. The boys gain their laughs by ganging up stooge style on the straight and on each other." All that they needed to "make the grade" was "a wow finish and some more polishing off"—and maybe losing the operation gag, in which one of the Howards wound up "showing his bare body." The reviewer decided that "it isn't funny, but rather objectionable to women present." As for the woman onstage? No objections. She was a "looker" who "tapped prettily in shorts."

The Billboard dispatched a reviewer to the Hippodrome a few weeks later. The verdict was that Ted Healy's former comic assistants had "set out to glorify the stooge" in an act that was "spotty and lacks a clever comedian as a pacer for their freakish comedy."

Ted Macke was seen as a "good contrast" to the "slovenly appearance" of the trio in their "misfit clothes and pale makeup" but "stands apart most of the time, working in with the trio in bits occasionally" while waiting to sing his one solo number. Ruth Goodwin's tap dance was the "punchiest single item in the act."

The reviewer from *The Billboard*, identified as "P.D.," also picked up on another aspect of the act, one that is quite significant and perhaps overlooked in the Three Stooges origin story. "Moe Howard," he wrote, "is the pivot of the act, spilling most of the gags and mauling his brother Shemp or Larry Fine whenever they interrupt him."

This was the seismic shift that literally set the stage for what would be one of the most successful comedy acts in the history of modern show business. Moe, the crafty, business-minded brother, was not only taking charge of the finances behind the scenes but also, as he would later brag, taking on the Ted Healy role for himself. The little fire hydrant of a guy who was hopping around behind his older brother Shemp at the Coney Island swimming pool, angling for attention from the newsreel camera, had edged his way to the center of the act. Moe was now the key player. He barked the orders and delivered the slaps, punches, and shoves. Ted Macke the straight man was no Ted Healy. He stood apart most of the time. Shemp, for so long the comic spokesman between Healy and the others, was now, with Larry Fine, one of Moe's whipping boys. This was the template for all the lineups of the Three Stooges for the next forty years.

Quite possibly, it was also setting the stage for Shemp Howard's exit from the team.

Twelve

Return of the Racketeers

Howard, Fine, and Howard worked with Ted Macke into the summer of 1931, and they managed to polish the act well. When they played the Albee Theatre in Cincinnati in July, the *Enquirer* awarded them "comedy honors." "Seen here previously as 'stooges' with Ted Healy, the boys find a ready welcome in their 'solo' attempt. Generally credited with originating the type of comedy they enact, the trio are masters of the art and easily throw the audience into gales of merriment."

By the fall, Ted Macke had been given his walking papers, and Howard, Fine, and Howard had a new straight man. Jack Walsh was a handsome, dark-haired Irishman with a decent singing voice. He, too, kept mostly to the side of the trio and got very small billing for a show they called *Cut the Acts*. When they played three days in September at the Orpheum Theatre in Sioux City, Iowa, between screenings of the Claudette Colbert drama *Secrets of a Secretary*, one of the local papers announced that "the stage 'stooge' has come into its own.

"When Ted Healy was in vaudeville, a lot of hilarious fun was provided by a quintet of stooges. They made so good that now they have an act of their own. . . . It is a combination of everything that can be classified as comedy. They enter and exit. There is a bit of burlesque business and a gag—a riot of fun without reason."

Walter D. Hickson at the *Indianapolis Times* piled on the praise when Howard, Fine, and Howard performed at the Lyric Theatre in the first days of November. "If you go in for goofy comedy, and I go in for it strong, when done by goofy experts, then do not miss Howard, Fine and Howard with Jack Walsh this week," adding

> The three comics of the act are the nearest approach to Olsen and Johnson that we have on the stage. Howard, Fine and Howard are not similar in any way to Olsen and Johnson in their comedy approach. The team at the Lyric this week goes in for extremely goofy and hokum comedy. Their makeup is the last word in the goofy dictionary. And their most repeated stunt is poking each other in the eye. Their burlesque singing trio is the last word. The

> three have the dumbest looking "maps," meaning faces, I have ever seen on living human beings. Yes, this act is the big hit on this bill and deserves to be.

"Poking each other in the eye." Eye pokes. This was new. The "twin-pronged eye poke" would become a staple of Three Stooges comedy routines and is a rare case in which Moe gave credit to Shemp for the gag—at least partially. "The poking in the eye was discovered in a card game, playing contract bridge," he told Philadelphia television host Bob Gale in 1973. "Larry claimed he had four honors when he only had three. Shemp proved to him that he had [three] and Larry still insisted that he had four, so Shemp threw his fingers and . . . poked him in the eyes. His fingers went about a half inch deep right into Larry's eyeballs. There were tears falling out of his eyes for a week. And it struck me so funny that I leaned backwards in the chair and went right through a glass window." Moe said that he introduced the eye poke to the act during the next matinee. That afternoon and from then on, he never warned the other two when it was coming. "It wasn't planned. . . . I just did it when I felt like doing it and when I felt like they deserved it."

Howard, Fine, and Howard continued with Jack Walsh on the RKO circuit into 1932, while their vaudeville agents Arthur Blondell and William Mack advertised the threesome in the trades as "Three Lost Soles." The agents misspelled the name, but by any name, Howard, Fine, and Howard, the Three Lost *Souls*, were rolling along well. When they opened as headliners at the Paramount Theatre, the palace on Peachtree Street in Atlanta, on June 26, the *Atlanta Constitution* described them as "three of the most eccentric comedians who ever played the circuit."

And this is where Ted Healy reenters the picture. After the failure of *The Gang's All Here* in February 1931, he made a pretty quick comeback thanks to the attention of Broadway producer, impresario, and showman Billy Rose. In April, Rose's Broadway revue *Sweet and Low*, starring his wife, Fanny Brice, and George Jessel, closed after 181 performances. Within weeks, Rose retooled the show into *Billy Rose's Crazy Quilt*, starring Fanny Brice, Phil Baker, and Ted Healy—or, as the savvy showman billed them, "The Transcendent Stellar Triumvirate of the Amusement Firmament." The new revue opened on May 19, 1931, at the 44th Street Theatre, ran for 79 performances, and then went on the road. This production, despite its so-so reviews in New York City, beat the Depression odds with a long, successful run in Chicago followed by a thirty-three-week tour that stretched 13,000 miles. The final performance took place on May 7, 1932, at the Irving Theatre in Reading, Pennsylvania.

By the end of the run, Healy had shed his wife—actually, he had been shed by her. Betty Healy filed for and received a divorce in March on the grounds of his adultery. The split was costing Ted Healy thousands of dollars; he had been ordered to pay Betty's legal fees as well as $150 per week in alimony. This time, the Shuberts tossed a lifeline with another Broadway show. Their musical revue *Hey, Nonny, Nonny!*, starring Frank Morgan (later in the title role in *The Wizard of Oz*), had opened at the Shubert on June 6 and made it two days into July. Rather than throw out the idea, the Shuberts announced a week later that the show would be retooled into *The Greenwich Village Follies*. That name was quickly scrapped in favor of blowing the dust off a title they had already used more than once. *The Passing Show* would go on the road, starring Ted Healy. Healy signed a deal in July that guaranteed him a salary plus half the net profits. He tore up the deal at the beginning of August. He wasn't happy with the cast, and because his payoff depended on the money that the show and its various acts brought in, he expected to have a say in casting.

And guess whom he wanted in the cast?

According to Moe Howard, if he's to be believed, Healy had not been in the best shape near the end of the *Crazy Quilt* run, drinking too much, missing performances, and even experiencing "the DTs"—delirium tremens, the most severe form of alcohol withdrawal. If that was the case, it's hard to believe the Shuberts would have entrusted him at the wheel of another expensive Broadway-bound production. It's even more surprising that in light of their experience with Healy and Fox Studios, Moe, Shemp, and Larry would agree to rejoin Ted Healy's act.

But they did.

Moe Howard would always have more than a few bad things to say about Ted Healy, and this was one period in his life when Moe's animosity toward his old friend and former boss had not cooled since Healy allegedly cost him, Shemp, and Larry a movie career. Yet Moe claimed that Healy had "begged us to go back with him" and that Moe, speaking for the team, said they would consider the offer if Healy went on the wagon. "Healy promised us he'd stay off the booze; it was one of the few promises he kept—for a while."

That sounds very forgiving, but Bill Cassara says the decision was more practical. "Howard, Fine and Howard didn't surface as big stars. They were a third-rate vaudeville act and vaudeville was dying. So when Ted Healy offered to have them come back to support him in his act, they all jumped because they'd have all the benefits of working with a bigger star and a better atmosphere. And Ted Healy in 1932 signed them all up for the year. They all had weekly paychecks for the year, and that was a major coup for them, for any actor back then, getting fifty-two weeks salary."

On August 7, 1932, two years after they had split from Ted Healy under the most acrimonious conditions, the Lost Souls returned to their roles as Healy's Racketeers onstage at the Keith Theatre in Boston. As reviewed in the *Boston Globe*, the show was like old times in more ways than one. "Ted and his 'Racketeers' appear between every act and invoke roars of laughter by their wisecracks and some not so wise, and also their ridiculous appearance. There's plenty of slapstick comedy, with much slapping of faces, squirting of seltzer water and knocking down." And there was something else: "A wrestling bear owned by the Stevens Brothers comes in for plenty of applause."

The following week, Healy and his original Racketeers were at Loew's State Theatre on Broadway and 45th Street, tuning up the act while also in rehearsals for their return to big-time Broadway. The week wasn't through before Ted Healy announced that he was quitting the Shuberts again. While a new contract was being drawn up after his first walkout, Healy had signed to play shows on the RKO vaudeville circuit. When he returned to rehearsals for *The Passing Show*, his attorneys claimed that the revised contract would keep him from working for RKO or anywhere else for an unlimited period.

That put the Racketeers in quite a pickle—but nothing compared to what happened next. On Friday, August 19, after finishing a week at Loew's State, Shemp Howard quit the act. He walked out on Ted Healy, and he walked out on Larry Fine and Moe "Harry" Howard. The scaredy-cat, phobic, dumb Shemp Howard, *The Billboard* reported, "intends on doing an act of his own."

"Shemp left the act because he was really afraid of Ted Healy," Joan Howard Maurer said in her brother Paul's documentary series *Hey Moe, Hey Dad!* "Ted, when he was drinking, could be very, well, mean. He never hurt anybody, but he was rather a frightening image and then Shemp being a little bit of a fraidy cat, it just took 'boo!' for him to run the other way."

Moe's daughter is far from the only person raised on Stooges mythology who has said or written that Shemp Howard ran away from his comedy team and Ted Healy because he feared more of the abuse he endured from his hard-drinking, ever more erratic, and unpredictable boss. Onstage there were the hard shoves, slaps, and hits. Offstage, there are stories of Healy setting fires in hotel rooms and pulling mean-spirited pranks on Shemp and others in his troupe.

Larry Fine said that Shemp was afraid of Ted Healy and that Shemp's wife, Babe, ever protective, urged him to walk away. In his 1973 memoir *Stroke of Luck*, Larry wrote that Shemp was so afraid of Healy that one encounter on the road left him so rattled that he urinated in the berth that he and Larry shared on the train ride out of town. Larry's book, according to Steve Cox, was an "abomination . . . riddled with errors . . . with little to no care for detail." In fact, Cox revealed, the book was written not by Larry, who had been disabled by a recent stroke, but by an abusive "collaborator." Despite the debunking, the train scene was dramatized in the 2000 television biopic *The Three Stooges*:

> MOE: Guys, guys! What's goin' on?
> LARRY: Ted Healy scared the piss outa your brother, and it landed on me!

In an oral narrative from 1960, Larry offered another version of Shemp's reason for quitting: rehearsals for *The Passing Show* had been postponed due to the illness of another of the stars. In the interim, Healy booked some lucrative vaudeville dates in Chicago. "Shubert was mad and sued. During the litigation, Mr. Shubert saw that he couldn't win the case, so he offered Shemp the starring part in the show at quite a lot of money. Shemp promptly gave Healy his notice."

Moe told a different story to show business historian Rick Lertzman over lunch at Moe's home in June 1973. Lertzman wrote that "Moe and Larry feared Healy. . . . They also retained a modicum of affection for him, at least when he was sober. Shemp, on the other hand, hated his former boyhood friend. More than once, the normally gentle Shemp told Moe that he wanted to kill Ted Healy. This stemmed from being on the receiving end of Healy's ferocious onstage slaps. . . . After one slap too many, he quit the act and pursued a solo career in movies."

Moe Howard produced a more detailed version of that story in his autobiography. He claimed that when it came time for Howard, Fine, and Howard to rejoin Ted Healy in August 1932, Shemp refused, saying, "Moe, Ted is not the wonderful guy you think he is; he's basically an alcoholic. He's only one drink from going back to his terrifying benders. Besides, I have a chance to play the part of Knobby Walsh in a Joe Palooka film for Vitaphone on the Coast." Moe wrote that Ted Healy "blew his top" when he got the news, shouting, "What the hell does Shemp mean by that? Is he trying to ruin my act? I need a drink!"

Cute story, but it didn't happen. Vitaphone didn't license the Joe Palooka character until late 1935. The nine Palooka film shorts were filmed in New York City.

None of the stories is true, not Moe's, not Larry's, not Larry's ghostwriter's story. Shemp Howard quit over money.

Ted Healy was making thousands of dollars per week, whether on the vaudeville circuit or, in this case, in another Broadway show. At this point, he was paying Shemp, Moe, and Larry a total of $450 per week, which the three of them had to split. One hundred and fifty dollars per week was not much more than they had received in the early days. As reported in *Variety* and other papers, Shemp believed that he deserved a larger portion of that pot and, during the run at Loew's State, demanded it. Moe and Larry, as might be expected, refused to give up any of their portions. Shemp gave Ted Healy one last chance to give him a raise. When Healy turned him down, Shemp quit.

"Shemp wanted a raise," says Cassara. "And Healy said, 'What? If you want a raise, get it out of Larry or Moe.' And wait a minute! That's not the story we have heard before. And of course, Moe and Larry were not going to go that route. In Healy's mind, he had established the base pay and no one was going to be above the other two."

"I suspect a big part of it was Healy's alcoholism and abusive behavior toward everybody, and the fact that he wasn't paying the Stooges very much relative to his own salary," says film historian and critic Stuart Galbraith IV. "And the impression that I got is that Shemp realized he was worth a lot more money. Shemp was talented in a way that was different from the other Stooges. It's hard to imagine Larry or Curly being anything other than Stooges. And even Moe, to some extent. When you see Moe's solo appearances in these very miscellaneous movies like *Space Master X-7* (1958) and *Doctor Death: Seeker of Souls* (1973), the stooge within him is still there. He never fully breaks away from it, whereas Shemp was a perfectly good character actor, primarily in comic parts, but he had a bigger range as well."

"I think it was very gutsy," Leonard Maltin, the film critic and historian, says. "I do, because he was leaving something certain for a world of uncertainty."

"Shemp was bold enough and had enough confidence that he was going to venture out on his own," Cassara adds. "And that really was a bold move."

Shemp was gone. Once there was a vacancy in the act, there was little sentimentality involved in filling it. In fact, even before the end of the month, the team was working with a replacement for Shemp while Healy's manager was threatening to file suit against Shemp to recover the $100 it cost to put the new man in place.

They didn't look far for the replacement. It was Jerome Howard: kid brother "Babe," soon to be known the world over as "Curly." At twenty-eight, Jerome wasn't yet the comic human cannonball with the shaved head but a slimmer, handsome man, with a lush head of hair and a waxed mustache. Despite his mother's reservations, Jerome had followed his brothers into show business after all. His most prominent job had been a couple of years earlier, working with Orville Knapp and His Orchestra. The orchestra was a dance band, and Jerome had a comic part in the shows. He would be introduced as a guest conductor, and once the music began, he would flail his arms wildly and go into all kinds of funny gyrations as parts of his tuxedo fell off around him. Ultimately, he would lose his pants, and the audience would lose its mind at the sight of the "conductor" in long underwear with the trap door on the rear end (held closed by a giant safety pin). Jerome Horwitz wasn't on the road with Orville Knapp during the tumultuous period of rehearsals and reversals for *The Passing Show*. He was there at rehearsals, on the sidelines, and in the shadows, working for the Shuberts, always on the edge of the action.

"Healy had Curly in the bullpen all that time at the Shubert!" Cassara exclaims. "And we know that because Joe Besser mentioned it." Joe Besser, who years later would replace Shemp Howard in the Three Stooges, was twenty-five years old and featured as a comedian in *The Passing Show*. "Joe Besser said that in 1932 at the Shuberts', Curly was there, fetching them sandwiches and Cokes—and so he could participate in the act, I'm sure. And it's a shame that no one ever interviewed Curly. No one ever interviewed Shemp, and if they did, would they have covered that part of their evolution? We're left with the newspaper clippings, but I think they're pretty illuminating."

And here we part ways, for now, with Moe, Larry, and Curly.

Thirteen

The Sex Symbol

So there stood Shemp Howard, in the last week of August 1932, a man alone. His walkout from the Ted Healy team was just being reported in the trades and causing an uproar throughout the entertainment industry. Ted Healy himself ankled *The Passing Show*. Moe Howard and Larry Fine followed him. They had no choice. They were part of the Healy gang package. The Shuberts also failed to close the deal with Healy's co-headliner, Sophie Tucker, but contrary to Larry Fine's recollections, the Shuberts did not offer Shemp the starring role "at quite a lot of money." The new leads were Broadway actor and comedian Lester Allen and Florence Moore, a wisecracking songstress, famous as the first female emcee at the Palace. Shemp signed his own deal with the Shuberts, as a solo performer.

J. J. Shubert's latest version of his "new revue of the events of today" began its tryouts far out of town on September 4, opening for a week at the Cass Theatre in Detroit, Michigan. There were high hopes for *The Passing Show* to succeed on the road and then open on Broadway at the Winter Garden Theatre, which for the past three and a half years had presented only talking pictures. The ads in the local papers read, "Don't Miss the Opening Performance!" Indeed, those who passed on the debut of *The Passing Show* in Detroit lost out on viewing a one-time-only spectacle. Len G. Shaw of the *Detroit Free Press* called the revival of the Shubert franchise an "orgy . . . filth . . . the rawest exhibition ever to parade the stage of a legitimate theater in Detroit for a third of a century, at least." The audience was, according to *The Billboard*, "shocked" by what was spewed onto the prestigious stage, and police censor Lester Potter moved in and began ordering that entire scenes and numbers be removed, lines written, and costumes altered. J. J. Shubert cooperated, and over the next couple of nights, the cast and crew struggled to get the show back on its feet—minus the dirty bits. The *Free Press* was very forgiving on Wednesday. "The objectionable numbers have been taken out, new sprightly ones added and the entire performance moves now with a zest." Shemp Howard was among the cast members singled out for the belated praise.

The show got out of town on Saturday and opened the next night at the Shubert in Cincinnati. The *Enquirer* critic wrote that the show had potential but, at more than three hours long and still containing a few "vulgarities," could use some pruning. As for the comedy element, the reviewer singled out "one uproarious character": Joe Besser. Shemp Howard was mentioned as part of the ensemble that was "effectively present for a large part of the show, but with three hours of presentation and the programmed sequence completely out of gear with production sequence, we cannot safely identify their activities."

Maybe word had traveled from Detroit (more likely it was the hard economic times), but there was little interest in *The Passing Show* in Cincinnati, and the show began losing money from the start. *The Passing Show* would have closed midweek if not for union and Actors' Equity Association regulations requiring a show to run—and actors to be paid—for a minimum of two weeks. *Variety* wasted no words and didn't even bother writing a complete sentence in the opening to its review: "A terrific flop." The trade critic blamed Ted Healy's departure and "the sad mistake of not readjusting the comedy material to the style of the talent at hand." The girls of the ensemble were tall, svelte, and charming. There were a novel acrobatic and contortionist dance and some fancy hoofers. Joe Besser again was recognized as "the best laugh grabber." "This lad, a burlecue grad, does an overgrown sissy character that in a way puts him in fast company."

But Shemp Howard? He was "strictly out of his metier. . . . One of the grimmest stooges ever to scowl behind Ted Healy's back, they got him with a clean face and dinner jacket." Shemp shouldn't have been surprised that he was basically sidelined from a show in which fifty acts had already been written and whose comic stars were already in place. He had originally been subcontracted for the show as one of Ted Healy's underlings, so his solo performance, all cleaned up and in a dinner jacket like some kind of swell, would go unheralded. Plans for *The Passing Show* to move on to Chicago and perhaps repeat the Shuberts' past success were discarded.

On the bright side, Shemp was on his own.

It's said that Shemp spent a few months on the road, trying out another act with his own set of stooges. Home, according to public records, was still at 8200 21st Avenue in Bensonhurst. That was his in-laws' house, and it must have been a bit crowded. Along with wife Babe and son Morton, now five, there were Babe's parents, Herman and Lena Frank; Babe's brothers Sidney and Harry; and her twelve-year-old niece Beatrice Frank.

In the new year, when Shemp found the key to his future, it was not a key to escape from the Frank house—not yet. For this new career opportunity in 1933, he did not have to hit the road. Just as kid brother Moses had done nearly a quarter of a century earlier, he needed only take the elevated train to the local movie studio in Flatbush, where the greatest portion of his career would get under way and where, under the bright studio lights, a face as unique, battered, and recognizable as any mo'ai on Rapa Nui would crater into shape.

More than a few things had changed at the Vitagraph Studios and Laboratory in the years since its construction phase, when young Moe was running errands and nabbing juvenile roles in silent film shorts. The studio went on to do well with full-length silent features and comedy shorts and in 1922 was among the nine original members of the Motion Picture Producers and Distributors of America (MPPDA), the trade organization set up to promote investment from Wall Street and to head off government censorship. Former U.S. postmaster general Will H. Hays was appointed president of the group. He would become known for the Motion Picture Code—the "Hays Code"—the set of self-imposed "moral guidelines" regarding sex, violence, and punishment that the major studios agreed to follow in Hollywood's golden era of censorship. Vitagraph's executives weren't so comfortable with the arrangement. Unlike some of the other MPPDA signatories, the studio did not have foreign distribution and didn't own theaters in which to release their product. In January 1925, Vitagraph pulled out of the MPPDA, claiming that it wasn't getting a fair shake as an independent studio. Monopolization was under way. Vitagraph couldn't keep up with the big boys.

By April, its president, Albert E. Smith, sold the company to Warner Bros., and the "original nine" became the Big Eight (which soon enough was whittled down to the Big Five). Warner Bros. changed the name of the studio to Vitaphone and set it up as an independent subsidiary to crank out short "two-reelers" to accompany feature film presentations. Many East Coast–based comedians, vaudeville entertainers, and Metropolitan Opera stars who would not or could not travel to Los Angeles for movie work were hired to populate them.

In the spring of 1933, Shemp Howard walked through the Vitaphone gates and got to work on the first of his "Big V Comedy" shorts. Most histories of Shemp's film career say that it took a couple of years for him to rise from "bit player" to "second banana" alongside some of Vitaphone's stars. A study of the first half dozen Vitaphone comedy shorts featuring Shemp tells a more complicated story. *Gobs of Fun, Close Relations, Paul*

Shemp's solo screen debut in the Vitaphone short Salt Water Daffy *(1933) teamed him with Jack Haley and introduced his signature nearsighted gag. Warner Bros./Photofest © Warner Bros.*

Revere Jr., Salt Water Daffy, In the Dough, and *Here Comes Flossie!* were all filmed between May and September 1933. Each demonstrates the different ways in which directors would use Shemp in various productions and showcase unique aspects of a comic persona that would become familiar in the years to come.

Those six Vitaphone shorts were released over a twelve-week period between September 16 and December 9, 1933, all but two in the order in which they were filmed. (According to Vitaphone production records, *Here Comes Flossie!* was Shemp's eighth role. His sixth and seventh, *Howd' Ya Like That?* and *The Wrong, Wrong Trail,* were filmed in July and August and released in January and February 1934, respectively.) *Gobs of Fun,* Shemp's first time in front of the Vitaphone cameras, was his fourth film to be released. *Salt Water Daffy* (working title *Ship-A-Hooey*), which was filmed in June, would be remembered as Shemp's solo motion picture debut.

The twenty-one-minute comedy (Vitaphone production reels 1561–1562) arrived in theaters to accompany feature-length films including James Cagney's latest, *The Mayor of Hell,* and *Song of Songs,* starring Marlene Dietrich. The star of *Salt Water Daffy* was Jack Haley, a thirty-five-year-old former vaudeville song and dance man who, in 1939, would play the Tin Man in *The Wizard of Oz* (seeing the two of them, side by side, immediately conjures the image of Shemp in the role of the Cowardly Lion). Haley got top billing—name over the title—but there was no doubt that Shemp Howard, listed on the next card along with chubby dialect comedian Charles Judels and Lionel Stander, the Bronx toughie with the distinctive gravel-gargle voice, deserved equal billing. From the very first scene, through every frame of the picture, Shemp was Haley's costar in what was essentially a "buddy film."

Haley and Howard are Edgar Wagonbottom and Wilbur the Kleptomaniac, a couple of well-dressed street hustlers who bump into a U.S. Navy captain on a Brooklyn sidewalk. Shemp the klepto swipes a prized antique pocket watch from the old salt, and within minutes, they're being chased around the corner by police. The pair duck into a U.S. Navy recruiting office, where they find themselves in line to be inducted. Despite their protests, they're bullied into undressing by the chief petty officer, played by Stander. While waiting for their physical exam, stripped down to undershirts with towels around their waists (in the style of the day, they have left their hats on), Edgar realizes a way out of the mess.

"If anything's wrong with ya, they won't take ya here!" he tells Wilbur. "I got an idea. You make believe you can't see anything. Stumble all around the joint. Ha! You can't see!"

Wilbur looks, dimly. "Ohhhh, I see."

"No, you don't see!"

"Ohhh . . ."

This leads into Shemp's first solo routine: feigning blindness as he enters the doctor's office for his physical. Feeling his way through the doorway, he shakes hands with the medical skeleton—"How are ya, doctor?!"—and finds his way to the doctor's desk, where he picks up the telephone. "Gosh, your hands are cold." The visually impaired character would become a familiar part of Shemp's bag of tricks (notably in the 1949 Abbott and Costello comedy *Africa Screams,* his last solo movie appearance).

Shemp asks the navy doctor for permission to "take a drink," then pours a pitcher of water onto the floor and guzzles from a jar of ink. "Your eyes couldn't be bad by any chance, could they?" the doctor asks. "They're a little bad, doc," Shemp replies. "Take a look at em!" An extended close-up of Shemp's face is edited to make it appear that his eyes are rolling in their sockets. The shot also gives the viewer a chance to study the iconic visage. Shemp is no longer the slim young man of his early stage days. He's already thirty-eight years old, his earlobes are thicker, pockmarks are evident on his cheeks, and there is a distinct, ridgelike lump about an inch below his left eye—right around where he took so many slaps and hits. Another, smaller welt and bump are developing under his right eye, and the nose could be a boxer's. A few more years of aging and work under the camera lights, and the face will settle into what the acclaimed portraitist Drew Friedman dubbed "the Boris Karloff-Rondo Hatton definition of handsome"—"one of those horrible faces that didn't need makeup," a "naturally beautiful, fascinating" mug that would one day earn Shemp the title of "The Ugliest Man in Hollywood."

The comedy in *Salt Water Daffy* continues as Haley and Howard enter the navy and cause all kinds of trouble for Stander, who turns out to be their basic training instructor. What's most notable is that Shemp Howard is Haley's equal throughout. It is a strong debut.

Moe, Larry, and Curly, meanwhile, were out west with Ted Healy, with a movie deal at MGM studios in Culver City. Their first short with Healy, *Nertsery Rhymes*, had been released on July 6, 1933. Credited not individually but as "Howard, Fine, and Howard," the three men were infantilized as a trio of pajama-clad babies, sleeping in the same bed, begging Papa Ted—in top hat and tails with cane—to tell them a bedtime story. In what is basically a version of the stage act (the short is intercut with long, elaborate stage production numbers), Curly's forehead gets the most attention as a target of slaps, pokes, and punches by Healy and the others.

Close Relations, Shemp's second short, was released on September 30. The star was Roscoe "Fatty" Arbuckle. Once one of the most popular and highest paid of Hollywood screen comedians, Arbuckle had been virtually blacklisted from the industry since 1921, when he was arrested and charged with rape and manslaughter in the death of actress Virginia Rappe at the St. Francisco Hotel in San Francisco. Although he was acquitted in a third trial in 1922, the scandal stuck. He directed some films under the name William Goodrich, but it wasn't until 1932 that Warner Bros. gave him the chance at an acting comeback as "Fatty," signing him to star in six Vitaphone comedy shorts. It was the first time in a decade that Arbuckle dared perform under his own name—and the very first time his voice would be heard on-screen.

In *Close Relations*, Arbuckle plays Wilbur Wart, called to visit a supposedly rich uncle who is seeking an heir. Shemp does three walk-on appearances, although the first is more of a "hop on," as, clad in a raincoat, his hair flapping, he bounces on a pogo stick through a drawing room scene. He returns, trudging along on snowshoes and wearing a long coat and straw boater. He stops midway, turns, tosses a handful of confetti into the air, and exits. (Rip Taylor was two years old when the film was released.) Shemp makes one last appearance in the final scene after the uncle's "farm" is revealed to be a "funny farm"—a sanitarium for "nuts." Dressed as an Elizabethan herald, he blows a trumpet fanfare and leads a gaggle of mental patients in a song and dance around a well. Shemp's role, also reminiscent of his vaudeville days, showcases him as a utility player, able to walk into any picture and add a bit of comedic flair, even if it's not connected directly to the plotline.

Shemp would always be good for a solo spot in any picture, as evident in *Paul Revere Jr.*, the musical comedy short released on October 7. Broadway comedian Gus Shy, known for his "drunk act," plays a drunk named Paul Revere Watson, who dreams he's the real Paul Revere on his midnight ride (the running gag is that his wife suspects he's out cheating—which he is). Shemp has one scene, separate from the musical numbers, as an attendant helping Revere onto his horse. It is, as expected, slapstick, in which Shy flies over the horse, lands on his bottom, tries again, and winds up on Shemp's shoulders, grabbing hold of Shemp's long, greasy hair as if he's holding the reins. "My goodness! I think you oughta get a haircut. At least you oughta get an estimate!"

Gobs of Fun stars the Dutchman Charles Judels as a French sailor and Russian-born Greek dialect comedian George Givot as a Greek sailor on shore leave, unwittingly romancing the same woman. (Film historian and critic Stuart Galbraith IV points out that both actors could also play Italians: Judels would provide the voice of Stromboli in Walt Disney's *Pinocchio*; Givot voiced Tony the restaurateur in *Lady and the Tramp*). Released on October 21, 1933, this was the first Vitaphone production in which Shemp was on the call sheet. He was being eased into the machine with a cameo role in a nightclub scene. Judels is canoodling with three women. Shemp, sitting at the next table with his date, taps him on the shoulder. "Sailor, you sure get the women. How do you do it?" Judels stands and demonstrates by stroking Shemp's gassed-back hair and kissing and stroking his cheeks. "And then you give a little kiss here, and then you say, 'I like you so much.'" Shemp's date suddenly stands says, "Would you two like to be alone?" and storms off. Judels jumps back. Shemp looks around in confusion. "Wait a minute! I'm innocent!" he grumbles in what sounds like the first of the ad-libs with which he would enhance many a comedy.

One of Shemp's most effective screen personas would be that of the comedic, "Runyonesque" gangster or thug. He gives the guise a tryout in his fourth picture. *In the Dough* was the last film in Fatty Arbuckle's Vitaphone deal. The disgraced comedian plays Slim, who takes a job at a bakery the day that a pair of gangsters—Toots and Bugs, played by Stander and Shemp—show up to demand protection money from the owner. Toots and Bugs are comic thugs. Shemp, shorter and a bit foggier than Stander, is the sidekick. In a running gag, Toots tells Bugs to straighten his bow tie and then slaps him in the face. When the crooks don't get their "dough," everything leads to chaos—an exploding cake and a big, messy, wet dough-, cake-, and pie-throwing fight (the Three Stooges, famous for their pie tossing, filmed a cream puff fight in the 1939 short *Three Sappy People* but didn't engage in a full-on pie fight until the 1941 short *In the Sweet Pie and Pie*).

Filming on *In the Dough* wrapped on July 28. That night, Arbuckle celebrated his first wedding anniversary with his third wife at a restaurant in Manhattan. The couple then returned to their suite at the Park Central Hotel on Seventh Avenue in midtown, where around 3:00 a.m. on July 29, Arbuckle suffered a heart attack and died. He was forty-six. *In the Dough* was released on November 25, 1933. Although at least a dozen actors were featured in the film, Roscoe ("Fatty") Arbuckle was the only one credited.

The last of Shemp's two-reelers to be released in 1933 had been filmed over five days, beginning on August 30, and earned him $175 for his work. *Here Comes Flossie!* might have stirred Shemp's memories of his days on the farm in Chatham. This comedy stars comedian Ben Blue (born Benjamin Bernstein) as a farmhand working for an old farmer and his two sons: Hank, played by Fred Harper, and Shemp as Ezry. Pa gives his sons $50 each to buy whatever they want. Hank wants to purchase a bride whose picture he saw in the *Farmer's Guide*. Ezry chooses a prize cow, also pictured in the *Farmer's Guide*. Both the woman and the cow are named Flossie. As might be expected, there's confusion when it's time for one to be taken to the bedroom, the other to be tied up in the barn. Shemp, loud, boorish, and muttering asides, makes comic hay out of shaving his face or wiping his shoes before entering the house. He's the chief laugh getter.

But ugly? In the final months of the "pre-Code era," *Here Comes Flossie!* gave Shemp the opportunity to play "the stud." The self-censoring Motion Picture Production Code had been adopted in 1930 but wouldn't be strictly monitored or enforced for another six months or so, which allowed a sex scene to slip through. Modern eyebrows might be raised at a scene in which mail-order bride Flossie Watson (an uninhibited Janet Reade) arrives at the farm after a bumpy car ride and says to the driver, "Well, hot stuff, whatta I owe you for the vibrator treatment?," but the payoff comes when Ezry heads to the barn, milking stool and bucket in hand, to milk his new cow, only to find the other, human Flossie restrained in a stanchion. He frees her and gets his first look.

"Say . . . you're kinda pretty."

"Ahh, you're kinda cute yourself," says Flossie.

"Thanks." Ezry looks away, aw-shucks style.

"C'mere, handsome."

When she goes for him, Ezry resists. "Now, wait a minute. I've been to the city once." He does a little dance. "Hotcha! Hey! Razzamataz! That's only a piece of the stuff I know."

"You know, I kinda like you."

Ezry is shy. "Thanks." He looks away, brushing back his mop of hair.

"What's the matter?" Flossie runs her hands along her hips. "Don't I *appeal* to you?"

"I have my moments," Ezry says defensively. "That was my brother that sent for you, not me. I wanted a cow."

"Oh, what's the difference?" Flossie places her hands on Ezry's shoulders and pulls him closer. "It's all in the family, anyhow."

Ezry resists. "Now I've been around! Cut it out, now!"

"C'mon."

"Cut it out lady, cut it out!"

Ezry continues to protest as she embraces and kisses him. The camera cuts away to a shot of Ezry's legs below the knees. His trouser legs roll up and down, accompanied by the sound of a slide whistle, while he moans. "Oh my gosh . . . oh, stop that."

Later, when Ezry staggers out of the barn, lipstick smeared all over his face, dazed and smiling, with a "Ro-cho-cheo-toe!" and a snap of the fingers, there's little doubt of what went on inside. *Here Comes Flossie!* (enough with the double entendres) was the perfect climax (no pun intended) to what does serve as a "Shemp cocktail" that whets the appetite for what was ahead: Shemp as comedian, Shemp as actor—Shemp as unlikely sex symbol even!

FOURTEEN

"Get Outta My Way!"

Those eight short Vitaphone comedies were not the only films Shemp acted in during 1933. There were still more than three months left in the year, and every couple of weeks, production on another one- or two-reeler was under way. There was more work with Charles Judels, George Givot, and Lionel Stander as well as two-reelers starring Jesse Block and Eva Sully (also known as the married vaudeville team of Block and Sully) and, beginning with *Mushrooms* in October, work with Harry Gribbon.

On November 1, Shemp filmed a scene in *Pure Feud*, the first picture in which he was a supporting player to a dummy. In this instance, it was an actual ventriloquist's dummy: Charlie McCarthy, who received equal billing with his partner and voice supplier, Edgar Bergen. Bergen plays a man who heads to the country for some rest and relaxation ("On my doctor's orders—nerves"), only to be caught in the crossfire of a hillbilly feud between the McCarthys and the Jenkinses. Shemp plays a relative of Charlie McCarthy. According to the Three Stooges website, he was paid $50 for a single day of work.

After his day on the set with the wooden actor, Shemp was again teamed with Harry Gribbon, this time in *Corn on the Cop*. Ten years Shemp's senior, Gribbon was a vaudeville and film comedy veteran. He got his start in silent films, working with Mack Sennett and Fatty Arbuckle in 1914, and was known in the 1920s as "Rubber-Faced Harry" and "Silk Hat Harry." Gribbon had top billing in *Corn on the Cop*, but he and Shemp were definitely a team as a couple of hobos who make a buck selling axle grease as a phony corn remover that they market as "Happy Feet Salve." Shemp "drums up trade" by hitting people on the foot with a mallet, leading to an encounter with a police officer with sore feet. Gribbon is the taller of the duo, more often than not reacting to Shemp's expert ad-libs, asides, and solo comedy bits—without any slaps or pokes.

Variety reviewed the short when it played at the Strand Theatre in New York City in June 1934. "Shemp Howard, a stooge from vaude, makes a perfect team-mate for Gribbon. They should be kept together."

Somehow, in the middle of all these productions, Shemp managed to fit in more work with a competing motion picture company. The Van Beuren Corporation had emerged in the 1920s as an animation studio and was still best known for its animated short subjects. Its cartoon *Dinner Time* was the first to include synchronized sound, but it was not a success, losing the credit to Walt Disney's *Steamboat Willie,* which was released about a month later. Van Beuren moved into live-action shorts in the early 1930s. With filming of the "Van Beuren Musical Comedies" taking place at the Fox Movietone Studios in Manhattan, it was an easy hop on the train for Shemp when he began to moonlight. In November 1933, he signed on for a role in *Henry the Ache,* a musical parody of the current hit film *The Private Life of Henry VIII.* Charles Laughton would win an Academy Award for Best Actor for *The Private Life.* Comedian Bert Lahr (the actual Cowardly Lion in *The Wizard of Oz*) plays Henry in the parody. Shemp is one of Henry's lackeys, and although the action is set during the Tudor era, this servant in the king's court is named "Artie." His hair is long and unruly, and he speaks Brooklynese. (Then again, Henry uses a telephone to invite his girlfriend Kitty on a date—"We can go to a hockey game and then after the hockey game, we can go to a nice Italian restaurant, and after that we'll go to a boilesque show written by a friend of mine, a guy named Shakespeare"—but who's counting?)

Shemp followed this sex comedy at Van Beuren with *The Knife of the Party,* a musical comedy about a vaudeville troupe forced to work in a hotel to pay off a bill. Media historian Hal Erickson wrote that filming was scheduled for December but moved to January 1934, when the short was shot over a four-day period. Shemp was paid $250 (about $5,800 today) for two days of work, on Thursday and Friday, January 11 and 12.

In this film, Shemp is credited as "Shemp Howard and the Stooges," and, in fact, he does lead a group of four sidemen. "Shemp had acquired a couple of stooges of his own named James Fox and Charles Senna," Erickson writes in his book *A Van Beuren Production,* "and in this film he and his new cohorts essentially duplicate Ted Healy's old act, replete with punches, kicks, eye-pokes, and salty expletives like 'I'm a little too quick for ya, ain't I?' and 'Ya see *that*?'" It has been written that this was an attempt to launch Shemp and his own cinematic team of stooges, but a viewing of the short makes it more likely that he was parodying, as Erickson observed, "Healy's old act" (which Moe, Larry, and Curly were continuing to work). He doesn't merely slap a stooge; he slaps four at a time. Later, there's an overhead shot of a five-way slapfest. Shemp's character in *The Knife of the Party* is the star of a vaudeville stooge team, and all the over-the-top hitting—including his wielding a golf club and using one of the stooges as a human golf ball—makes the sly parody more apparent.

Even before *The Knife of the Party* was released on February 16—"three weeks after completion," according to Erickson—Shemp had one more Van Beuren short under his belt. Erickson's research showed that Shemp was paid $250 for three days portraying a "goofy detective" in *Everybody Likes Music*. Originally titled *So You Won't Talk*, the short "has seldom been exhibited since its March 9, 1934 release date (a little over a month after production wrapped)."

The Vitaphone comedy team of Gribbon and Howard was reunited in January 1934 in *The Nude Deal* as a pair of house painters who substitute for a couple of rich kids who don't want to travel to Paris to study art—and stumble into winning a major art prize. The short had been retitled *Art Trouble* by the time it opened on June 23 and is notable for introducing Mary Wickes, the tall and wisecracking comedienne and actress. Her long career would include the role of Shemp's girlfriend in *Private Buckaroo*, the 1942 army musical comedy starring Harry James and the Andrews Sisters (and extend into the 1990s to include Whoopi Goldberg's *Sister Act* comedies and Gillian Armstrong's *Little Women*). Also making his film debut in *Art Trouble* (and, like Wickes, uncredited), was twenty-five-year-old James Stewart, who would also go on to a long career in pictures. Stewart played one of the rich kids. He'd been working onstage in New York City and rooming with Henry Fonda when, he later said, he was attracted to Vitaphone by the paycheck.

"I wasn't thinking I could break into pictures," Stewart said. "I was offered the job at fifty dollars a day and that was a lot of money to me at the time, so I just accepted it as a job." Stewart reminisced that Vitaphone shorts contained "no plots that made any sense and that anyone could remember a minute later, but they were lively and they moved! And some wonderful comedians were in them," adding,

> Working with people like Harry Gribbon and Shemp Howard and Eddie Quillan was sheer, undiluted pleasure. Everything moved so fast, there was no opportunity to learn what they call "film technique." We just got up there in front of the camera with our learned lines—what there were of them—and played it all by ear. I did it because I didn't believe they actually paid fifty dollars a day. There were damn few days, but fifty dollars was fifty dollars.

Gribbon again had star billing, but when *Art Trouble* played the Strand in September, *Variety* tagged Gribbon and Shemp as "a comical couple" and referred to the short as the latest in "the Harry Gribbon-Shemp

Howard series." Shemp was singled out in the positive review for "the not-unexpected Apache routine . . . funnied up when Shemp Howard and a girl try to go through the same motions."

In all, nineteen motion picture shorts (including the three from Van Beuren) featuring Shemp Howard were released in 1934. And there were many more in the pipeline.

One of Shemp's more memorable shorts of 1934 was another pairing with Harry Gribbon. In *My Mummy's Arms*, they're most definitely a team as Kenneth and Harry, a couple of boobs hired as aides to an expedition "to the inner tomb of the greatest Egyptian king, Phooey the Third." Yet Gribbon again had billing above the title, and Shemp led the supporting cast—Russell Hicks, Louise Latimer, and, in his first film role, Sheldon Leonard. Not yet typecast as a tough-guy gangster, Leonard played Abdullah, an Egyptian.

Described by one character as "imbeciles and very incompetent," Kenneth and Harry are introduced as such inside the tomb when curtains are

Boxed in with Sheldon Leonard and Harry Gribbon in My Mummy's Arms *(1934)—Harry got top billing, but Shemp was more than his equal. Warner Bros./Photofest © Warner Bros.*

parted in what is supposed to be the grand reveal of the mummy, only to reveal the two of them playing a game of cards atop the sarcophagus (and literally "cutting the cards" with an ancient ax). The short is full of one-line groaners, as when Shemp gets his first look at the mummy of King Phooey III:

SHEMP: Boy, he must have met with a terrible accident. Look the way he's bandaged up. What's that 5000 BC?
GRIBBON: That must be the number of the truck that hit him.

Shemp goes all out with his asides and ad-libs. Early on, after he and Gribbon are sent packing from the tomb, the soundtrack segues into a version of Al Jolson's showstopper "My Mammy," led by a comedic wah-wah trumpet:

SHEMP: So that's an Egyptian rummy.
GRIBBON: No, no, Egyptian *mummy*.
SHEMP: Well, they can have it. I'd rather see mah old Alabamy mummy.

In a nod to Jolson's weeks in Chicago with *A Night in Spain*, Shemp looks past the camera into the distance, as if he can see his mammy—er, mummy—there. Gribbon can see her as well. "I can see mah old mummy now!" Shemp exclaims. "Mummy! Mummy! This your little Sonny!" He pauses. "But my mummy don't knows me. But you *will* knows me, mummy! You'll knows me by the tattoo on my chest. *Bool-ya!*"

He tears open his shirt, exposing his bare, hairless, tattooless chest.

"Your mammy don't knows ya," Gribbon says. *Mammy?* Gribbon should have said "your *mummy*." But schedules are tight. He goes on. "Have ya got anything else to show your mammy?"

Shemp, downcast, shakes his head.

"Show her your vaccination."

Shemp brightens. "The old vacky!" He grabs the left shoulder of his shirt and tears open the sleeve, displaying his bicep. Gribbon leans down to get a look:

GRIBBON: You have no vaccination.
SHEMP: I been robbed!
GRIBBON: Have ya got anything else to show your mammy?
SHEMP: I got it!
GRIBBON: He's got it, Mammy!
SHEMP: The old operation! *Boolya!*

Shemp reaches down to pull up his shirt, but before any more of his body is exposed, the picture cuts to an animation of the Sphinx, shaking with laughter.

The short entered theaters on June 28.

Around the time that Shemp was filming *My Mummy's Arms*, Howard, Fine, and Howard's contract with MGM had expired. They had already split with Ted Healy, who this time wasn't so enraged to see them go. In addition to the shorts and features he had filmed with his stooges, Healy was achieving some success in a number of solo movie appearances, and both he and the studio were confident that he could go out on his own. According to Moe's recollection, on the very day the trio was cut loose from MGM, a young agent walked him, without an appointment, into a meeting with Columbia Pictures' tyrannical boss Harry Cohn and his production chief Sam Briscoe. Moe walked out with a contract that would pay the Stooges $1,500 to appear in a two-reel comedy with an option for a long-term contract. Simultaneously, Larry Fine, who had also claimed authority to deal on behalf of his fellow stooges, was walked by another hungry agent into the office of Carl Laemmle Jr., head of production at Universal Studios, and signed a deal there. The fact that Moe had signed a few hours earlier meant that Columbia got the Stooges—and, despite the fact that they had finally broken free from their servitude to the increasingly drunk and personally abusive Ted Healy, they retained the identity as "stooges." They would be "The Three Stooges." Moe, as might be expected, wrote that he came up with the name ("I said, 'Listen boys, if we stick with Ted we'll be getting our measly one hundred dollars a week. . . . Right now we are *three* fairly good comics, and we were Healy's Stooges, so let's call ourselves The Three Stooges!'").

Moe quickly established himself as "boss" and chief punisher of the team on-screen. Off-screen, he convinced Larry and Curly to sign an agreement giving him sole ownership of the name "The Three Stooges" and the authority to "sign all contracts." The agreement also gave Moe the power to replace either or both of them "at his discretion." If either Larry or Curly were to quit the team, he would have to pay Moe $2,500.

An interesting footnote: Moe also claimed credit for the movie career of the Abbott and Costello comedy team, claiming in his book that "I doubt very much if they would have joined Universal if fate had us sign there first." He added that years earlier, when both acts were performing in Atlantic City, "at every opportunity, [Abbott and Costello] would come backstage and watch us perform from the wings. I always felt there was much of Curly—his mannerisms and high-pitched voice—in Costello's act in feature films."

"Yeah, I've been hearing that for years," says Nick Santa Maria, coauthor of *The Annotated Abbott and Costello*. "Let me tell you one thing about Lou Costello. In 1929, he did his very first audition for a burlesque company in the Midwest. He's twenty-three years old. He gets the part. He gets the role of a Dutch comedian. That same year, he's getting singled out in reviews for being a song and dance man and 'the funniest comic we've seen come along and blah blah blah.' He was a natural. He didn't need Curly."

The first Three Stooges short, *Woman Haters*, was filmed between March 27 and March 30, 1934, on the Columbia Studios lot on Gower Street in Hollywood. It was released on May 5. This was one of the few among many Columbia shorts in which their characters had different names. Moe was Tom, Larry was Jim, and Curly, who was billed as "Jerry Howard," was Jackie. As part of Columbia's *Musical Novelties* series, all dialogue in *Woman Haters* was in rhyme, recited to the beat of the jazzy music that played throughout.

While the Stooges went to work in California, Shemp continued his busy and varied schedule on the East Coast. Late in June 1934, he stepped away from his three-day Vitaphone shoots to work in a feature film with location shooting in Atlantic City, New Jersey. *Convention Girl* was produced by the Falcon Pictures Corporation, a Hollywood "Poverty Row" outfit, so tagged because it was one of the independents that churned out features at a fraction of the cost and taste of the major studios. The Poverty Row studios also didn't necessarily subscribe to the voluntary Motion Picture Code of morals, and *Convention Girl* is a good example of that rebellion. Rose Hobart plays Babe Laval, a cabaret "hostess" in Atlantic City who clearly is a call girl who provides other prostitutes for visiting conventioneers and businessmen. Babe is in love with a gambler who is not so hot on her. Shemp Howard is Dan Higgins, one of the gangsters in the gambler's orbit.

Convention Girl has been billed as a comedy drama and musical, and it does indeed feature elements of those three genres. Shemp, just being Shemp, can't help but inject some natural humor into his role of a tough-talking wise guy. He's funny, but not in a Jerry Lewis *Family Jewels* way. Shemp is funny in a Joe Pesci, *Goodfellas* "How am I funny?" way. He not

"Get outta my way!" Shemp showed unexpected range as a bad guy in Convention Girl *(1935). Photofest*

only talks tough and acts like a ruthless thug but also engineers a blackmail scheme, and when his partner in crime demands his share of the loot, Shemp barks, "Get outta my way!" and shoots him!

Shemp's effectiveness as a comic gangster makes one wish he would have made it back to Broadway in *Guys and Dolls*—but *Scarface*? Who knew? The film was released in the United Kingdom as *Atlantic City Romance* on May 15, 1935, but didn't make it to theaters in the United States until Halloween.

Shemp's involvement with baseball legend Honus Wagner in the "lost" film *Spring Fever* may be unconfirmed, but his role in a historic comedy short with a pair of World Series heroes survives in its black-and-white glory. Shemp, as nearsighted pitcher Lefty Howard, is clearly the star of *Dizzy and Daffy* despite top billing going to brothers Jerome and Paul Dean, better known as Dizzy and Daffy Dean, pitchers for the St. Louis Cardinals. On October 9, the Cardinals had won the 1934 World Series over the heavily favored Detroit Tigers. The Dean brothers, who each had pitched two winning games in the best-of-seven series, became overnight heroes. Less than three weeks later, on October 29, they signed a deal with Warner Bros. to star in their own Vitaphone comedy short. Filming on *Dizzy and Daffy* began at Vitaphone Studios in Brooklyn a mere three days later. Warner Bros. planned to have the two-reeler in theaters in time for Thanksgiving.

The press release announcing the project stated that "Roscoe Ates and Shemp Howard will be featured with the Deans." Ates had been coasting on a "stuttering" act since vaudeville. He had appeared in *Soup to Nuts* and starred in several Vitaphone shorts, including *Let Them T-T-T-Talk,* that Shemp had filmed in the beginning of July. Ates was cast as speech-impaired umpire "Call-'Em-Wrong Jones," who calls a wild pitch a "strike" because he can't spit out "b-b-b-ball." (Coincidentally, on November 1, when the camera was set to roll on the Vitaphone lot, *Let Them T-T-T-Talk* was released into theaters. *Variety*'s review of the "slapstick" short mentioned Shemp Howard's "physiognomy . . . a pan no one could forget.")

Dizzy and Daffy is a fictionalized account of the Deans' road to the championship. The film opens in the locker room of the minor league Farmer White Sox, where the brothers are among the teammates listening to Lefty, who, the sign says, has come "direct from the Big League" to "positively" pitch against the Shanty Town No Sox. Shemp, in full blowhard mode and a head shorter than most of the others, is bragging and braying about his fastball.

"Why, I whiz 'em past so fast, all the batters do is get up and sit right down again," he brags, then is interrupted by Jerome. "How do you throw a curve?"

"I usually use a baseball!" Lefty snaps. "Hahaha! Now, where was I before I was so rudely interrupted. Oh yes . . ."

Jerome butts in again. "I'm having trouble with my curves."

"Why don't you go on a diet!" Lefty barks. As Jerome's teammates laugh, Shemp turns to another player. "Hey, who is this pest?"

"That's Dean."

"Dean? Dean? The only Dean I ever hoid of was *Gunga*!"

A locker room pitching demonstration reveals that Lefty is nearsighted—near *blind,* actually. "My eyes went back on me," he explains. "Not both of them, just one is bad. The other is just about . . . about that much off . . . but with my glasses, I'm just as good as I ever was!" As the team files out, Shemp puts on another impressive display of his slapstick abilities, walking into a doorframe, tripping over a bench, and smashing his head into the wall of lockers. "Somebody left a two-by-four out here," he mutters.

On the mound, Lefty puts on a solo show of comedic windups and pitches, mistakes a picture on a billboard for the left fielder, and, when he's taken out of the game after aiming a pitch in the wrong direction, comes up with the nicknames Dizzy and Daffy. The brothers are then hired by the Cardinals and go on to win the World Series.

The short didn't make it into theaters for the November holidays but did arrive on December 15, in plenty of time for Christmas. (On Thanksgiving eve, Shemp returned to the stage—he was one of the Vitaphone stars who performed at the Flatbush studio in a dance and frolic for the Brooklyn unit of the Warner Club, a national beneficial organization and social club for employees of Warner Bros. movie theaters.)

Dizzy and Daffy was directed by Lloyd French, who had begun his career at Hal Roach Studios in 1919. Lloyd had worked his way up as a comedy writer, assistant director, and director. After working as assistant director on many Laurel and Hardy silent comedies, French directed half a dozen of their shorts before moving to Vitaphone in 1934.

French would work with Shemp on a dozen two-reel comedies. The first was in June 1934 when Shemp was teamed with Daphne Pollard in *Smoked Hams*. Shemp would make three Vitaphone shorts with Pollard, a tiny forty-two-year-old Australian dancer and physical comedy performer who had appeared in Mack Sennett's silent comedies (and would later play Mrs. Hardy in a couple of Laurel and Hardy films). At four feet nine inches, tops, Pollard was, at last, a costar whom Shemp could tower above but also an experienced, versatile screen partner. They shared top billing as "Daphne Pollard and Shemp Howard" in *Smoked Hams*. The order was switched in *A Peach of a Pair* and *His First Flame*.

In *A Peach of a Pair*, filmed in August 1934, Howard and Pollard play a vaudeville team named Butler and Cook who mistakenly take jobs as—a butler and a cook. The short may be best remembered because the final scene has been edited out of some showings on television: a formal dinner where a plum pudding that has been doused with gasoline instead of brandy is lit and explodes into flames. When the smoke clears, everyone is "corked up" in blackface (and the rich white hostess says, "Yowsah!").

According to Stuart Galbraith IV, Shemp by this time had proven to be more than a utility player on the Vitaphone lot. "Shemp reportedly punched up their weak scripts with ad-libbing, more Popeye-like asides really, but he certainly contributes to what fun there is," Galbraith wrote. "Unlike the Arbuckle shorts which frequently ventured out of the studio to interesting Brooklyn exteriors (a welcome contrast to overly familiar Hollywood backlots and nearby neighborhoods), most of the shorts here fall back on cheap soundstage exteriors with painted backdrops which add to their impoverished look. And, while in Hollywood Warner Bros.

(majority owners of the Vitaphone facilities) was a bigger studio than Columbia, Columbia's short subject unit contemporaneously lavished more time, money, and attention on their shorts."

In October, Shemp played a firefighter named Smokey Moe in *His First Flame,* a two-reeler that did feature some impressive exterior footage in an extended segment in which Moe's house burns to the ground. Included is a scene in which a fireman played by Fred Harper wrestles and is dragged around by a runaway fire hose, a gag that had been a useful fallback since the silent comedies (Laurel and Hardy, for example, go airborne in 1927's *Duck Soup*) and was borrowed in 1958 by writer and director Frank Tashlin for *Rock-A-Bye Baby,* starring Stan Laurel acolyte Jerry Lewis.

FIFTEEN

Knobby

June 15, 1935, is a notable date in cinema and comedy history. It was opening day for *Serves You Right*, the first film in which Shemp Howard received solo star billing. Records show that the comedy short (Vitaphone production reels 1835 and 1836) had been filmed in February and that Shemp was paid $750 for his work. The supporting cast included Nell O'Day, Donald MacBride (as "Don MacBride"), Eddie Hall, Connie Almy, and Fred Harper. Lloyd French directed.

Serves You Right is not among the best of Shemp's oeuvre, but it is the first in which he demonstrates the slapstick potential of attempting to walk in women's high heels. He portrays Johnny Spivens, a process server (for the law firm of Summers, Summers, Winters & Summers—the laughs never end) attempting to hand a summons to a local racketeer named Muscle Bound Pete (played by Vitaphone regular MacBride). Many had tried, many had failed, and many had been beaten to a pulp. In his first go, Johnny takes a punch from Pete that knocks him out of his shoes and through a wall. When he is told that Pete "wouldn't dare hit a woman—he's afraid of anything in skirts," Johnny trades clothes with his fiancée and eventually succeeds by disguising himself in drag (Shemp's long, greasy hair comes in handy). Aside from the edgy cross-dressing angle, it's standard vaudeville slapstick throughout, with most of the action taking place inside Pete's watering hole, Ye Old Oaken Bucket of Suds saloon.

When *Variety* caught up with *Serves You Right* at the end of September, the reviewer described Shemp as "one of Ted Healy's original Three Stooges out for starring honors and missing the support of his former partners. At this stage he's not ready to carry the full burden." Reviewer "Chic" was obviously late to the game and, like Moe a decade earlier, had missed out on a couple of years of Shemp's work in various pairings and modes. But Chic's words were prophetic. As Shemp moved forward in his solo career, he would star in more short comedies but would make his biggest impression as a supporting player in full-length features.

The Vitaphone short Serves You Right *(1935) gave Shemp his first solo star billing—and his first chance to walk in women's high heels. Warner Bros./Photofest © Warner Bros.*

Shemp was billed as the solo star in two more Vitaphone comedy shorts: *The Officer's Mess,* released on November 9, and *While the Cat's Away,* which followed on January 4, 1936. He shared top billing with Roscoe Ates in *On the Wagon* in theaters on August 24, 1935, and with Johnnie Berkes in *Absorbing Junior,* filmed in February 1936 and released on May 9.

By that time, Shemp was already on a new trajectory in his career. In late 1935, Warner Bros. bought the rights to film a series of comedy shorts featuring a very popular character from the funny papers. Shemp was about to become part of a franchise.

Joe Palooka was a comic strip following the exploits of a heavyweight boxing champion by that name: a big, blonde, good-natured galoot with muscles and a cowlick. Created by Ham Fisher, the comic first appeared in newspapers in 1930 and grew in popularity throughout the decade. It was eventually syndicated to 900 newspapers. The character of Joe Palooka was introduced into each paper as "a young man of great physical strength, without making any pretenses to mental superiority." The comic's more interesting and comedically complex character was Joe's manager, Knobby Walsh, "who is hard-boiled, clever about money matters, and does not always tell Joe the truth. He wants Joe to win back the position of acknowledged champion of the world, partly for the glory of Joe, but mostly for the profit of Knobby Walsh."

Joe Palooka inspired a radio series in 1932 and a feature-length movie two years later. *Palooka*, a United Artists comedy, featured Stuart Erwin in the role of Joe but starred Jimmy Durante, the all-round entertainer with a prominent nose that earned him the nickname "Schnozzola" (an Italian twist on "schnoz," Yiddish for "nose"). Durante played Knobby Walsh, a rascal as colorful and entertaining as Palooka was simple and bland (so entertaining and central, in fact, that the film was released in the United Kingdom as *The Great Schnozzle*).

Warner Bros. would produce nine Joe Palooka shorts on the Vitaphone lot. Robert Norton played Joe in every one. Norton is a "whatever happened to?" candidate. His only other role listed on the IMDb website is an appearance in the 1938 Paramount short *Touchdown Army*, and that role is uncredited. As Joe, Norton looks not unlike Ryan Gosling as Ken in the 2023 movie *Barbie* and, as historian and critic Galbraith wrote, "proves to be a miserably bad actor who makes Buster Crabbe look like Olivier." Top billing in the series of shorts went to the fictional Joe Palooka (as in "Vitaphone presents Joe Palooka in . . ."). Norton's credit followed. Shemp Howard came next in most of the seven films in which he appeared (sometimes behind Beverly Phalon, who played Joe's gal Ann Howe), but like Schnozzola, he dominated the series. Up against that lightweight palooka, how could he not?

For the Love of Pete, the first of the Palooka series, was filmed in Brooklyn over five days, beginning on October 31, 1935. The two-reeler opens very much like *Dizzy and Daffy*, with attention on a poster advertising an upcoming sporting event—in this case, a heavyweight boxing bout—and the voice of Shemp regaling a crowd of men. He's on a railway station platform, dapper in a striped suit, vest, and bowler hat, bragging about his glory days. "Fightin' use'ta be my racket before I went in the haberdashery business. . . . I'll never forget one particular fight in Salt Lake City. There was Dempsey sittin' in his corner. He give me a dirty look! What did I do? I give him a dirty look right back! Then the bell rang—*BONG!*—and he come rushing out of his corner with his left like that! And he crosses it with two rights like this!"

Shemp throws punches in the air.

"Hey," one of the men interrupts, "do you mean to say you fought Jack Dempsey?"

"No, I was sellin' peanuts in the arena."

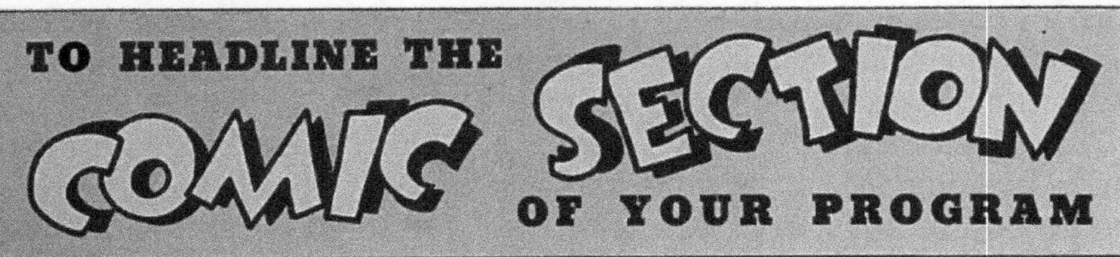

Less than two years into his solo film career, Shemp was a star of Vitaphone's comedy shorts. Courtesy of the Media History Digital Library

For the Love of Pete was released on March 14, 1936, with Shemp center stage as a scheming loudmouth who happens to deal a lot of slaps and hits to his subordinates. Reviewing the Vitaphone Joe Palooka collection, a writer for the *Out of the Past* film website commented that in this and other Palooka shorts, "Shemp often has moments where he appears to be playing the 'Moe Howard' role, in that he is or thinks he is in charge and verbally and/or physically bosses his cohorts around."

Comedy shorts that were added to showings of feature films didn't get much critical attention in daily newspapers, but the trade paper *Variety* had reviewers on the beat. One of its watchers labeled the first in Warner Bros.' Joe Palooka series "no more than mildly amusing" but added that "Shemp Howard in the cast . . . tends to make the short palatable."

With the exception of *Absorbing Junior* (with *Palooka* costar Johnny Berkes), all of Shemp Howard's work at Vitaphone from October 31, 1935, through January 18, 1937, was dedicated to the Palooka series. After *For the Love of Pete,* six *Palooka* two-reelers followed: *Here's Howe* (released on June 6, 1936, and introducing Beverly Phalon as Ann Howe), *Punch and Beauty* (released on August 6, 1936), *The Choke's on You* (released on September 12, 1936), *The Blonde Bomber* (released on November 28, 1936), *Kick Me Again* (released on February 6, 1937); and *Taking the Count* (which was filmed in March 1937 and in theaters by April 24, 1937). Shemp's image appears, although he is not credited, in *Thirst Aid* (June 12, 1937). He did not appear in *Calling All Kids,* which was released on November 20, 1937—the final installment in the series.

That was it. The Joe Palooka comic strip character had only gotten more popular and was even being held up by some as a national hero (the comic would run in newspapers until 1984), but Warner Bros.' Vitaphone series burned out quickly. It may have been time. The shorts were, like Robert Norton, forgettable. A viewing of the final installment led Dick Pitts of the *Charlotte Observer* to observe, "Mystery of the week. Why can't something be done about many of the unforgivable short subjects forced on the public? One of the worst examples of these monstrosities is Joe Palooka in *Calling All Kids,* which played a local theater last week. . . .There was neither rhyme nor reason for the Joe Palooka subject. The office boy could have written a better script. If there was anything funny about it, I wish someone would kindly draw me a picture and explain it in detail. Gloom seemed to settle over the audience, and, with the exception of several kids, not a laugh was heard."

At least Shemp could not be blamed for *Calling All Kids* or *Thirst Aid* (the plot of which concerned Knobby's kidnapping). After he completed four days of work on *Taking the Count* in January (Vitaphone production reels 2093 and 2094), Shemp collected his check for $1,500 (minus taxes) and left the Vitaphone Studios for good.

Perhaps it was a year and a half of playing the same character to diminishing returns while losing out on other opportunities. Shemp would have realized by then that Warner Bros. was cutting back on its short subject units, getting more bang for its buck by supplying movie houses with low-budget double features. Maybe he had the inside track on the studio's plans to close the Brooklyn Vitaphone Studios and do all its filming in sunny California (the Vitaphone lot would be shuttered in 1940). Then there was his wife, Babe, always there to offer support and sometimes a push.

Whatever the impetus, Shemp made the decision. With Babe and ten-year-old son Mort in tow, Shemp boarded the *20th Century Limited* train (you didn't expect him to fly, did you?) at Grand Central Station. It was on to Chicago, where they would switch to the Santa Fe Railway's *Chief* for the final leg of the trip to La Grande Station in downtown Los Angeles. Shemp was moving west. He was going Hollywood.

Sixteen

The Stage 1 Café

When Shemp Howard arrived in Hollywood in 1937, he didn't waste much time before resuming his career and stepping into a wide array of feature films as well as a mixed bag of comedy shorts.

Over the next decade, Shemp would appear alongside and would often upstage some of the top movie stars of the era—not only comedians but also screen idols of Hollywood's Golden Age. And the work he had been doing for the past four years at Vitaphone Studios was perfect preparation for a variety of roles, from cameos to costar. In those sixteen- to twenty-minute shorts he had been knocking off in a matter of days in Brooklyn, Shemp had honed a number of distinct characters and bits ready to be pulled out, depending on what the role called for—or what a picture might be able to use.

Shemp's first work on the West Coast was with Columbia Pictures, the studio on the corner of Sunset Boulevard and Gower Street, where his brothers Moe and Curly and Larry Fine had been making two-reel comedies for producer and director Jules White's short subject division since 1934. Shemp began filming his first Columbia feature in September 1937, just as the Stooges' latest short, *Cash and Carry,* was being delivered to theaters. The team's next two-reeler, *Termites of 1938,* would be produced under something of a new regime. White's low-budget comedy operation had become so prolific and successful that he had split it into two filming units. White would commandeer one unit, while business manager Hugh McCollum was promoted to producer to run the other. McCollum had joined Columbia in 1929 as Harry Cohn's secretary. At age thirty-seven, he was actually six months older than Jules White but younger in spirit, among the few in charge who did not have experience in silent movies. As the two units alternated in producing Stooges shorts, McCollum gave his directors and writers a longer leash, and as a result, the "B" team's work didn't seem so tired. After all, *Termites* would be the Three Stooges' twenty-eighth Columbia short.

While Moe, Larry, and Curly waited to read the script from writers Elwood Ullman and Al Giebler, Shemp was on location at a movie ranch about twenty-five miles north in Chatsworth. He had a plum supporting role in another of Columbia's experiments, a full-length western—well, not exactly a western, more like a movie about the *making* of a western. *Hollywood Round-Up* was the third of three Columbia pictures set behind the scenes of a western movie production. The first of the series, *The Cowboy Star*, starring Charles Starrett as the cowboy, had been released in November 1936, followed in September 1937 by *It Happened in Hollywood*, with Richard Dix in the saddle and a poster that read, "Hollywood turns the camera on its own gay, glamorous, glittering self!" *Hollywood Round-Up* starred Buck Jones, a veteran movie stuntman and cowboy who had been making westerns since the silent days and for Columbia since 1930. Jones plays a stunt double for a pompous, pampered western movie star (Grant Withers) who is fired and gets hoodwinked into joining a bank robbery. The meat of the picture is his friendship with the character played by Shemp.

As assistant director Oscar Bush, Shemp is not only the sparkplug pushing production of the movie within a movie but also the comedic center of the film, a full-fledged parody of a movie set's "A.D.," barking orders the director has whispered, shouting for everyone to take their places, blowing his whistle, and reaching for his mini-megaphone, his long, greasy hair flying and swirling like a wet mop head as he works himself into a frenzy of ad-libs and asides. Shemp's performance, a valentine and challenge to Hollywood, helps place this forgotten B-movie alongside pictures like *Singin' in the Rain*, *Hail, Caesar!*, and *Babylon*.

With *Hollywood Round-Up*, Shemp also displayed what would become a habit of delivering the best line in the movie. Les Adams, the prolific plot summarizer for the IMDb, pointed it out:

> A mid-point sequence has hotel clerk George Beranger, who dreams of being a western star, performing a twittering, ballet-slippering audition for the checking-in film company by quoting lines from a western and asking them to identify the film. Shemp Howard guesses, "*Little Women*."

Hollywood Round-Up began playing in theaters on November 6. A review of the picture in the *New York Daily News* singled out Shemp as "the comic relief": "As an excitable assistant director, he gets, and is entitled to, a number of hearty laughs." *Variety* also noticed. "Shemp Howard tries like a Trojan to make effective rather stale comedy material in the part of an assistant director. That he largely succeeds is much to his credit."

Another Buck Jones western, with another twist, followed. In *Headin' East*, Jones saddled up as a cowboy who heads to the big city—New York—for a showdown with the gangsters who are putting the strong arm on his father's lettuce farm. Shemp is again the comic relief as a warehouse worker who also coaches kids in a boxing gym. One of the young boxers is played by Leo Gorcey of "The Dead End Kids," the young actors who had appeared on Broadway in 1935 in Stanley Kingsley's play *Dead End*. Samuel Goldwyn had recently brought the group to Hollywood for the movie version, directed by William Wyler. Shemp would soon meet up and begin a lifelong friendship with another Dead End Kid, Gorcey's future movie comedy partner, Huntz Hall.

Headin' East headed to theaters on December 13. "Comedy comes with Shemp Howard, late of the two-reelers," *Variety*'s Barn wrote. "Howard's best fun-making comes with his appearance in gym clothes on the main street, and running races with a cop."

Ted Healy, whose solo career was moving along nicely at MGM (despite his spiraling drinking problem), made news more than once that week. The studio had recently loaned him out to Warner Bros. for the musical farce *Hollywood Hotel*. The picture, featuring what Healy biographer Bill Cassara says "may be considered his best role," was slated to open in January.

On the night of December 17, 1937, Healy became a father for the first time. His second wife, who like his first was named "Betty," gave birth to an eleven-pound, two-ounce boy at University Hospital in Culver City.

On the morning of December 21, Ted Healy died.

The two incidents were connected. On the birth of John Jacob Nash, new father Ted Healy went out to celebrate, embarking on what turned out to be a two-day boozing binge. At around 1:00 on Monday morning, he staggered into the Trocadero, a swinging nightspot on the Sunset Strip, and allegedly got into something of a fight with a twenty-eight-year-old producer named Albert "Cubby" Broccoli (who would go on to produce the James Bond movies). The drunken Healy was hustled out of the joint and about an hour later was treated by a doctor for a cut over his left eye. On Monday evening, Healy attended a preview screening of *Hollywood Hotel* at the Warner Hollywood Theatre. He then went home to 10749 Weyburn Avenue in the Westwood neighborhood, where, according to the *Los Angeles Times*, he became very ill and was "convulsed by vomiting attacks." On Tuesday, half an hour before noon, with his wife still in the hospital with their newborn son, Healy died. He was forty-one. In light of his notorious bender and Monday morning punch-up, rumors began flying immediately that he had been beaten to death and that MGM was covering it up. Decades later, Bill Cassara put that lie to rest.

"If MGM covered it up, that's the worst job of covering up anything I could ever imagine," he says. "Medical examiners are trained to identify failings of the bodily functions, specifically in this case, the heart, the lungs. and the kidneys. The medical examiner diagnosed that Healy died of acute toxic nephritis caused by acute and chronic alcoholism, which weakened the heart, kidneys, and liver. He declared no injury to the skull or brain caused by the blow resulting in the laceration. There was no evidence of cerebral hemorrhage."

Moe, Larry, and Curly were on the road, performing in Boston and about to board a train when they received word that their old boss—and Moe's old friend—was dead. In his book, Moe says that he cried uncontrollably. (He also wrote that Healy died of a "brain concussion.") "When sober, Ted was the essence of refinement; while under the influence, he became a foul-mouthed, vicious character. . . . The strain of his life in show business got him started and once he started drinking he was never able to stop."

A requiem funeral mass took place on December 23 at St. Augustine Roman Catholic Church in Culver City across the street from the MGM studios. The crowd of more than 300 included a who's who of Hollywood and Healy's first wife, Betty Braun. Stuck on tour, Moe, Larry, and Curly were unable to attend. The three of them, especially Moe, might not have been happy when they picked up the local newspaper in whatever city they rolled into and read the Associated Press report on the funeral services, which included these lines:

> Healy's original three stooges, who formed a comic background that aided his climb to success, also attended the rites. They were Dick Hakins, Sam Wolfe and Paul Garner.

If you wanted to look up Shemp Howard in 1938, you could do so by looking him up—literally—in the Beverly Hills phone book. Shemp's phone number was WO-62386, and his address was 128 North Stanley Drive. When he arrived in Los Angeles, he had rented the house just north of Wilshire Boulevard and settled in for the time being with Babe, son Mort, and Babe's niece Beatrice. On the Columbia lot, Shemp was a contract player, and the studio execs were still experimenting, moving him around to see where he would fit in. Jules White had already been working with Shemp's brothers in the Three Stooges. That summer, White grabbed Shemp for his comedy shorts unit and paired him with one of their tried-and-true stars.

Andy Clyde, born in Scotland in 1892, was a vaudeville veteran who had worked in silent comedies with Mack Sennett. He was among the first batch of comedians—including the Three Stooges—whom White had signed up when Harry Cohn tasked him with starting the short subject department in 1934. Shemp would go up against Clyde in *Not Guilty Enough,* a remake of *Half-Baked Relations,* the last short that Clyde made for Educational Films of America before signing to Columbia. Filmed over five days beginning on July 29, the picture opens with Clyde as a man on trial for beating up his brother-in-law. In a flashback, the brother-in-law is revealed to be an obnoxious and havoc-wreaking character played by Shemp. Slapstick chaos follows, and Andy is found not guilty. The short began showing up in theaters on the last day of September. It was obvious that there was more comic gold to be mined from what Clyde film expert James L. Neibaur called "the conflict between the quietly befuddled Andy and the noisy and abrasive Shemp Howard . . . so the idea was revisited in *Home on the Rage.*"

For the encore, the dynamics and roles were the same. *Box Office* described the plot succinctly in its Shorts Index: "Andy's buttinsky brother-in-law creates a lot of excitement when he sells Andy an insurance policy." *Home on the Rage* was released on December 9, notable because the part of "Mr. Lent" was played by Vernon Dent, the character actor who would be best known as the adversary and sometime ally of the Three Stooges in ninety-six shorts (beginning with *Half Shot Shooters* in 1936) and whose most memorable and affecting appearance would be at Shemp's funeral.

If you wanted to run into Shemp Howard near the end of 1938, you might be able to find him around the corner from his house, at 8635 Wilshire Boulevard. Between filming the two Andy Clyde shorts, Shemp became part owner of a nightclub. The Stage 1 Café was a restaurant, bar, and showplace on the edge of Beverly Hills. And this was no corner sandwich shop. There were tables for 300 people, a stage, and, in one corner of the room, an imitation movie set (a perfect place for Shemp to reenact his Oscar Bush). It was a hangout where Shemp and his friends could meet up—and perform.

Shemp had partnered with Jack Edelstein and Wally Vernon. Edelstein was the businessman, described by *Variety* as "a one-time Long Island entrepreneur." Vernon was a comic actor and dancer who had signed to 20th Century Fox. He was riding high on his featured song and dance, "This Is the Life," in *Alexander's Ragtime Band,* a musical starring Tyrone Power, Alice Faye, and Don Ameche that had turned into a big success since its release in August.

The Stage 1 Café was launched on October 13 with a $1 minimum, "plain drinks" for fifty cents, and a stage revue called *Retakes of 1938. Los*

Angeles Times reporter Read Kendall covered the debut in his "Around and About in Hollywood" column: "Yverta Gartor, soprano and ballerina, is featured, and her performance should remind folks of Jimmy Durante's Mlle. Fifi." That must have been a taste of Read Kendall's sly humor. Mademoiselle Fifi was no dainty ballerina but a busty burlesque dancer. Back in the Roaring Twenties, Fifi was the comic foil for Durante and his partners Lou Clayton and Eddie Jackson when they played the tough Dover Club on West 51st Street in Manhattan. The comedy and entertainment at the Stage 1 Café was a bit rough and tumble as well—after all, it was Shemp's joint.

The grand opening a week later attracted a Hollywood crowd with reservations made by film folk, including Power, Ameche, Faye, her husband Tony Martin, Milton Berle, Brian Donlevy, Joan Davis, and the Ritz Brothers. Kendall gave the Stage 1 Café lots of mentions in his column in the weeks after the opening, dropping the names of Hollywood celebrities who had stopped in. Jack Haley, Shemp's partner in comedy in *Salt Water Daffy*, partied with a group in December. A weekend later, it was Bert Lahr from *Henry the Ache* along with his date, Ray Bolger, and Bolger's wife, Gwendolyn. Haley, Lahr, and Bolger were currently filming *The Wizard of Oz* at MGM. Kendall named Wally Vernon as the Stage 1 Café owner—he didn't mention Shemp—but many of the celebrity patrons were Shemp's new Hollywood pals: people like the joke writer Morey Amsterdam as well as Phil Silvers, another vaudeville veteran who had done some work at Vitaphone and was now seeking character parts.

Shemp got his Stage 1 Café plug on December 10 with the lead story and banner headline, "Stooging to Success," on page 1 of *The Billboard*:

> Despite the axiom that working as a stooge marks said stooge as a stooge forevermore, there is, upon investigation, an impressive list of such acts which, in one way or another, have made good on their own.
>
> Probably the best example is the trio which graduated from vaudeville's classic stoogery, the late Ted Healy's act, and became a national name. This is the Howard-Fine-Howard circus billed as the Three Stooges. After leaving Healy to be starred in Columbia shorts, trio became a high-priced vaude and nitery act. Shemp Howard is now part owner and featured act at his Stage No. 1 Cafe in Hollywood.

New Year's Eve 1938 was the big night for the Stage 1. The ads promised "an all new gala show that is the maddest and craziest show in town," starring the club's emcee Cully Richards, a singer and actor who had done some work in Poverty Row pictures and had a role in the Ritz Brothers' first feature, *Sing, Baby, Sing*—and Shemp Howard himself. Tickets were two dollars for "fun like you never had before. Plenty favors, hats, noise makers."

A down-and-dirty assessment of Shemp's place—and most likely that New Year's Eve lineup—was delivered by *Variety*, whose editor sent a spy to check out the show on Sunday, February 27, 1939. Shemp was leading a comedy revue and playing for a small crowd of drunks—or, as *Variety* put it more delicately, "those with a few on board."

"To the stone sober and discriminating, it's no go. Rowdy, rough, carefree and come-what-may, there's no rhyme or reason to the Stage hijinks.

"Cully Richards performs the m.c. duties and he rates a better break," according to the *Variety* review. He has a warming personality and knows how to drop off a gag." The Four Squares, "four very unfunny fellows" on piano, guitar, bull fiddle, and trumpet, were supplied with "a stage full of props, mostly hats, which they utilize for laffs that don't come." Henry Galante, "a run-of-the-mine baritone," played piano and sang at intermission—in the delightful language of the trades, he "ivories his own accompaniment at intermish."

Then there was Shemp:

> Howard does a shirt-tearing turn with Billy Young that's just as funny as it ever was. It's the old gag of meeting up with a pal and moping about the clunk that made off with his frau, then putting on the works to show what he'll do with the hoss thief if he ever catches up with him. Shemp, of course, plays the sucker.

Shemp's appearance was apparently worth wading through the rest. After all, the Stage 1 Café was like his living room (and not far from his actual living room), and it would be a treat to see a star tuning up for his screen or theatrical appearances (as comedy clubs would become a testing ground for top stand-ups decades later). But *Variety* reviewer "Helm" predicted that the room would continue to struggle because dancing was not allowed—a petition from neighbors had stopped the city from issuing a permit. "No matter how bad the music, or how small the floor, the celebrants must have their terping. It's the shank to the evening's fun, or are they going to change nature."

Late in 1939, *Variety* continued to list the Stage 1 Café as Shemp Howard's nightclub and home base. Meanwhile, his actual home base had moved a few blocks west. Shemp had rented a three-bedroom house at 201 South Hamel Drive in Beverly Hills, where he lived with Babe, Morton, and niece Beatrice.

Shemp was seeing a lot of action at Columbia Studios during this period, recognized as a very adaptable player fitting into a diverse collection of comedic and even dramatic film roles. In May 1939, he was cast in *Behind*

Shemp—with Dick Powell, longtime pal Murray Alper, and babies—was an uncredited highlight of Another Thin Man, *the 1939 adventures of married sleuths Nick and Nora Charles. MGM/Photofest © MGM*

Prison Gates, a drama with Brian Donlevy as a police detective who assumes a dead man's identity in order to infiltrate a prison in search of bank robbers. The movie went into production as *Escape from Alcatraz*. Shemp had a small, uncredited role as a kitchen worker, a trustee dishing out the slop.

Behind Prison Gates was released on July 28. Around that time, Columbia had loaned out Shemp to MGM for the second sequel to *The Thin Man*. William Powell and Myrna Loy starred as Nick and Nora Charles, a playful pair of sophisticated sleuths who love cocktails and banter; their scene-stealing costar was a wirehaired terrier named Asta. *Another Thin Man* (delayed by Powell's bout with cancer) added a baby, Nick Jr., to the mix. Shemp is not credited, but he had another standout role in a subplot: one of Nick's underworld connections, a comical ex-con named Creeps (played by Harry Bellaver), insists on throwing a first birthday party for Nick Jr. Near the end of the film, the Charleses' apartment is suddenly filled with ex-cons and hoods, each carrying an infant. Creeps and the boys have finished a chorus of "Happy Boithday" when Shemp, as an ex-con named Wacky, pokes his head around the door. One of the men rushes over with his baby.

"Hey, wait a minute, you can't come in here!"

"What do you mean I can't come in?" Wacky says. "Why? Why?"'

"You heard what Creeps said. You gotta have a kid!"

Shemp steps around the door, revealing that he's carrying a baby, too. "Well, I got a kid!"

Nick steps over. "Hello, Wacky!" he says, shaking his hand. "I didn't know you were married."

"Married? They didn't say you had to be married. They just said you hadda have a kid."

Shemp walks forward with his wailing child and is stopped by Creeps, with his baby. "Hey, hey," Creeps says, pointing to Wacky's boy. "You didn't snatch that, didja? We don't wanna put the heat on this party."

"No, I got it legitimate," Shemp says. "I rented it for a buck."

Once again, Shemp was given the best line in the picture. The actor who supposedly had an unnatural fear of dogs also had a scene with Asta.

Another Thin Man was released on November 17, 1939, by which time Jules White had grabbed Shemp for another short subject. Filmed over four days beginning on October 3, *Glove Slingers* was the first in a series of boxing comedies. Shemp was very likely cast because of his recognition as Knobby Walsh in the *Palooka* shorts at Vitaphone, and here, as fight promoter Pat Patrick, the former Sam Horwitz was playing a character who was even more obviously an Irishman. Hair trimmed and sporting eyeglasses and a mustache, Shemp left most of the comedy and about all of the slapstick to Paul Hurst, a large actor best known for his work in westerns, and Noah Beery Jr. as Terry Kelly, the reluctant young boxer.

Glove Slingers hit theaters a week after *Another Thin Man*. Over the next three and a half years, there would be a dozen films in the series—and three actors playing Terry Kelly. Shemp appeared only once more, in the next installment, *Pleased to Mitt You* (released on September 6, 1940), in which Guinn "Big Boy" Williams and a bland David Durand took over for Hurst and Beery Jr.

Shemp's final *Glove Slingers* appearance is remembered by many Stooges fans as proof of his off-the-cuff ad-libbing. It's a scene in a kitchen where Shemp is teaching "Big Boy" Williams how to peel potatoes. He has already sliced up a loaf of bread and played it like an accordion (director Jules White would reuse the gag with the Three Stooges at least twice, beginning in 1943) when he notices that Williams is butchering the taters. "What are you makin? French fries? I said peel the spud!" Shemp barks. "What're ya doing? I'll chop your hands up! Put the potatoes down. You don't know how to cut a potata!" He picks up a large knife to demonstrate. "You start this way"—Shemp fumbles the knife as he chops a potato and pretends to cut off his thumb. He drops the knife: "Wait a minute. You got some alum?" As Shemp walks away, thumb to his mouth, Williams laughs. And keeps laughing. He flings his knife, which sticks into the counter—*doink!*—and looks into the camera and laughs heartily. White left in what usually would have been an outtake—an early "blooper" that did not have to be saved for sixty years until DVDs came along.

On January 27, 1940, Shemp began work on another Columbia short with Andy Clyde. In *Money Squawks,* Shemp was not the antagonist. Andy and Shemp were railway station workers guarding a payroll from crooks. On February 15, they were in more familiar territory in *Boobs in the Woods,* an all-out, crash-bang, slapstick comedy in which Andy goes camping with his loudmouth brother-in-law Gus. Amid the mayhem, Clyde and Howard were becoming quite the team. It was, however, their last short together.

Shemp filmed a scene for a Columbia feature in March. *The Lone Wolf Meets a Lady* was the latest adventure of Mike Lanyard, a reformed jewel thief played by Warren William. Shemp is a loud, fast-talking pickpocket named Joe, who walks into a meeting between Lanyard and an informant who fences stolen goods. Shemp plays it for laughs, talking tough and repeating every few words (very much a model for "Jimmy Two Times" in *Goodfellas*). It's less than a minute of screen time. He enters down a staircase screen left, does his bit, and exits screen right—but it's an effective bit that fits into the picture and adds some levity to the mystery yet is not out of place in the milieu.

Columbia next loaned Shemp to RKO Radio Pictures, the studio located a mile south on Gower Street at the corner of Melrose Avenue, for a more substantial role. *Millionaires in Prison* was another drama with comedic overtones about just that—a group of millionaires trying to adjust to life in the pen. Shemp is one of the convicts they meet. He's introduced as "The Professor . . . quite a ladies man until he retired to this joint. Married three dames at the same time." "Bigamy, ay?" a millionaire asks. "No," Shemp says. "Two wives is bigamy. Three is *trigamy*! Ha ha ha!" The Professor takes a serious turn as one of four inmates who risk death as medical guinea pigs, testing a cure for a killer virus called "Malta fever."

In July 1940, it was a drive through the Cahuenga Pass from Hollywood to the San Fernando Valley and Universal City. Shemp had been tapped by Universal Pictures for a role in a feature film. At first glance, the role of Sailor McNeill was a simple case of typecasting. *The Leather Pushers* was a boxing comedy. Cribbed from Universal's 1922 silent movie serial starring Reginald Denny, it was the latest vehicle for the "Aces of Action," the team of actors Richard Arlen and Andy Devine. For Shemp, who had played the loud, hustling boxing figure so many times before, it should have been a breeze. Only this time, the role called for a slight twist. *Sailor McNeill was a mute.* Shemp would play this entire film in pantomime. *Variety* noticed. Its review singled out Shemp and Horace McMahon as "a pair of slap-happy vets who create some laughs."

Shemp would repeat the mute act for Universal in December as a character named "Gabby" in the Leon Errol-Lupe Velez musical comedy *Six Lessons from Madame La Zonga.* The author and film historian Edward Watz noted that although it was a "not-so-bright idea to have Shemp portray a mute"—for the second time in a year—"he still shines. Watch the conga line scene, where Shemp's fancy gyrations are the sole highlight of the film."

The difference was that Shemp now had a contract with Universal after some outstanding performances capped by a costarring role in a film that would come to be regarded as a comedy classic.

But first there was work at 20th Century Fox Studios on the west side of Los Angeles. Once again, Shemp was called in for a single scene, although this one would be something of a tour de force. He would be featured in *Murder Over New York,* the latest among the dozens of pictures in the series that followed the fictional Honolulu police detective Charlie Chan. The Chinese American character was portrayed by Sidney Toler, a Caucasian American actor who had taken over the role after the death of Warner Oland, a white Swede. (Toler would play Chan in twenty films; Oland had appeared in sixteen Charlie Chan features and also played other stereotypical Asians, including, in 1929, the starring role in *The Mysterious Dr. Fu Manchu.*)

Toler worked in "yellowface," a practice that would come to be condemned along with the racist blackface routines that were still showing up in mainstream pictures at the time. In *Murder Over New York,* Shemp appears in "brownface," at least temporarily, as part of a police lineup assembled for "Number Two Son" Jimmy Chan. After Jimmy gets a look at a murder suspect who appeared to be East Indian, the police inspector orders his men to "round up every Hindu in town." The inspector, played by Frank MacBride, who had roles in eight of Shemp's solo shorts and two features, repeats the casual racism in the police lineup scene, asking a subordinate, "Hey Frank, how many more of these Ali Babas are there?" When Jimmy Chan, played by Victor Sen Yung, is unable to identify the perpetrator among the eleven men standing before him, he utters what could be a sly line: "They're all beginning to look alike to me."

In the Charlie Chan mystery Murder Over New York *(1940), Shemp is Shorty McCoy, aka The Canarsie Kid, "feeding suckers" as a "phony Hindu." Twentieth Century Studios/ Photofest © Twentieth Century Studios*

Shemp, in a long raincoat, is dead center in the lineup of suspects, although, with his darkened skin, turban, mustache, and beard, he's not immediately recognizable. He has already caused a commotion by sitting cross-legged on the floor when he's ordered to step forward. The Inspector walks to the stage and looks up at him:

> INSPECTOR: Well, what's your racket?
> SHEMP: Racket? I do not understand, sahib. I am Hindu fakir.
> INSPECTOR: Faker's right!
> *Shemp opens his coat, revealing harem pants and no shirt, and strikes a model's pose.*
> SHEMP: My dear sir, you are laboring under a delusion. You have the honor of addressing the great Rashid, grand lama of the sacred cult of psychic believers. Through me, souls are cleansed.
> INSPECTOR: Wait a minute, buddy. (*motions over a cop with a bucket of soapy water*) We're gonna start with a little cleansing of your mug!
> COP (*to Shemp*): Come on, sit down!

Shemp sits, cross-legged. The Inspector removes his turban. The cop peels off Shemp's phony mustache and beard and with a wet sponge begins scrubbing the paint off his face. There's laughter from the "Hindus" in the lineup as Shemp's pale skin is revealed and he loses the formal foreign accent and sputters in Brooklynese—*Shemp*-ese:

> SHEMP: Cut it out! I'll get a habey corpey on you! Cut it out! Wait a minute, I'm a citizen! Cut it out, cut it out, will ya!
> *The cop stops scrubbing.*
> COP: This is Shorty McCoy, the Canarsie Kid! He makes a living feeding suckers phony religions!
> SHEMP (*standing, soaked*): A guy can't make an honest living no more!
> INSPECTOR: Get him outta here!
> SHEMP: I'll go, but this is my bread and butter!
> INSPECTOR: Get out!
> SHEMP: I got connections, don't forget that!

Back on the Universal lot in late August 1940, Shemp had a substantial supporting role in *Give Us Wings*. The adventure-comedy was the first of three films (along with *Hit the Road* in 1941 and *Keep 'em Slugging* in 1943) that he would make under Universal's "Dead End Kids and Little Tough Guys" brand, which featured five of the original Dead End Kids (with the exception of Leo Gorcey, still under contract to Warner Bros.). Huntz Hall was one of the originals and, of all the Kids, the one with whom Shemp connected. Shemp saw real comic potential in the young actor and coached him through the comedy scenes that were important to the series.

"The youthful and aspiring twenty-year-old Hall lacked something Shemp's years had given him; namely, extensive vaudeville experience," Jim Manago wrote in *Behind Sach*, his 2015 Huntz Hall biography. "Shemp most certainly had a deeper well of gags to draw upon than Hall. Therefore, Shemp could offer valuable pointers to Hall on timing and other aspects to comedy performance."

"Huntz Hall always gave Shemp credit for his comedy sense," comedy historian Nick Santa Maria says. "Shemp took him under his wing, according to Huntz, and coached him with the comedy. But if you notice, in those films in the early forties that he made with Shemp, Huntz is still kind of that wise guy kid who occasionally elicits a snicker. He doesn't become fully funny until about 1950, almost ten years later. It took a long time to gestate within, but when you watch Huntz in the Bowery Boys films, where he's a full-out comedian, it's remarkable. He's funny. I think he's funnier than Jerry Lewis."

Give Us Wings *(1940) was the first of three films Shemp made with the "Dead End Kids," including Huntz Hall, who would become his comedy protégé and lifelong friend. Universal Pictures/Photofest © Universal Pictures*

It's said that Shemp and Huntz Hall would visit each other's sets while working at Universal. They became such good friends that Hall began to refer to Shemp as "my father in this business."

"My father thought Shemp was the funniest man who ever lived," Hall's son Gary told Manago. "Though Shemp died when I was five, I remember him well. My parents considered Shemp (and his wife, Babe) to be my godparents. I do remember my father saying that he was on set when they were shooting the W. C. Fields movie *The Bank Dick*. Shemp did many hilarious scenes that Fields cut out because they were too funny and therefore competition for Fields."

Shemp jumped into *The Bank Dick*, the Universal feature written by and starring the great stage and film comedian W. C. Fields, as soon as *Give Us Wings* wrapped. When he went to work on the Fields project in September 1940, there would be no loud, obnoxious outbursts, slapstick routines, or muttering comic asides from Shemp. That was W. C. Fields's territory. If Fields did indeed excise Shemp's "hilarious scenes," it was to his credit. As Joe Guelpe, bartender at the Black Pussy Cat Café, Shemp's was probably the most human, realistic character in the outrageous comedy.

Shemp's low-key role as bartender Joe Guelpe in the W. C. Fields 1940 classic The Bank Dick *was among his most highly praised performances. Universal Pictures/Photofest © Universal Pictures*

"Fields gave him his moment in the sun," the film critic and historian Leonard Maltin says. "It's such a wonderful film, I would think he would have been happy just to be in the company of Fields and the director Eddie Cline." *The Bank Dick*, Maltin adds, is his favorite of Shemp's solo work.

The movie premiered on November 29, 1940. Although Shemp did not deliver the "best line," he would be the essential straight man when Fields leans over the bar and asks, "Was I in here last night and did I spend a twenty dollar bill?"

"Yeah."

"Oh boy, what a load that is off my mind." And after a beat, "I thought I'd lost it."

(Incidentally, in the original script, the bar was named "The Black Pussy," leading to an immediate rejection from Joseph Breen, who administered the industry's self-censoring Motion Picture Code. Fields argued that his friend, the comic Leon Errol, ran a bar by that name—and he was telling the truth. Errol's Black Pussy was located at 8253 Santa Monica Boulevard in West Hollywood. An apparent compromise was reached. The signs and window of the bar were marked "Black Pussy Cat Café," but whenever Fields' character mentioned the place, he called it "The Black Pussy.")

Give Us Wings and *The Bank Dick* began showing up in movie houses near the beginning of December 1940, sometimes, as at the State Theatre in Waterbury, Connecticut, paired on the same bill. Readers of the movie ad in the *Waterbury Democrat* might notice Shemp Howard's name listed among the supporting cast in both films. Those who bought tickets and stayed through the double feature would see two sides of Shemp's movie persona.

Shemp's role in *The Bank Dick* rated a mention in his old hometown paper, the *Brooklyn Eagle*, on December 10. Under the headline "No Matter Where You Go 'Brooklyn Touch' Leaves Its Imprint," columnist Clifford Evans wrote,

> *Bank Dick*, the W. C. Fields film now showing at the RKO Albee Theater, is an old-time comedy. One of those who helps Fields obtain the laughs is Shemp Howard, another Brooklyn product. Shemp is a brother of Moe and Curly Howard, two of the Three Stooges. Years ago, when the Howard brothers first started in show business, Shemp played with them. Eventually they separated. Moe and Curly teamed up with Larry Fine and the trio reached the big time as stooges to the late Ted Healy. Shemp Howard is from Bensonhurst, the 86th St. sector.

Shemp was a long way from Brooklyn. And thanks to his work in *The Bank Dick*, he was about to go much farther.

SEVENTEEN

Universal Soldier

Even before *The Bank Dick* was released, executives at Universal knew that they had a solid player in Shemp Howard. They signed him to a contract that would not only keep the comic actor busy for at least half the year but also provide him with the most memorable roles in the most artistically satisfying portion of his career.

Between September 1940, when *The Bank Dick* was filmed, through the summer of 1943, when he did his last work at Universal in *Moonlight and Cactus*, Shemp would be cast in a wide variety of films, many B-movies but with a distinguished group of actors, in roles that ranged from costar to featured player to cameo spots.

In the final days of 1940, Shemp showed up in *The Invisible Woman*, a comedy in which John Barrymore (once the stage's greatest Hamlet, now a debauched drinking buddy of W. C. Fields and Errol Flynn) starred as the inventor of an invisibility machine. Shemp was "Hammerhead," one of a trio of comedic thugs who steal the device for their gangster boss, who is holed up in Mexico and hoping not to be seen.

Shemp had an uncredited role in *Lucky Devils*, another Richard Arlen-Andy Devine "Aces of Action" mystery. This time he wasn't a mute, but he did have something of a stutter as a pickpocket the pair meet in a jail cell. Shemp does a short, funny monologue; throws in an ad-lib at the end; and then probably headed home for dinner. *Lucky Devils* opened in theaters on January 3, 1941. *Six Lessons from Madame La Zonga*, which was highlighted by Shemp's revival of the mute routine, opened two weeks later.

A review of his filmography shows that Shemp's movies were being released at about the same rate as some of his short subjects at Vitaphone, often more frequently than biweekly. There was *Road Show* for Hal Roach Studios (February 18), starring John Hubbard as a rich playboy who escapes marriage to a gold digger by faking insanity and then running off with a carnival. Shemp shows up as a lion tamer named Moe Parker. He does not share the scene with any actual lions.

His show-stopping appearance as the fake "Ali Baba" Shorty McCoy in *Murder Over New York* got a replay of sorts in *Mr. Dynamite* (March 7). Lloyd Nolan is a Major League Baseball pitcher on the eve of the World Series, running with Irene Hervey from foreign saboteurs in a carny section of New York City called Baghdad Way. The pair are being chased by bad guys when they approach a fortune-teller booth, where Shemp, in Arab headdress and robes, is scamming a widow. "Everything is clear now," Shemp says, peering into his crystal ball. "Abdullah sees tall man, dark woman. They come into your life." Suddenly, the fleeing couple is reflected in his crystal ball, and he does a Shempian double take. We next see Abdullah emerging from a closet (where Nolan had stuffed him and the woman after taking their clothes for disguise). He's in long underwear, surprising his mark as he vows revenge in a thick Brooklyn accent. "Why those lowdown, no good, doity crooks! I'll get the Williamsboig Protection Association to get after them! Leave it to me!" (Shemp would go full "Ali Baba" as Sinbad in *Arabian Nights*, released on Christmas Day 1942—his sole appearance in Technicolor—annoying Billy Gilbert with his constant tales of the sea told in a Brooklyn accent.)

There were other forgotten B-movie gems, like *Cracked Nuts* (released on July 1, 1941), with Shemp and Mischa Auer as a pair of con men with a scheme to sell a phony robot. Auer is Boris Kabiloff, the phony inventor. Shemp, as Eddie, pretends to be Ivan the robot. Ernie Stanton plays the scenes in the full robot suit, so most of Shemp's work is in voice-over, but he has his moments while Auer is fitting him into the metal suit:

> EDDIE: I thought you were gonna get into this sardine can and let me be the inventor.
> KABIKOFF: Do you look like an inventor? No.
> EDDIE: Do I look like a dummy?
> KABIKOFF: Yes.
> EDDIE: Yeah . . .

Later in the scene, Eddie reveals that he's afflicted by a "phobia," just as Shemp was supposedly phobic in real life—that will lead to complications (even though he has a little trouble with the definition):

> EDDIE: Wait a minute, I can't go this afternoon. I got a date.
> KABIKOFF: You better forget about your date. This is more important.
> EDDIE: Oh no, this is a date with a blonde.
> KABIKOFF: Blonde? Why don't you forget about blondes?
> EDDIE: Oh, no, I can't forget about blondes. I got blonde-phobia.

KABIKOFF: Blondaphobia?
EDDIE: Sure. Some guys got a phobia for getting drunk. Other guys collect stamps. And some other guys save string. Me, I chase blondes.
KABIKOFF: What for?
EDDIE: I don't know. I never caught one yet.

The film includes some very funny scenes with the robot and Black comic actors Mantan Moreland and Hattie Noel. In *The Strange Case of Dr. Rx*, a mystery filmed at Universal in October 1941 and released on April 18, 1942, Shemp plays a detective in need of a drink. In recognition of their talents and chemistry, the script takes a break from the plot to allow Shemp and Moreland to work some stand-alone comedy scenes that could have come straight from the vaudeville stage.

Shemp was cast in two films starring the comedy team of Ole Olsen and Chic Johnson. *Hellzapoppin'* was filmed at Universal Studios between June and November 1941. It was the screen version of Olsen and Johnson's wild, long-running musical comedy revue that had opened on Broadway in 1938. The movie opens with a shot of a formally dressed crowd gathered outside the "Universal Theatre," dissolving to a scene inside the theater's projection booth. Shemp is Louie the projectionist, handling reels of film to be screened for the crowd. When he has trouble unspooling a reel, he merely tears off a piece of film and throws it on the floor. "This a fine pickledilly," he grumbles. "Fifteen years I been runnin' these pictures and now all of a sudden, I gotta be an actor!" He flicks a switch and watches the film play on the big screen below: a dozen and a half singing chorus girls, all in gowns, descend a marble staircase. As they near the bottom, the stairs flatten out, and all the women scream as they slide down out of frame. There's an explosion, and then, under the credits, the dancers fall against a backdrop of flames. They are going to hell!

Cut to a musical number set in hell, with lots of devils sharpening pitchforks and jabbing people in the rear ends, people boiling in cauldrons, and three very pretty women roasting on a spit. Then there's another explosion. A taxicab appears. Olsen and Johnson, announced as "our prized guests," slide out the back. "That's the first taxi driver that ever went straight where I told him to!" says Johnson. Like the stage show, the movie is full of corny jokes, pre–Ernie Kovacs sight gags, singers, dancers, specialty acts, and wild concepts come to life.

Shemp returns for a bizarre scene in the projection booth that pushes the fourth wall into the next soundstage. He's got a guest, a quite large usherette who demands, "Are you more interested in that picture or in me? I've wasted all day up here with you! I could've had a good date this afternoon!" Suddenly, she's on the attack, reels are flying, film is unspooled—and the movie's framing goes out of rack. On-screen, Olsen and Johnson notice and yell at the projectionist, "Hey Louie! Will you keep your mind on your work?" Louie, knee-deep in film and dodging hits from his gal pal, slaps on the wrong reel. Suddenly, cowboys and Indians are fighting it out. Chic Johnson orders, "Will you take those phony Hollywood Indians off the screen!" just as one of the Indians aims his rifle and fires, hitting Johnson in the seat of his pants! *Hellzapoppin'* was, *Variety* decreed, "a good escapist comedy. . . . The title is a natural in itself, and the laughs are plentiful enough in the madcap helter-skelter of corny hoke to rate the picture extended runs," adding,

> One of the picture's saving graces is the originality of presentation of screwball comedy. That business of O. & J. talking from the screen to comic projectionist Shemp Howard is one such detail.

Hellzapoppin' premiered at the Rivoli Theatre on Broadway on Christmas Day 1941. Shemp was featured in Olsen and Johnson's *Crazy House* in October 1943. In this outing, the pair are rejected by Universal Pictures, so, as Les Adams explained, "they decide to rent a movie lot and make their own films . . . financed by a 'millionaire' who hasn't got two nickels he could rub together." Shemp plays one of Olsen and Johnson's flunkies, Mumbo (teamed with Fred Sanborn as "Jumbo") and has a role in the film within the film—as a street hustler who approaches the pair from all directions. "Wanna buy a clock? On time? . . . Do you wanna buy a deck of cards? It's a good deal. . . . Wanna buy a stove? It's hot! . . . Wanna buy an anchor? Right off the boat!" In what would be his penultimate film with Universal and amid a cast crammed with popular comedians and Universal stars, Shemp stands out.

"He was hilarious," says the critic and historian Stuart Galbraith IV.

As Three Stooges history has been passed down through the decades, Shemp has also been credited for a dramatic role in *Pittsburgh*, a film in which John Wayne and Randolph Scott portray coal miner buddies who rise to the top of the steel industry while fighting over Marlene Dietrich. It was the second teaming for the threesome in 1942 (*The Spoilers*, which had them brawling in Nome, Alaska, landed in theaters in June) and was, according to Caro Ness of *Eye for Film*, "an unashamed propaganda film to inspire workers to work harder in order to help the War effort." Shemp, as a tailor named Shorty, plays it "straight"—but as only he can. He most definitely serves as comic relief during a segment in which Wayne's character walks out of Shorty's shop wearing a suit he neglects

Shemp definitely was a comedic bright spot in the 1942 drama Pittsburgh, *sharing the screen with stars Randolph Scott, John Wayne, and Marlene Dietrich. Universal Pictures/ Photofest © Universal Pictures*

to pay for and heads across the street and into a theater where there's a boxing challenge that turns into a free-for-all (and where Shemp shows how a vaudeville-trained professional reacts when a chair is smashed over his head).

But of all the work Shemp did as a contract player at Universal, two movie brands stand out as showcases for his best and most lasting work, whether solo or later with the Three Stooges. They were two genres of comedy that complemented each other, and in one picture, actually came together.

Abbott and Costello were the quintessential burlesque comedy team (not vaudevillians, as commonly believed, historian Travis S.D. clarified, but "strictly burlesque men who came to prominence in that industry's final years"). Both were veterans of the burlesque "wheels" (circuits) when they first teamed up in 1935 at the Eltinge Theatre on 42nd Street in New York City. By then, burlesque, once the affordable "vaudeville for the working class," had become what it's known as today: a showcase for strippers and comedians, including legendary strippers like Gypsy Rose Lee and Sally Rand and legendary comedians like Jackie Gleason, Red Skelton—and Abbott and Costello. Bud Abbott, born in 1897, was the oily straight man; Lou Costello, eight years his junior, was the roly-poly, childlike clown who would moan "I'm a b-a-a-ad boy." Their combination of slapstick and snappy patter—but mostly that three-card-monte wordplay—set them apart and made them a hit on radio as well as onstage. Their calling card routine was "Who's on First?," a back-and-forth flummox bit in which Abbott explains to Costello the names of players on a baseball team. The catch is that each name is also the basis for a question:

> ABBOTT: I'm telling you: Who's on first, What's on second, I Don't Know is on third.
> COSTELLO: You know the fellows' names?
> ABBOTT: Yes.
> COSTELLO: Well then, who's playing first?
> ABBOTT: Yes.
> COSTELLO: I mean the fellow's name on first base.
> ABBOTT: Who.
> COSTELLO: The fella playin' first base . . .

Not only was the routine not unique, it wasn't even new, having worked its way through burlesque and vaudeville circuits from the early days. In fact, the vaudeville team of Bert Wheeler and Robert Woolsey trotted out a version in *Cracked Nuts*—not Shemp's 1941 robot comedy but a movie they made ten years earlier for RKO Radio Pictures. The two of them are studying a map, discussing battle plans:

> WHEELER: . . . proceed in a northerly direction to the town of What.
> WOOLSEY: What?
> WHEELER: That's right.
> WOOLSEY: What's right?
> WHEELER: What's right.
> WOOLSEY: That's what I said. What's right?
> WHEELER: Well, I agreed with you, didn't I?
> WOOLSEY: On what?
> WHEELER: Yes.

Abbott and Costello signed to Universal in 1940 and made their movie debut in the romantic comedy *One Night in the Tropics*. They were supporting players, typical comic relief, but got to show off half a dozen routines, including a taste of "Who's on First," ten years after Wheeler and Woolsey. *Variety* decided that their appearances were "the brightest spots in the picture." In fact, they ran away with the picture. *Tropics* premiered on October 30. On December 13, Abbott and Costello were already back on the Universal lot, filming *Buck Privates*. The picture was originally written as a romance, with Abbott and Costello providing the comedy spots, but as shooting progressed, it was clear that the pair were the center of the story. More of their burlesque bits were added to the script.

With the popular swinging, close-harmony singing trio the Andrews Sisters providing musical interludes, *Buck Privates* was cheerful propaganda, promoting the new peacetime draft—the first in the nation's history. Hitler's army was crushing its way across Europe, Japan had joined Germany's alliance with Italy, France had fallen, Great Britain was about to be under siege, and it was inevitable that the United States would eventually enter a war that had been spreading around the world since 1937. Now it was a matter of getting American audiences in the mood, putting a happy face on the nightmares ahead.

Buck Privates opens with a pre-credits sequence showing a theater audience watching newsreel footage of President Franklin D. Roosevelt signing the draft into law on September 16, 1940, and the defense secretary drawing, at random, the number of the first draftee. The credits are set to a tune that the Andrews Sisters will sing more than once: "You're a Lucky Fellow, Mr. Smith"—lucky to be born in the United States, lucky to be conscripted, and—unsaid but apparent—lucky to die for your country.

Abbott and Costello's introduction in *Buck Privates* is very similar to Shemp and Jack Haley's entrance in *Salt Water Daffy*: they're a couple of street scammers who run from a pursuing policeman into a movie theater, not realizing that the venue is being used as an army induction center. Abbott and Costello join the army and move on to basic training (with that police officer as their drill instructor).

Shemp shows up in the picture as "Chef," an army cook, in a musical number with Lou Costello, "When Private Brown Becomes a Captain." Costello raps about the changes he would make if he were in charge, Shemp joins in, they dance a rhumba, and flour is tossed through the air and into faces. "There's no doubt Shemp is one of the true one-offs of comedy," Matthew Cumian and Nick Santa Maria wrote in *The Annotated Abbott and Costello*, "capable (especially when his brothers are not around) of a surprisingly wide range of effects. . . . He's a delight here."

In an interview, Santa Maria adds, "The Abbott and Costello films were star comedies, built around Lou Costello with the great straight part by Bud Abbott in support. There wasn't much room for a lot of other

With Buck Privates *(1941), Shemp became a prized member of Abbott and Costello's on-screen comedy troupe. Universal Pictures/Photofest © Universal Pictures*

comedy, let's say. I think Shemp was kind of like the paprika that you put in the tomato sauce to give it that kick. That was Shemp."

The Universal suits liked what they saw, and once *Buck Privates* wrapped on January 11, 1941 (over budget and over schedule), they assigned director Arthur Lubin to knock out another Abbott and Costello B-movie. This time, it would be a horror comedy. Cameras rolled ten days later on *Oh, Charlie!*, in which Abbott and Costello were a couple of service station pump jockeys stranded in a haunted house. Shemp was written into a scene as a soda jerk. ("It probably took him half a day," Santa Maria says.) Then, on January 31, 1941, plans changed once again. That was the day *Buck Privates* was released.

The movie was a hit! Audiences ate it up—and so did the critics. Theodore Strauss, second stringer to Bosley Crowther at the *New York Times*, wrote that the film was "an hour and a half of uproarious monkeyshines. Army humor isn't apt to be subtle and neither are Abbott and Costello. Their antics have as much innuendo as a 1000-pound bomb but nearly as much explosive force." *Variety* agreed: "Geared at a zippy pace and providing lusty and enthusiastic comedy of the broadest slapstick, it's a hilarious laugh concoction that will click solidly in the general runs for profitable biz." *Variety*'s reviewer added two predictions: "A natural for the family and hinterland trade, *Buck Privates* might easily surprise in the key houses," and "Picture has a good chance to skyrocket the former burlesk and radio team of Bud Abbott and Lou Costello into the top flight starring ranks as a comedy duo." Both predictions would be proven correct.

Executives at Universal were quick to switch gears to capitalize on the success of service comedies and their new star duo. *Oh, Charlie!* was shelved for the time being, and by the beginning of April, a sequel to *Buck Privates* was scripted and rushed into production. *In the Navy* reunited the boys with the Andrews Sisters and sent them all off to sea. Shemp Howard was again recruited, this time in a more prominent role as Dizzy, a sailor who again shares kitchen duties with Costello's character.

"Shemp was included in a few of the key routines," Nick Santa Maria says. "In fact, he was prominent in them, and so I have a feeling they looked at the previous two films and said, 'Yeah, we've got to give this guy some more stuff. He works well with these guys.' You've got to give credit to Universal for noticing that. He made five pictures with Abbott and Costello, but *Africa Screams* (in 1949) is the only film among those that Bud and Lou had any say over casting. By that time, they were casting friends, they were casting Joe Besser, they were casting Shemp. They were casting the Baer brothers. They're all buddies, all friends, so I have a feeling that they did cross paths. They were at Universal from 1940, before they worked together in 1941, so maybe they hung together in the commissary and had lunch. The only thing is, in those early films, they didn't have any say in casting Shemp. Shemp was a contract player. He was cast, really randomly, in the film. He was a funny guy going into a funny film."

In the Navy was released on May 30, 1941. As in *Buck Privates,* "You're a Lucky Fellow, Mr. Smith" played over the opening credits. *Oh, Charlie!* had been rushed back into production a few weeks earlier. When preview audiences asked why the Andrews Sisters were missing, wraparound nightclub scenes were added to include songs by Patty, Maxene, and LaVerne Andrews—and Ted Lewis, whose numbers include his racist song-and-dance version of "Me and My Shadow," in which an uncredited Black dancer (Eddie Chester in a "shadowlike" all-black tuxedo and top hat) mimics his every step and movement (Lewis performed the bit with various Black "shadows" into the civil rights era of the 1960s). *Oh, Charlie!* was retitled *Hold That Ghost* and made it into theaters on August 6 as the Abbott and Costello—and Shemp Howard—steamroller rolled on.

The executives at Universal had gold with their new comedy team, but there was only so much Abbott and Costello to go around. So the studio began making Abbott and Costello pictures *without* Abbott and Costello. In late May 1941, around the time extra scenes were being shot for *Hold That Ghost*, a low-budget, black-and-white musical comedy went into production. *San Antonio Rose* starred Eve Arden, Jane Frazee, and Robert Paige in a story of two entertainment groups and a gangster competing to reopen an abandoned roadhouse. Filling in for the Andrews Sisters were the Merry Macs, a close-harmony foursome made up of the McMichael brothers—Judd, Joe, and Ted—and Mary Lou Cook.

(The Merry Macs would sing in a real Abbott and Costello picture, *Ride 'Em Cowboy*, in 1942. The youngest McMichael brother, Joe, was inducted into the army in 1943 and died the following February. Some biographies state mistakenly that he was killed in action during World War II; Joe died not in battle but in Santa Ana, California, of "an improperly taken dose of sulfa tablets for a cold.")

Shemp Howard had a major supporting role in *San Antonio Rose*, and he was teamed with an unlikely comedic partner, Lon Chaney Jr. Son of the legendary actor known as the "Man of a Thousand Faces," Chaney Jr. had been signed to Universal earlier in the year. A veteran of more than fifty pictures in the past decade, Chaney was not known for comedic skills.

In San Antonio Rose *(1941), Universal tried out Shemp and Lon Chaney Jr. as an ersatz Abbott and Costello. (Shemp and Eve Arden might have been a better match.) Universal Pictures/Photofest © Universal Pictures*

His most notable role was as Lennie, the hulking, autistic, accidental killer in the 1939 Hal Roach feature *Of Mice and Men*. Nevertheless, Universal immediately assigned him to two musical comedies—musical comedies that Shemp was also slotted in.

The first time Shemp and Chaney shared the screen was in *Too Many Blondes*, which began filming on April 2, 1941. Rudy Vallee and Helen Parris star as a married couple. Shemp is a hotel manager and Chaney a cab driver, enlisted to help save them from a Mexican divorce. Shemp and Chaney had some funny scenes, but it was clear that Chaney was not a natural comedian. So it may be surprising to learn that at the end of May, after Shemp had wrapped work on *In the Navy*, he and Chaney were reunited. This time, they were—or were supposed to be—a real comedy team in *San Antonio Rose*. While Bud and Lou were filming the wrapround material for *Hold That Ghost*, Shemp and Chaney Jr. were teamed as Benny the Bounce and Jigsaw Kennedy, a pair of ex-con racketeers looking to muscle in on the nitery business. There was talk that Universal executives were considering the team of Howard and Chaney as "the new Abbott and Costello." There's even a segment of the film in which they're hired on as waiters and wreak havoc in the reopened roadhouse—just as the new scenes penned in for *Hold That Ghost* had Abbott and Costello's characters serving tables.

There was one problem with the teaming: Lon Chaney Jr. was not funny. His character was mean, dour, scary, and too often smacking Shemp around with a shocking intensity. The hits and slaps weren't comical or amped up with silly sound effects. They were real, brutal, and harder than anything Moe had dished out in the Three Stooges shorts—harder even than the ones from that guy from the vaudeville days.

The abuse did not go unnoticed. Days before the release of *San Antonio Rose* in June 1941, syndicated columnist Harold Heffernan dedicated part of his column to the battering Shemp takes on-screen and the "art to this business of absorbing a mauling": "We don't know a more experienced professor to handle this lesson than Shemp Howard. You must remember Shemp—chief sock and kick assimilator of the famous Three Stooges. Shemp is turning both cheeks these days to Lon Chaney Jr. in *San Antonio Rose*. He's cast as a dumb stooge and Lon wallops him in practically every scene—with no pulled punches." Heffernan added a quote from Shemp himself:

> You can't pull a slap in the face and make it sound real. The way to take an open-handed clout is to be certain it lands in the right spot. Full on the cheek, you take it, as high on the cheekbones as possible without striking the eye, and far back enough so the force of the blow is absorbed by the jawbone. That and rolling with the slap—and you can take 'em.

Heffernan ended the item with a warning:

> But, cautious Shemp, watch your cues—or you're headed for a slap-happy old age.

"I saw the movie recently for the first time, and no," Nick Santa Maria says, denying any chance that a Howard–Chaney comedy team would ever be a serious consideration. "Again, it's just two contract players being put in the same film. We see they have no chemistry. And with Lon's slaps, Shemp's head should have been across the set. I'm sure Shemp was longing for Ted Healy at that point."

Chaney's biographer Don G. Smith agreed that "as Jigsaw Kennedy, Lon is a gruff, powerful but comically inept gangster. . . . Lon Chaney is no comedian. . . . He would never have been a candidate to become one of the Three Stooges. According to his wife, Patsy Chaney, Lon never liked slapstick, anyway." Later that year, in the title role of *The Wolfman*, Chaney would begin a legendary run in horror films. He would play the Wolfman in several pictures, including, in 1948, *Abbott and Costello Meet Frankenstein*.

"I love what Bud Abbott said about Shemp," Santa Maria adds. "He was talking about the importance of a straight man and what he does for Lou in the act. And he was very proud of what he did for Lou, and he said, 'You know, there's a comic working now, Shemp Howard, one of the funniest guys in the business, but he's stuck making those crappy shorts because he doesn't have a decent straight man.' That's what Bud thought about Shemp."

Shemp fared far better in the ersatz Abbott and Costello genre when he was cast in *Private Buckaroo*. A genuine bastard child of *Buck Privates*, the musical comedy was ordered up after the United States entered World War II in response to Japan's attack on Pearl Harbor on December 7, 1941. *Private Buckaroo* had its premiere in Los Angeles on May 25, 1942. On its New York City opening, Theodore Strauss of the *New York Times* described the film as "a jam session with patriotic overtones . . . another story of what an assortment of crooners, band musicians and jitterbugs can do to the Army."

In *Private Buckaroo*, jazz trumpeter and big-band leader Harry James, playing himself, finds out he has been drafted and heads off to basic training (in real life, an old back injury got him classified 4-F). That's basically the plot in a picture that's little more than "enlistment propaganda."

But it's entertaining propaganda, packed with talent, and a high point in Shemp Howard's career.

The Andrews Sisters are in their usual places—and there's even more jitterbugging, courtesy of the Jivin' Jacks and Jills, a teenage dance group assembled by Universal and led by seventeen-year-old Peggy Ryan and Donald O'Connor, who at sixteen was a movie veteran. Joe E. Lewis plays nightclub comedian Lancelot Pringle "Biff" McBiff. Shemp's good friend and "student" Huntz Hall shows up as "Corporal Anemic," an army recruit who teaches Harry James how to play a bugle. The only missing piece in the flag-waver is the team of Abbott and Costello. Shemp, as army sergeant "Muggsy" Snavel, fills in nicely in what many Stooges fans and critics alike say is his best performance.

The film opens as Sergeant Snavel and his (much taller) fiancée, Bonnie-Belle Schlopkiss, played wonderfully by Mary Wickes, arrive at the packed nightclub where Harry James is headlining. Muggsy bribes their way in and to a table, which turns out to be located in a hallway between kitchen doors far from the show. After some deft slapstick, the couple carries the table into the showroom and plants it ringside, where emcee McBiff begins hitting on Bonnie-Belle.

Shemp's showstopper with the Andrews Sisters in Private Buckaroo, *the 1942 musical comedy that's "the closest thing to a feature film starring Shemp." Universal Pictures/ Photofest © Universal Pictures*

According to Edward Watz, Shemp was not supposed to have the leading comedic role in the film—but he took it, pulling out all the comedic stops in every scene he played. Once again, somebody noticed:

> A bonafide studio genius realized that Shemp was walking away with the film, so all of his scenes were included in the final cut, making *Buckaroo* the closest thing to a feature film starring Shemp. The nominal star of the film, Joe E. Lewis, though lionized in his day, can't hold a candle to what Shemp creates in his scenes.

It's the picture's finale, an army camp variety show, that provides a transcendent Shemp moment. The Andrews Sisters, backed by Harry James and His Music Makers, are onstage, singing and dancing a swinging version of "Don't Sit Under the Apple Tree." Arms linked, Maxene, Patty, and LaVerne sidestep toward the wings, screen right, and when they move back toward center stage, Sergeant Snavel is linked with them. Shemp's surprise appearance—dead serious, ramrod straight, in uniform with his hat in the crook of his left arm, sure footwork, and a bit shorter than the women—may give the viewer an unexpected lump in the throat along with a laugh. In the pantomime that follows, Shemp's the one who has been "sitting under the apple tree." Patty gives him a Ted Healy slap, and Maxene shoves him back to the wings. But when the sisters dance over to the bandstand, Shemp emerges from the opposite wings, screen left. Maxene gives him another slap, sending him stutter-stepping backward into the wings. The boys in Harry James's band are watching Shemp, and they're all cracking up.

Eighteen

The Ugliest Man in Hollywood

Damon Runyon was a newspaper journalist and short-story writer. He was born in Manhattan, Kansas, in 1880 and in the 1920s and 1930s became the prime chronicler of the colorful underworld in the Manhattan located in New York City. Runyon's turf was Broadway (or a mythical Broadway he conjured), a stretch populated with characters with names like Joe the Joker, Madame La Gimp, and Sorrowful Jones. They were characters who spoke in a unique, deliberately formal style of speech (described by literary editor Sam Leith as "an inimitable slang that is at once vernacular and almost comically circumlocutory"): hustlers and fraudsters, gangsters and gamblers, bookies and boxers, shysters and showgirls. Runyon columnized about these denizens of a particular romanticized setting and wrote funny short stories that he collected in a volume he titled *Guys and Dolls*. The stories and characters inspired a Tony Award–winning Broadway musical and many Hollywood films, including one based on that musical. Runyon's work was so popular and singular that it became its own genre. You hear *Runyonesque*, and you think gangsters in pinstriped suits and big hats, gum-snapping dancing girls, and comical thugs laying odds on the ponies. Shemp fit right in.

Shemp's official entrance into Runyon's world was set in motion by Jules Levey, a producer who had been with Universal Pictures for years. Levey had started out in sales in 1919 and twenty years later hung his own shingle, Mayfair Productions, as an independent producer at the studio. In October 1940, Mayfair bought the rights to two Damon Runyon stories: "Tight Shoes" and "Butch Minds the Baby." Levey right away set up *Damon Runyon's Tight Shoes* at Universal, scheduled for a fifteen-day shoot beginning on March 20, 1941. Universal just happened to have a contract player who had stepped right out of the Runyon milieu. Twenty-nine-year-old Broderick Crawford, then billed as "Brod," would star as

With Broderick Crawford in Tight Shoes *(1941), the film in which Shemp first stepped into Damon Runyon territory—a shame he never made it to* Guys and Dolls. *Universal Pictures/Photofest © Universal Pictures*

Speedy Miller, a racketeer with big feet who buys a pair of shoes that are too tight. The tight shoes will get the blame for all the troubles that will befall Speedy in the days to come. Universal slotted Shemp into the picture in between his work as a waiter in the Marlene Dietrich romantic comedy *The Flame of New Orleans* and double duty in April as the hotel manager in *Too Many Blondes* and his expanded role with Abbott and Costello in *In the Navy*. In *Tight Shoes,* he was cast as a mug named Okay, who, along with Edward Gargan as "Blooch," is one of Speedy's hoods. Shemp gave the character a stammer.

Tight Shoes was released on June 13, 1941. *Variety* was impressed that the filmmakers managed to retain "the strong flavor of Damon Runyon's wit and comedy, specifically the New Yorkese brand of slang so ably expounded to the American public through Runyon's syndicated column." More to the point, the picture was "a whirlwind laugh-getter, studded with hilarious episodes and rolling along at a zippy pace."

"Crawford hits consistently as the flashy ward boss . . . Shemp Howard and Ed Gargan provide broad comedy as Crawford's stooges."

❖

January 22, 1942, marked day one of a three-week shoot for *Damon Runyon's Butch Minds the Baby*. Brod Crawford was back, this time as Aloysius "Butch" Grogan, a reformed safecracker and ex-con who babysits the infant son of a young widow. When he reluctantly signs on to another safecracking job on a night he has to watch the baby, Butch takes the kid along with him. Shemp plays Blinky Sweeney, a member of the gang who happens to be nearly blind. The role gives him the best stage yet for his "nearsighted routine," and he takes advantage of the opportunity, walking into closed doors ("Ooh! Who closed that door?") or walking into the door after it's been opened for him ("What is that? A revolving door?"). Blinky is a more defined character than Okay. He even has a backstory that he reveals while riding in a taxicab with his fellow mug, Harry the Horse (Richard Lane):

> BLINKY: Where are we goin'?
> HARRY THE HORSE: We're going to pay a call on Butch, the poor fella. He's got to make that parole board think he's a janitor.
> BLINKY: Hey, I see in the funny papers Flash Gordon is doing all right.
> HARRY: You see? With your eyes?
> BLINKY: Yeah, the doctor told me in five years I'll be able to see as good as before.
> HARRY: Before what?
> BLINKY: Before Prohibition. Before I sampled my own gin. Before I went blind. He says I only got a . . . a cute stink-a-matism.

Shemp also has a comic fight scene in which Blinky and Harry the Horse brawl with Butch. Blinky, "fighting blind," punches his partner, the door, a coffeepot, and various kitchen items before Butch tosses both flunkies into the hallway. When he's next seen, Blinky is in a bar, and both his hands are bandaged into mitts. Butch holds Blinky's glass so that he can drink.

The picture was released on March 20, 1942. *Variety* called it "an effervescing and spontaneous piece of entertainment for widest audience appeal . . . typically Runyonesque in both story and dialog and . . . retains all of the delightful flavor of the author's original," adding,

> Shemp Howard plays the pants off a Runyon characterization—an ex-bootlegger mug with bad eyesight who continually stumbles into people and doors.

This role alone would have been enough to enshrine Shemp in the Damon Runyon Character Hall of Fame, but there was more to ensure his place. In the days after the film's release, a story began to spread throughout the country.

And it wasn't pretty:

> The ugliest man in Hollywood is Shemp Howard! This distinction has been made official, with balloting, judges and a certain amount of formality. Mr. Howard is now undisputed owner of the title, to have and to hold for the next twelve months.
>
> (*Kenosha Evening News*, April 24, 1942)

The release of Damon Runyon's *Butch Minds the Baby* by Universal Pictures in March 1942 was accompanied by a publicity campaign that included a press release that appeared in newspapers in cities from coast to coast:

> Election Was Held for Ugliest Man
> *Ugliest Movie Actor Selected*
> He's the Ugliest Man in Movies
> *Ugly Man in Runyon Film*
> "Butch Minds the Baby" Has Ugliest Movie Actor
>
> One of the most unusual elections ever staged in Hollywood took place on the lot at Universal Studios during the filming of *Butch Minds the Baby*, a Damon Runyon production now playing. It was to choose the ugliest man in Hollywood and the "honor" was accorded Shemp Howard, who plays the part of "Blinky" in the picture.
>
> Judges in the contest were Virginia Bruce, Priscilla Lane, Anne Gwynne and Carol Bruce, who concocted the idea. They were visiting the set when a mob of Broadway "muggs" were assembled to welcome their pal "Butch," portrayed by Brod Crawford, who was being released from serving a stretch in Sing Sing.
>
> For this scene, the Universal casting office had scoured Hollywood for "rugged" character types, and the roundup netted about fifty former prize-fighters, tough guys, muggs and individuals who would never have a chance in a male beauty contest. Tom Kennedy and Frank Moran, both of whom sport cauliflower ears as a result of years in the prize ring, were placed second and third to Howard, who won his first place on strictly natural points.

The story and contest were a press agent's concoction. The opening scene in which Butch Grogan's pals welcome him home from a ten-year prison stay with a testimonial dinner at the Pioneer Athletic Club featured no more than two dozen actors. Only a few faces were seen on-screen, and none, with the exception of costars Kennedy and Moran (Philly the Weeper and Jack the Beefer), came anywhere near the plug-uglies who

With a face like that, how could Shemp's role in Butch Minds the Baby *earn him the title of "The Ugliest Man in Hollywood"? Universal Pictures/Photofest © Universal Pictures*

showed up for the baby birthday party that Shemp crashed at the end of *Another Thin Man*. Would Virginia Bruce, a star of the film, have giggled while watching the shooting of the scene, then stopped the music to hold an "ugly man competition"? Not likely. It was, however, a good way to drum up publicity for the film in a very Runyonesque fashion, with a nod to Shemp's prominent role.

More to the point: Was Shemp Howard really the ugliest man in Hollywood?

Leonard Maltin is quick to answer. "No." He pauses. "For a world that included Rondo Hatton, to single him out . . ." Maltin goes silent. He has no words.

The "honor" may seem cruel in retrospect. For all the punches, slaps, and hits he took—and continued to take in this film and others—Shemp Howard had earned that face, and in all seriousness and for all the wonders of its terrain, that face was far from "ugly." But in 1942, the title of "ugliest man" was actually one that some celebrities sought.

At the time the Shemp story appeared, Johnny Dickshot of the Hollywood Stars in the Pacific Coast League was laying claim to being the ugliest man in baseball, while wrestler Maurice Tillet, aka "The French Angel," was on a U.S. arena tour, billed as "The Ugliest Man in the World" ("Tillet's head and face are more than twice the size of the ordinary human being's"). As Leonard Maltin points out, Rondo Hatton would seem to be the prime candidate for the "ugliest actor" title. Hatton was afflicted with acromegaly, a pituitary gland disorder that causes the body to produce too much growth hormone, resulting in enlarged hands, feet, and facial features that include forehead bulges, widened cheekbones, and enlarged lips, tongue, and nose. Hatton's frightening looks were his ticket to a career in Hollywood pictures, and in 1944, Universal would enshrine him among its horror movie icons as a monstrous killer, the "Hoxton Creeper." But Hatton had stiff—and vocal—competition in the ugly department from British actor Harry Wilson. Wilson, who had some characteristics of acromegaly but never received an official diagnosis, had billed himself for years as "the ugliest man in Hollywood."

In May 1942, a feature story on wrestler and actor Mike Mazurki stated that "his ambition is to succeed to the long-vacant title of 'ugliest man in Hollywood,' once held against all comers by Bull Montana." Mazurki and Wilson would double the ugly when they were teamed as gangster Spats Colombo's henchmen in Billy Wilder's 1959 film *Some Like It Hot*.

"Bottom line, it was a way to get Shemp's name in the papers. And it worked," says the archivist and author Jeff Abraham, who as a publicist has represented some of the biggest names in comedy. "Shemp was a comedian, but even more so, he had great face for comedy, like Joe E. Brown, Ben Blue and Bill Wolfe. He wasn't trying to be Errol Flynn or Clark Gable. The best part of the campaign? Shemp loved it."

In some ways, being named "The Ugliest Man in Hollywood" was an honor. Shemp Howard did accept it as such.

"I'm probably not only the ugliest man in Hollywood, but in the whole country," he said. "I'm a groundhog, and every time I look in the mirror I have to face the fact."

On September 28, 1942, with the "ugliest man in Hollywood" story still working its way across the amusement sections of various metropolitan and small-town newspapers, cameras rolled on the latest Abbott and Costello comedy. *It Ain't Hay* was a bright racetrack comedy based on "Princess O'Hara," a story by Damon Runyon.

Lou Costello is Wilbur Hoolihan, a New York City taxi driver who feeds candy to the horse that pulls his friend King O'Hara's hansom cab through Central Park, accidentally killing it. The horse that Wilbur rescues and gives King as a replacement turns out to be a famous racehorse named Tea Biscuit. The fun begins.

Shemp is in a supporting role, as a, well, as a "Damon Runyon character," and it's in his introductory scene that he's given a gift that, in most cases, Lou Costello would have insisted on keeping for himself. Shemp shows up about six minutes into the film as part of a trio of horse race gamblers very similar to Nicely-Nicely Johnson, Benny Southstreet, and Rusty Charlie, the "Fugue for Tinhorns" trio from *Guys and Dolls*. There's no singing, however, for Eddie Quillan as Harry the Horse, David Hacker as Chauncey the Eye, and Shemp as Umbrella Sam. The author and film historian Edward Watz offers this reminiscence from Quillan:

> Shemp and I played a couple of wiseguy racetrack characters. In our opening scene, Shemp is asked why he always carries an umbrella when the sun is shining. Shemp's scripted line was, "How should I know? I'm a Damon Runyon character." Our director (Erle Kenton) thought the joke might go over the heads of the audience. We did another take, and this time when Shemp was asked why he always carries an umbrella, he answered, "Have you seen the size of the flying elephants they got around here?" The whole set just collapsed in laughter. Abbott and Costello came over after hearing all the commotion. When told what it was all about, Lou said, "Shemp, you know I think you're terrific, but come on, I've got to be the funniest guy. You gotta get your own movie!"

"It ain't rainin'. Why the umbrella?"
"Who knows? I'm a Damon Runyon character!"

Nick Santa Maria knows the film and the story well. That line, the one that had been originally scripted and that Shemp would deliver in *It Ain't Hay*, was more than enough. "People give Lou Costello a lot of crap about, 'I'm the comedian, I get all the laughs.' He gave Shemp the best line in the movie!"

Nineteen

Toluca Lake

In 1942, Shemp Howard filed his income tax for the 1941 calendar year. "Samuel Horowitz aka Shemp Howard," resident of 201 South Hamel Drive in Beverly Hills, California, declared a total income of $7,654.16, which, after deductions, resulted in a net income of $6,209.95. With wife Gertrude claiming half of the earnings, that reduced Shemp's net income for 1941 to $3,104.98. Adjusted for inflation, net income for the Howard household in 2024 would be around $135,000.

Federal income tax was due on March 15, 1942. Six weeks later, on April 26, forty-seven-year-old U.S. Army veteran Shemp Howard arrived at the office of Local Board No. 247 of the U.S. Selective Service at 426 North Canon Drive in Beverly Hills and once again registered for the draft. (Following Japan's surprise strike on the U.S. naval base at Pearl Harbor in Honolulu, Hawaii, President Roosevelt required able-bodied men between the ages of eighteen and sixty-four to register for military service, although the only ones drafted were between the ages of eighteen and forty-five.) Shemp gave his birth date as March 17, 1895. His official name was listed as Samuel Horwitz, with a note that he was "professionally Shemp Howard." His place of residence was listed as 201 South Hamel Drive in Beverly Hills. The "person who will always know your address" was Gertrude Horwitz ("known as Howard") of the same address. Phone number: CR-67404. His employer was Universal Pictures in Universal City.

Shemp signed the draft card twice: as "Samuel Horwitz" and "Shemp Howard." The registrar's notes indicated that Shemp was White and approximately five feet six inches tall, weighing 150 pounds with blue eyes and brown hair. His complexion? Registrar Rosalind D. Brown checked off "ruddy" and "freckled." She also noted a "cyst on right shin."

(Shemp's friend Huntz Hall noticed the protuberance on the lower part of Shemp's leg one morning on a movie set. "We were changing into our wardrobe and I noticed a huge, ugly carbuncle on Shemp's leg," Hall recalled. "I said, 'Shemp! You should see a doctor and have that thing removed.' He just shrugged and said, 'Nah, it holds up my socks.'")

In the end, Shemp was not recalled into the armed forces and so was spared more of his younger brother Moe's jokes and jibes about bed-wetting, but he did do his part in supporting the war effort. Edward Watz says his father witnessed Shemp's wartime work in action on the first anniversary of the Pearl Harbor attack. Watz's father was eighteen years old and working in the sprawling Brooklyn Navy Yard, where the day of infamy was being commemorated with a weeklong war bond drive. To drum up enthusiasm, the drive was accompanied by lunchtime concerts for the thousands of workers. On Monday, December 7, the final day of the drive, Watz's father and a friend arrived late for the show ("due to problems they experienced fitting an escape hatch onto a submarine conning tower") and were surprised to be ushered to seats in the fifth row. They were excited, anticipating another musical performance that was accompanied by the invigorating presence of scantily clad chorus girls. Instead, "the workers were told that they were going to watch a sketch stressing safety in the workplace, titled 'Never Play in the (Navy) Yard.'"

There was, the senior Watz recalled, "an audible groan" from the crowd. Onstage, several men were dressed as shipyard workers, while a "safety director" instructed them on how to perform their tasks without injuring themselves or others:

> But one man, dressed as a welder and wearing a metal face shield, was ignoring the advice. Instead, he kept dropping his tools, and bumped into a gym locker, causing the surrounding lockers to fall over, domino-style. "Hey, you!" called the safety director. "What do you think you're doing?" The "welder" stepped up to the footlights and lifted his mask. "Why, I'm woikin'," he replied. It was Shemp!

The groans turned to laughter. The crowd realized they had been "set up." Meanwhile, Shemp and the safety director argued. Cream pies were somehow produced from one of the lockers, and suddenly there was a pie fight. Watz quotes his dad: "It was a very cold day, and Shemp took a bunch of pies square in the face. I was laughing, but also felt sorry for the poor guy. The cream from the pie looked like it had frozen solid on his face! Right then and there, I bought a twenty dollar war bond, mainly as a thank-you to poor Shemp!"

Edward Watz says that his father was drafted into the U.S. Army in March 1943 and went on to fight in the Battle of the Bulge and serve in General George S. Patton's Honor Guard. In Germany, after the war, Watz Sr. attended shows by many celebrity entertainers, including Bob Hope, Jerry Colonna, and Frances Langford. "But he told me, 'Nobody gave as good a show or was as funny as Shemp. He was the best!'"

By 1943, Shemp and his family had left the flats of Beverly Hills and moved across Los Angeles to the edge of the San Fernando Valley. Tucked away in the valley's southeast corner, with Burbank on its eastern border and North Hollywood to the north, the neighborhood of Toluca Lake was just north of Universal City, where Shemp was working at least half the year. Toluca Lake was developed in the 1920s as the valley's first bedroom community, and it was not unlike a small-town movie set plopped into the middle of a growing city. The "Main Street," Riverside Drive, was a collection of small shops. There were no sidewalks in the quiet, tree-lined village. The houses were relatively large, with lots of various sizes and shapes with lawns and many with curved driveways. Toluca Lake seemed a world away from the activities of the big city but was close to the studios and main roads into Hollywood and so attracted many folks from the movie industry. Stars like Frank Sinatra, Bette Davis, William Holden, and Bing Crosby had homes in Toluca Lake. Bob Hope's estate on Moorpark Street was about a three-minute drive from Shemp's home at 4604 Placidia Avenue, with a view of the looming bell tower of the St. Charles Borromeo Roman Catholic Church on the corner of Moorpark and Lankershim Boulevard. Hollywood legend has it that Hope's wife, Dolores, forced him to fund the church in order to atone for all the mistresses he had set up in bungalows across the valley.

Shemp, Babe, and Morton lived in a four-bedroom, English-style ranch house on the corner of Placidia Avenue and Sarah Street. Their home in this small-town, middle American oasis was close to Shemp's work at Universal Studios and, since he didn't drive, an easy taxi ride down Cahuenga Boulevard to get there. (For all his fear of automobiles, Shemp was very comfortable being driven around by strangers in taxicabs.) His family has said that Bob Hope would sometimes give him a lift to the set, but that's a legend that is not likely to be confirmed.

"He bought the house in Toluca Lake because Curly lived around the corner and Moe lived around the other corner, about two blocks away, so they were all close together," said daughter-in-law Geraldyn Howard Greenbaum. "They were all close." Morton, who according to family lore graduated from high school at the age of fifteen, is listed as a junior in the Beverly Hills High School yearbook of 1942 but transferred to North Hollywood High School after the family moved to Toluca Lake. He is listed and pictured at age seventeen among the North Hollywood High School graduating class of 1944.

Former Brooklynite Shemp Howard was the suburban squire in Toluca Lake. He and Gertrude contributed to the war effort by heeding a request by the Department of Agriculture and planting a "victory garden"—vegetables, fruit, and herbs in the backyard to supplement their home food supply. This helped lower the price of vegetables needed by the War Department to feed the troops. Along with the garden, they kept chickens.

Babe also volunteered as an air raid warden. You can picture her in a helmet, wielding a flashlight as she walked through the quiet neighborhood at night and enforcing air raid drills in case the Germans or Japanese decided to fly over the valley and bomb Toluca Lake.

"It was her duty to patrol the streets of their Toluca Lake neighborhood at the midnight hour," granddaughter Sandie Howard-Isaac wrote in 2012 in *Stooges Among Us*:

> The residents were instructed to tightly shutter their homes and not let a single ray of light pierce the darkness. The air raid siren would sound—its deafening roar sent chills up and down the spines of anyone within earshot. When that alarm went off, Shemp would dart under the piano with lightning speed. He huddled there, shaking with fear.
>
> "Babe, is it safe yet?" he would yell out. "Can I come out now?"
>
> Shemp, Babe said affectionately, was just a "Big 'fraidy cat."

Through the 1940s and into the 1950s, Shemp and Babe Howard opened their home to guests and entertained a group of friends that included some of Shemp's pals from the studio lot and the Stage 1 Café and others of similar status in the comedy and show business hierarchy. The regular crowd included Morey Amsterdam, Phil Silvers and his brother (and manager) Harry, Milton Berle, Martha Raye, actor Murray Alper (who had appeared with Shemp in *Another Thin Man* and *Moonlight and Cactus*), and Dead End Kids Gabe Dell and Huntz Hall.

"I can see them at Shemp's house," Nick Santa Maria says. "Right from the top, Morey Amsterdam, who was a joke machine—and a ghostwriter for Will Rogers, in fact. Phil Silvers, his brother Harry, these are all—how can I put this? All of them were very funny, and all of them were, whether performing or writing, all kind of second-tier. And that was pretty common in those days. If you were a character actor in a film, even a respected one, you were not expected to be invited over Irving Thalberg's house for the big MGM party. Abbott and Costello suffered from it. They didn't hang out with the elite. They'd hang out with their burlesque friends. The elite didn't want anything to do with them. They were from burlesque. And the Stooges were from two-reelers, which was in a way almost worse. Do you know how looked down upon those two-reelers were? It was kind of like Poverty Row. People just looked down on them in the echelon of Hollywood."

"Shemp was a sweetheart," Huntz Hall recalled, "until you got him into a serious card game. Then he was all business. If Shemp didn't like your play at pinochle, he'd kick you under the table . . . hard! He was ruthless that way; it didn't matter if you were a friend or not.

"But he also had this manner about him, like no other actor. Shemp was naturally funny."

Huntz Hall wasn't the only young performer Shemp had taken under his wing. Sometime in the early 1950s, a mutual affection for gambling and horse racing led to a friendship with Shecky Greene. The wild improvisational comedian was born Fred Sheldon Greenfield in Chicago in 1926, and before his career took off in Las Vegas in the mid-1950s, he received attention working at Martha Raye's Five O'Clock Club on Collins Avenue in Miami Beach. In March 1953, Greene opened at Billy Gray's Band Box, a nightclub and eatery on North Fairfax Avenue (the new "Jewish heart" of Los Angeles). Gray, a comedian and actor, had bought the club from Lou Costello, and Shemp's pals, like Maxie Rosenbloom, performed their acts there.

At the time he and Shemp became acquainted, Greene was on his way to becoming, according to the preeminent comedy historian Kliph Nesteroff, "comedy's great non-conformist . . . experimental beyond belief, possessing a kinetic and forceful dynamism that spilled off the stage into his everyday life." Had he emerged in recent years, Nesteroff wrote, Greene "would be considered the leading voice in what is vaguely defined as alternative comedy." Greene was known as a heavy drinker and gunslinger whose well-documented escapades offstage included driving his car, while drunk, into the fountains of Caesars Palace on the Las Vegas Strip. Yet Shecky Greene expressed an affinity not for his boundary-breaking peers but rather for old-school greats, including his friend on Placidia Avenue.

"I was very fond of Mort Sahl, but I never laughed," he told Gerald Nachman. "I was never into social satire. I just said, 'That's good, that's good, that's good.' [Shelley] Berman and [Bob] Newhart never made me laugh. Nichols and May, I would sit there and love 'em to death, but they would not make me guffaw. I would say, 'Wonderful, clever, clever, clever, wonderful.' But Shemp Howard of the Three Stooges going 'Nyuk, nyuk, nyuk'—*that* would make me laugh." Well, yes, Stooges aficionados will point out that it was Curly Howard who was known for his "Nyuk, nyuk"—when called on, Shemp had the "Hee bee bee"—but the point was taken.

By the fall of 1943, Shemp's time at Universal had come to an end. "I remember when Shemp's contract was not renewed with Universal," Moe's sister-in-law Clarice Seiden told the Lenburgs, "the partygoers that were always at the house disappeared. When his contract was renewed, everyone would come back." That could be expected. It wasn't a matter of good friends turning their backs on a pal; when belts tightened, the canapes got put in the freezer. Along with Cole Porter music, games of cards, funny stories, and a wonderful hostess in Babe Howard, 4604 Placidia Avenue remained a center of Shemp's crowd and on occasion was enlivened by visits from his brothers Moe and Curly Howard. By the final week of 1943, the two of them and older brother Jack were what was left of Shemp's original family. Parents Jennie and Solomon had moved west in 1937 around the time that Shemp pulled up stakes. According to Howard family lore, they had no real choice; Jennie's real estate business had gone under, so Moe and Curly set up their parents in a house on the edge of Beverly Hills. Jennie arrived kicking and screaming and never really settled into the land of sunshine and orange trees. Bensonhurst was her world. Afflicted with high blood pressure and other ailments, she was sixty-nine when she died on September 9, 1939 (three weeks after eldest son Irving, the only brother to keep the Horwitz name, died back in Brooklyn at forty-eight of a burst appendix). Solomon took greater advantage of Tinseltown, appearing as an extra in at least half a dozen Stooges shorts. He died of pneumonia on December 21, 1943. He was seventy-one and had been living with Moe.

By this time, Moe Howard, Larry Fine, and Curly Howard—Moe, Larry, and Curly, the Three Stooges—had reached their cinematic peak after filming dozens of short comedies for Jules White's department at Harry Cohn's Columbia Pictures. The trio had been accepted into the Hollywood comedy community early on when, in 1935, their third Columbia short, *Men in Black*, was nominated for an Academy Award. (It lost in the "Short Subject, Comedy" category to the Technicolor musical *La Cucaracha*.) Their comedy highs had been repeated time and again, the most recent probably being *A Plumbing We Will Go*, their forty-sixth short for Columbia and the last short they filmed in the 1930s. Moe, Larry, and Curly, fleeing a policeman, pose as plumbers and wreak havoc in a fancy mansion, digging up the lawn, and connecting the water supply to the electrical system, causing water to pour out of kitchen appliances, flummoxing Dudley Dickerson as the cook. The short is perhaps best remembered for the scene in which Curly goes to work in the bathroom and winds up entrapped in a maze of water-spurting pipes but also includes a scene in which the hostess invites her guest to watch a transmission from Niagara Falls on her new television set, only to have everyone get drenched when a cascade of water gushes through the screen.

A Plumbing We Will Go was also notable as an example of producer Jules White's frugality and recycling abilities, as it was a remake of a 1934 Columbia comedy short, *Plumbing for Gold,* starring George Sydney and Charlie Murray. *A Plumbing We Will Go* would be remade with Shemp and El Brendel in 1944 as *Pick a Peck of Plumbers;* in 1949 as *Vagabond Loafers,* with Moe, Larry, and Shemp (and Shemp re-creating Curly's prison of pipes in the bathroom); and, incorporating a lot of stock footage and a day of filming less than eight weeks after Shemp's death, in 1956 as *Scheming Schemers,* featuring Joe Palma as the "fake Shemp."

The Three Stooges were not often celebrated for their social commentary or witty parody beyond some Yiddishisms sprinkled among their routines, but their political and historic relevance were probably ensured with *You Nazty Spy!,* an eighteen-minute two-reel comedy that has been recognized as the first Hollywood film to satirize Nazi Germany and Adolf Hitler. Filmed over four days in early December 1939 (and wrapped four days before shooting began on *A Plumbing We Will Go*), *You Nazty Spy!* was released on January 19, 1940, nine months before *The Great Dictator,* the feature-length Hitler satire starring and written and directed by Charlie Chaplin. *The Great Dictator,* which was Chaplin's first talking picture, had gone into production months earlier than the Stooges' short and had been on the boards as early as 1937, but in this case, timing was everything. Chaplin's character Adenoid Hynkel, fascist dictator of the country of Tomainia, took second place to Moe Hailstone, Curly Gallstone, and Larry Pebble of Moronika in the history of anti-Hitler satire. This would be the one time that the acknowledged master of film comedy had been outdone and one-upped by the lowly two-reel-dwelling Stooges, a trio that had many fans but little respect in the film industry.

Comedically, everything centered on Curly, and by the early 1940s, Curly was on the decline. During all their performing years, from the seediest rungs of vaudeville gigs to the lights of Broadway and Hollywood, Moe and Shemp Howard never had reputations as heavy drinkers, carousers, or womanizers. They were known to gamble, but only their partner Larry Fine was caught up in the web of betting too often and too much and always being the poorer for it. Even while working and traveling with the notorious boozehound and skirt-chaser Ted Healy or rooming in hotels and traveling on trains with dozens of willing chorus girls, the Howards had the reputations as nice Jewish mama's boys, good husbands away from home. They were tough talking, "rough around the edges" types, and they would play a game of cards or place a bet, but there aren't legendary tales of wild scenes in speakeasies or the brothels that were part of the late-night underworld of show business during the Roaring Twenties and Prohibition.

Baby brother Jerome was a different story. Certainly by May 1936, two years into the Three Stooges' solo career, when the studio finally began billing him as "Curly" and not "Curley" (in the comedy short *Disorder in the Court*), the youngest Howard brother was unquestionably the star Stooge. Moe had gazed into the mirror early on and realized where he stood. At five feet three inches (Moe made sure that his Columbia Pictures employee ID card, the one that allowed him onto the studio lot, listed his height as five feet three *and a half* inches), Moe didn't have much to go on beyond his angry, screwed-up mug, and he made the best of it, taking the driver's seat as the disciplinarian, the "boss" on both sides of the camera. How many times did Moe say something along the lines of "I was smart. I took Healy's place," doling out the punishments? Larry Fine would have his solo spots, but he wasn't the focus by any means. They called him "the Stooge in the middle," but he was the stooge on the sidelines. Curly was a quintessential larger-than-life, comic force of nature, a man who was far more nimble and graceful on his feet than his size would indicate and whose unleashing of pure id brought joy and laughter. He acted like a baby man, barked like a dog, dropped to the floor and spun around in circles, and took the pokes, nose twists, smacks, and repeated hits to his big fat shaved head with a "Nyuk, nyuk, nyuk!" or a "Woowowoowoo!" His off-screen appetites reflected his on-screen indulgences, and like Fatty Arbuckle before him and screen comics like John Belushi, John Candy, and Chris Farley to follow, the excess would take its toll. Moe and Shemp had stable marriages; each was headed toward twenty years in the early 1940s. Curly married a woman in 1930, when he was twenty-six. The marriage was annulled a year later. According to his niece Joan, it was his mother, Jennie, overprotective and holding the purse strings, who convinced him—forced him—to end the union. Curly had three more marriages in his future.

In 1937, he married Elaine Ackerman, a fur store model and daughter of a Los Angeles jeweler. He was thirty-three; she was twenty-two. Their daughter, Marilyn, was born in December 1938. This wasn't a happy marriage, either. Elaine complained that she never really got to know her husband. He spent most of this time at the studio or on the road, making personal appearances with the Three Stooges. And when he was on the road, who knew what he was up to? In 1940, Elaine took the baby and left their home on Highland Avenue in Hollywood. On June 13, she sued for divorce. She said that he left her alone too often. She was lonely. He was jealous. According to one newspaper report, "She complained he struck her only a month after the ceremony, remained away from home at night, associated with other women and demanded she leave him." Curly responded to the divorce suit and the loss of his child by carrying on much as he had always done, only with something of a weary vengeance.

He drank more, smoked more big expensive Havana cigars, went in for more expensive clothes and fancy cars, and grabbed at and pulled more women. Only now he was doing it without a smile.

Art Seid was a film editor who worked on a few of the Stooges shorts at Columbia and, though a decade younger than Curly, not only befriended the star but also became one of his drinking buddies. "We got drunk a couple of times together," he said. "We'd go out after work together, to a couple of saloons around Columbia—Brewer's, Brittingham's, up the street. . . .The way I would describe him mostly, he seemed to be a very unhappy guy. There was a moroseness about him. Just like most clowns, he rarely laughed," adding,

> Mostly I would see him by himself, a loner. I think most of it was that he wasn't very well. His leg used to drive him crazy. As the years went by, I could see the pain on his face increasing. Even on the screen, I could see that the man wasn't well. He'd be dragging that foot. I could see it on the Moviola. He didn't crack jokes . . . he wasn't a high energy person and he didn't hang around very long. He'd have a couple of drinks and then go. . . . Other times there was always a girl with him. He was a real womanizer.

By 1942, the strain on Curly was evident and could be seen on-screen. He registered for the draft like everyone else, though. On February 17, he showed up at the Selective Service office on Riverside Drive in Toluca Lake. He gave his name as Jerome Lester Horwitz and his address as Moe's home at 10500 Kling Street in North Hollywood (Toluca Lake). He also listed "Moe Horwitz" as "the person who will always know your address." His employer: Columbia Pictures at 1438 North Gower Street in Hollywood. The registrar checked off the boxes: blue eyes, brown hair, light complexion. Height: five feet five and a half inches. Curly was thirty-eight years old, within the drafting parameters. His weight was listed as 200 pounds. That was heavy for a man under five feet six inches tall. That was obese. Uncle Sam wasn't going to take him.

Curly signed up for the draft a week after production wrapped on Shemp's latest film, *Butch Minds the Baby*. The next sixteen months or so would provide rich work for Shemp the actor, who was yet to be named "The Ugliest Man in Hollywood." He would work with bandleader Ozzie Nelson on *Strictly in the Groove*, stand out in high-profile roles in *Pittsburgh* and *Arabian Nights*, and make more pictures with Abbott and Costello, the Andrews Sisters, Olsen and Johnson, and his protégé Huntz Hall.

But by the end of 1943, as independent as Shemp was from his brothers' careers, he was not completely free of the influence of younger brother Moe, who knew that Horwitz blood was thicker than Hollywood water and that, when push came to shove, big brother Shemp would be there. Moe, at least in his head, was the astute businessman, keeping Curly and Larry busy with personal appearances on the road when they weren't filming. So it's not inconceivable that at this point, he could sense that his comedy team and career were approaching a crossroads. Curly's situation was obvious, and if he needed to be replaced—well, events would take a bizarre twist.

Just as it was convenient for Moe in 1932 to have another brother on deck in case the problematic one fell out, so it was ten years later that Moe knew that he had a potential fallback in the family. Sounds crazy that the brother who had been replaced without skipping a beat would return, stepping in for the brother who replaced him! In 1943, it was just wishful thinking, something for Moe to keep in his back pocket if worse came to worst. In 1944, the wishful thinking became more realistic than ever, when Shemp signed up at a studio where he had worked before, the very studio where his brothers Moe and Jerome had held court as the top, if not top-paid, comedy stars on the lot. Shemp was heading back through the Cahuenga Pass and returning to Columbia Pictures. And as Moe's machinations came into play, there he would stay until his final cigar—no, he would be there, even beyond.

TWENTY

On Hold at Columbia

Production on *Crazy House*, the second film starring the barrier-breaking comedy team of Ole Olsen and Chic Johnson, wrapped at Universal Studios after a thirty-day shoot on July 17, 1943. Shemp returned to the studio in late August for a role in *Moonlight and Cactus*, a wartime comedy about a merchant marine who returns to his cattle ranch to find it's being operated by women—including the singing Andrews Sisters—and menaced by a neighbor played by Leo Carrillo. Shemp leads the comedy contingent as "Punchy Carter," one of three pals of leading man Tom Seidel (Eddie Quillan is Stubby Lamont; Murray Alper is simply "Slugger"). His role is notable for a scene in which he dresses in drag, impersonating Patty Andrews.

Moonlight and Cactus, which wouldn't be released for another year, would be Shemp Howard's last work at Universal, the studio that had offered his most fulfilling and memorable work in the movies. Although the partying at his home in Toluca Lake was said to be put on hiatus, everything would soon be back on track, and the house would be full of the sounds of music, laughter, and eating. By April 1944, Shemp was back in the movies—working at two separate studios.

One place was quite familiar—maybe even too familiar. At the age of forty-nine, Shemp returned to the corner of Gower Street and Sunset Boulevard when he signed on with Columbia Pictures. The studio had a variety of roles lined up for him both in feature films and in comedy shorts. Jules White had slotted Shemp in several shorts in his first go-round at the studio and, with Shemp's return, appeared to have first dibs on the actor, who had made a name for himself as a versatile player at Universal Studios.

Shemp arrived for work on April 3, two weeks and two days after the release of the most recent Three Stooges short. *Busy Buddies* had been produced by Hugh McCollum and directed by Del Lord over five days, beginning on November 1, 1943. On November 8, the camera rolled on another Stooges short—their seventy-ninth at Columbia—*The Yoke's on*

As "Mumbo" in Olsen and Johnson's Crazy House *(1943), with "Jumbo" Fred Sanborn, xylophone virtuoso and fellow veteran of Ted Healy's Gang and* Soup to Nuts. *Universal Pictures/Photofest © Universal Pictures*

Me. With the shorts department's two units lobbing production back and forth, Jules White produced and directed *The Yoke's on Me*. It was in the can, ready to be released in May.

And now Shemp was going to compete against his brothers and Larry Fine with his own series of comedies. The first to be released was *Pick a Peck of Plumbers*. When Shemp read the script, he could see the opportunity to pull an ace from his sleeve—actually, his coke bottle glasses from his bag of tricks—because the character was myopic. But if Jules White had indeed planned for Shemp Howard to be a Columbia star distinct from his brothers' team, he had come up with a strange way of kicking things off. The Shemp short that he would produce and direct was a remake of the 1940 Three Stooges classic *A Plumbing We Will Go* (another Hugh McCollum–Del Lord triumph and, as mentioned earlier, also a remake). Although this was to be the first of Shemp's solo shorts, he was teamed—and shared top billing—with El Brendel, the fifty-four-year-old Philadelphia vaudevillian making his way through the movies with his "Swedish act." Jules White said that he teamed Shemp with the "Swedish little country bumpkin" character because "Shemp was overloaded carrying a short series by himself. . . . I tried Shemp and Brendel together. They didn't click well."

In *Pick a Pick of Plumbers*, Brendel does his "Yumpin Yiminy" routine (he actually utters the phrase) as "Axel Swenson," while Shemp's character is named Elmer Peabody. "Elmer" was Brendel's actual first name. And if the premise of phony plumbers trying to retrieve a diamond ring from a sink drain and destroying a house in the process wasn't familiar enough, the supporting cast included Beatrice Blinn, Heinie Conklin, Judy Malcolm, Al Thompson, and John Tyrrell, all recognizable from roles in many Three Stooges shorts.

Pick a Peck of Plumbers would turn out to be funny but not great. It was also, in retrospect, a little creepy when one learns that in a scene that was filmed but not included, Joe Palma played a policeman. Jules White would later use Palma to stand in for (and pretend to *be*) Shemp in four comedy shorts filmed after Shemp's death.

In April 1944, Shemp didn't have much time to obsess over whether he was being served reheated goods. A week after the last setup for *Pick a Peck of Plumbers* on April 6, he had an appointment farther east on Sunset Boulevard at Monogram Pictures, one of the more cash-rich operations among the low-budget Poverty Row studios. Shemp had a freelance deal with Sam Katzman, a producer who for years had been doing very well for himself, making money on low-budget westerns, crime movies, action pictures, and serials. At Monogram, Katzman teamed with producer Jack Dietz under the banner of Banner Productions and cranked out B-movie horror flicks starring Bela Lugosi and crime comedies starring the East Side Kids—the latest morph of the Dead End Kids and Little Tough Guys—including *Spooks Run Wild*, which teamed the East Side Kids with Lugosi.

(The East Side Kids brought Leo Gorcey from *Dead End* back into the fold, reuniting him with Huntz Hall. When in 1945 the group again jumped studios and became *The Bowery Boys*, the films shifted from light crime drama to straight comedy, and Gorcey and Hall, now clearly adults, became a comedy team. By the early 1950s, they had moved to pure slapstick, heavily influenced by the Three Stooges, with many of the films written and/or directed by Edward Bernds, the longtime sound editor who in the mid-1940s began to write and direct Shemp and Three Stooges shorts.)

Katzman had seen the success of teams like Abbott and Costello and Olsen and Johnson, so in 1943, he created a Poverty Row version by signing Billy Gilbert and Frank Fay to star in four wartime comedies. Gilbert was the rotund comic actor who had grown up in vaudeville, was "discovered" by Stan Laurel, and had appeared with Shemp in several films, playing off him, memorably, in *Arabian Nights*. Fay, a stage and screen comedian recognized as "the first stand-up comic," was in that career dead zone between flop movies and revival as an American fascist. *Spotlight Scandals,* with Fay as a down-and-out vaudeville actor who finds success by teaming up with singing barber Gilbert, opened in September 1943. *Variety* said that the picture could use some editing but was "surprising" in that "the work of Gilbert and Fay carries it along fairly successfully." That bode well for the next three Gilbert and Fay pictures, but it was already too late. Fay, always a prickly type, had walked away. Katzman rebounded quickly. He knew from funny, and he knew how to make hay with it. Gilbert and Shemp Howard got along well. Shemp was available. He was hired in Fay's place.

In the short term, this looked like a good investment. Gilbert and Howard had worked together before, and Katzman obviously saw something in the union. But what did he see? Another Abbott and Costello? An Olsen and Johnson? Or was it another Three Stooges? Katzman was either hedging his bet or doubling down. The film they would begin shooting on Thursday, April 13, was *3 of a Kind,* and there was a third wheel to the arranged comedy marriage. "Slapsie" Maxie Rosenbloom is billed along with Gilbert and Howard, with the faces of all three shown on a hand of playing cards (all aces) in the opening credits. Rosenbloom was a former light heavyweight boxing champion who had moved into movies playing big, often punch-drunk tough guys (the nickname "Slapsie" referred not to dizziness or chronic traumatic encephalopathy but to his boxing style of slapping opponents with an open hand).

In this picture, at least, Gilbert and Howard work as a team, as a couple of stooges for a vaudeville acrobat. When the boss falls to his death onstage, they're left to care for his young son. The pair has some very funny scenes, entering a radio quiz show, being mistaken for science professors on an inventors' show, and, in a kitchen, when they're hired as cooks by restaurateur Rosenbloom (the film was also released as *Cookin' Up Trouble*).

Katzman trotted out the Gilbert–Howard–Rosenbloom trio for two more goes at Monogram. *Crazy Knights* (also released as *Ghost Crazy*) was knocked off in less than a week, beginning on August 7, 1944, a mile and a half west of Gower Street at the Chaplin Studios on North LaBrea Avenue. The horror comedy focused on the Gilbert–Howard pairing as a couple of carnies who work with a live gorilla billed as "Barney from Borneo, the Gorilla with the Human Mind." Rosenbloom is a chauffeur who joins up with them in what seems to be a haunted house.

Shemp was paid $1,050 per week for *Trouble Chasers,* which began a twelve-day shoot on March 12, 1945. This film had Gilbert, Howard, and Rosenbloom as three idiots in the middle of a hunt for a stolen necklace. With Slapsie Maxie as a boxer, Shemp in a familiar role as his trainer, and

By the time they make Crazy Knights *(1944), Shemp and Billy Gilbert seemed to have the makings of a comedy team—and, with Slapsie Maxie Rosenbloom also on board, a comedy trio. Monogram Pictures/Photofest © Monogram Pictures*

Gilbert as the manager, this was the first picture in which they were truly a team throughout—"three stooges" or, as the ads read, "Three looney characters that can chase your blues away in double quick time!" *Trouble Chasers* was released on June 2. By then, it was Sam Katzman who had moved on. This was the last of the teaming for the trio.

Work on the Monogram films had to be squeezed in on Shemp's days and weeks off from Columbia, where there seemed to be a lot cooking.

Over the next two years, Shemp would be slotted in supporting roles in four feature films at Columbia. In early June 1944, he filmed a cameo in *Strange Affair*, a comedic murder mystery starring Allyn Joslyn and Evelyn Keyes. Shemp is a laundry truck driver who happens to be near-sighted. He's got a couple of funny scenes with Joslyn, working along the sides of the plot. In the next two films, he played the comic gangster. Filming on the B-movie musical comedy *Lullaby of Broadway*, starring Bob Haymes and Hillary Brooke, took place in October and November 1945. An extant contract shows that Shemp was paid $750 for the role of Marty.

The film was released in February 1946 as *The Gentleman Misbehaves. Dangerous Business,* filmed in March 1946, featured Shemp as a thug named Monk, one of a trio of kidnappers. He brings his usual comic touch to the role in this comedy drama while revealing shades of the frightening criminal he played in *Convention Girl.* In December 1945, Shemp also was part of a crooked threesome—a racketeer con man, along with Pinky Lee and Jerome Cowan—in the crime-comedy *One Exciting Week,* directed by William Beaudine of *Crazy Knights* at Republic Pictures.

Shemp would take out the coke bottle glasses in 1946 for one last solo role in a Columbia feature film—but none of the feature parts being sent his way had the weight of his work at Universal. Much of it seemed to be random, as if the execs were filling a space on the call sheet with a contract player with an open schedule. For Shemp, the focus was on comedy shorts, where Jules White seemed intent on establishing Shemp as a solo star.

Or was he?

Open Season for Saps, another Shemp short produced in 1944 and the second to be released, at least gave him solo star billing and introduced a new character with the potential to take him to new places comedically and commercially. This was the debut of Woodcock Q. Strinker, a loud, crass womanizer. Strinker would appear in three shorts in the next two years. In this first comedy, produced and directed by Jules White, Strinker, a member of the Hoot Owls fraternal organization, arrives home from a night out, in bowler hat and tuxedo, at five in the morning. He tries, unsuccessfully, to sneak in and not awaken his wife, who has been waiting for him on the couch. When she says she's had enough of his philandering and complains that he spends more time at the lodge than he does with her, he offers to take her on a belated honeymoon. But when Strinker arrives at the hotel, he runs into a lodge buddy who gets him caught up between a blackmailing blonde and her hot-tempered Latin husband.

Galbraith found the short to be "very funny. . . . Shemp is amusing (and indescribably ugly) disguised as a señora." There was one slight catch, however. *Open Season for Saps* was a remake of *Grand Hooter,* a 1937 Columbia short starring Charley Chase, a comedian, writer, and director who had done a lot of work at Hal Roach Studios before Jules White took him into the fold in 1937. At Columbia, Chase starred in his own short comedies and directed and produced others, including half a dozen Three Stooges shorts. He died young (at age forty-six) of a heart attack in June 1940, but his scripts were not buried with him at Forest Lawn.

Open Season for Saps was released on October 27, 1944. It was followed by *Off Again, On Again* on February 16, 1945. Shemp was again in the role of Woodcock Q. Strinker, with White producing and directing. "Routine, but Shemp is funny," Galbraith wrote, "and there's some irony in future Shemp impersonator Joe Palma playing the assassin trying to kill him." Funny, but again, Shemp was not bringing originality to the comedy world. *Off Again, On Again* was not only a remake of the Charley Chase short *Time Out for Trouble* but also included footage from the 1938 original.

The "B" unit handled Shemp's next outing. *Where the Pest Begins* went into production in October 1944, produced by Hugh McCollum, written by Edward Bernds, and directed by another veteran of Three Stooges shorts, Harry Edwards. Here, Shemp is a loud, lazy, grating idiot who offers to help his new neighbor, a government inventor played by Tom Kennedy, and in the process destroys the inventor's car, his garage, and, by the end, his house. It was, at least, original.

Two comedy shorts filmed in 1945 stand out as highlights in Shemp's solo career and should have been highlights in the history of film comedy—if only. Jules White was in charge on January 3, when filming began on *A Hit with a Miss*. Shemp is a mild-mannered waiter named Rameses who becomes an unstoppable, unbeatable boxer when he hears the tune "Pop Goes the Weasel." It's very funny and would have stood out even more had it not been a remake of the 1934 Three Stooges classic *Punch Drunks*. Shemp is playing a character and re-creating some of the exact scenes that his brother Curly had aced almost eleven years earlier. White was even more explicit in his recycling of footage from the original, including shots of the boxing match timekeeper, played by Arthur Housman, who died in 1942, and a sequence in which the 1934 Larry Fine can be identified.

Then there's *Mr. Noisy*. Edward Bernds directed this short over four days, beginning on August 17. Shemp portrays a boisterous, obnoxious sports heckler who is hired by gamblers to distract and rattle a star baseball player during a game while they bet on the opposing team. It's classic Shemp. The downside? *Mr. Noisy* is a very faithful remake of *The Heckler*, a Charley Chase two-reeler from 1940. The new model is close enough to Chase's that historian Nick Santa Maria is not alone when he says, "I prefer the Charley Chase version. I think the original is usually the better version."

On August 30, 1945, Bernds directed Shemp in *Society Mugs*, which again paired him with Tom Kennedy and would have to stand up against a hailed predecessor. It was a remake of the Three Stooges' short *Termites of 1938*.

One week after *Society Mugs* wrapped a four-day shoot, Jules White called "action" on *Jiggers, My Wife*. Galbraith calls it "the best of the Woodcock J. Strinker shorts."

Bride and Gloom, an action-packed comedy of errors, was filmed over four days beginning on February 20, 1946. It would be the last of Shemp's solo shorts at Columbia and his final appearance as a solo star. Bernds directed and wrote the screenplay, which opens with Shemp late for his own wedding. Rushing to the church where his bride waits, Shemp's taxi is stuck in the mud. He borrows a car with no brakes and slams into a fire hydrant that gushes water and drenches (regular Three Stooges supporting player) Christine McIntyre, who hops into his car and undresses to get dry. "Still without brakes, Shemp and a half-naked Christine keep circling the block where the church is," Galbraith wrote in his review. He added that it was "too bad" this was the last one. "Shemp's solo shorts were really getting good during 1945–46."

They were getting good, and Shemp may have gone on to greater heights, but, Galbraith tells the author, there were limits, and those limits were set by Jules White. "A lot of people have seen the Three Stooges shorts over and over again, but they're not as familiar with Columbia's other two-reel comedies. Over the last twenty-five years or so, these other comedies that were long unavailable were released to DVD. The two-reel comedies that Buster Keaton and Charley Chase made at Columbia came out, and some other miscellaneous stuff, including the Shemp solo shorts. And when you look at all those, it's really interesting, because although Keaton and Charley Chase were able to, to a greater or lesser degree, continue doing the kinds of comedies that they had been making before, for the most part Jules White had this very rigid concept of what type of comedy Columbia was going to do:

> He would hire these people to come in and start a two-reel comedy, but it was always a Jules White type of slapstick comedy. They were never really tailored to the specific talents or persona of the people they brought in. It was, "Okay, you're going to come in and do this, but you're going to do it our way." And in Shemp's case, it was interesting because they tried all these different things, and a lot of what he was doing were remakes of other shorts. *Mr. Noisy* is a remake of *The Heckler*, which was one of Charley Chase's last films. And he's really good and it's really funny, but it's also a remake, so he didn't really have that much opportunity to develop a specific kind of character, whereas in some of the short comedies made by other companies, they were able to nurture it along a little bit better. Certainly that was true at Hal Roach and then later at RKO with the Edgar Kennedy two-reel comedies and the Leon Errol comedies. They were more suited to their particular talents and I think were a little more character-driven, and less the violent slapstick kind of humor.

Edward Bernds blamed the decline in quality and the repackaging on production costs. He told film historians Edward Watz and Ted Okuda that the average budget for a two-reel short was $35,000 back in the 1930s—and stayed there into the 1940s. "Costs rose sharply and the dollar simply didn't buy as much, So the budgets remained the same, but you weren't able to stretch them as far as they could in the 1930s."

Leonard Maltin, who recalls "a long correspondence and eventual friendship with Edward Bernds," agrees that the shorts division was in a predicament. "Bernds was a big booster for Shemp. He thought Shemp was hilarious and very talented; thought the world of him and really enjoyed working with him. The problem was that theater owners over the years got used to paying a certain amount for cartoons and shorts and newsreels, and they never wanted to pay more. So for the studios, it was a losing proposition. Costs were going up. Costs never go down. The cost of making this stuff was going up and their customers weren't willing to pay more."

All that makes sense but there may have been something else on the Columbia lot that was keeping Shemp's work in low gear since his arrival at Sunset and Gower in 1944. That was the drama surrounding his younger brother Curly and concern over the future of the Three Stooges.

Twenty-One

The Curly Conspiracy

By the time Shemp Howard had returned to the Columbia Pictures lot in the spring of 1944, everybody involved with the Three Stooges knew that the star of the act, Shemp's brother Curly Howard, wasn't somehow going to get better miraculously and become the wild comic presence of the past. He was, in the words of Edward Bernds, "a hard liver and he drank too much," and his health was fading fast. It was suspected that Curly had already suffered more than one "mini-stroke" (a brief blockage of blood flow to the brain that causes stroke-like symptoms, including numbness, paralysis, and slurred or garbled speech). And it wasn't as if he had any downtime to recuperate or recover in a spa or sanitorium. When the Stooges weren't filming their shorts at Columbia, they were out of town, making personal appearances arranged by Moe Howard. The businessman and "brains" of the operation, Moe kept the Stooges on the road on an endless tour of movie theaters, vaudeville houses, nightclubs, fairs, and USO Stage Door Canteens. Sure, the Three Stooges had remained on yearly contracts at Columbia for the past decade, and Moe supposedly never once demanded a raise, but he had to know what he was doing.

In the case of Curly, Moe at least thought he knew. The Stooges filmed the comedy short *Idiots Deluxe* with Jules White in October 1944 and in December headed to the Columbia Ranch in Burbank to make a feature film. For the Three Stooges, a full-length motion picture was unusual. Unlike many contemporary comedy teams, the Stooges had never "graduated" from shorts in the 1930s. Moe had said it was hard enough "inventing, rewriting, or stealing gags" for the two-reelers. When they did appear in film, the Stooges had cameo roles where they could provide some comic relief in a scene or two. *Rockin' in the Rockies* was different. It was a low-budget musical comedy western, and Moe, Larry, and Curly were the stars. But this was not a "Three Stooges" comedy. Moe had his hair greased back to play a character, a ranch foreman named Shorty Williams, while Larry and Curly were a couple of vagrants—named Larry and Curly. Critic Stuart Galbraith IV suggests that the Stooges may have been slipped into roles originally written for other actors. (He also notes that "Curly's small strokes affect his line delivery.") The cast also included Hollywood's "King of Western Swing" and future wife murderer Spade Cooley and, as ranch hands, the comedy swing band, the Hoosier Hotshots. The picture began to make the rounds of movie theaters in April 1945. When it showed up in New York City in July, Wanda Hale of the *Daily News* described the plot:

> All these comedians and entertainers, plus several straight players, somehow get together on a ranch in the West while the owner is away on business, go through a lot of noisy, discordant monkeyshines and those who do not get rich on a valuable mineral discovered on the ranch get signed up by a Broadway producer for a New York musical show.

The film was, she concluded, "Columbia's mistake."

The Stooges completed work on *Rockin' in the Rockies* on December 22, 1944. While the shoot made it all the more obvious that Curly's health issues needed to be addressed, Moe did not give his brother a break. The Stooges made a lot of their money by taking their act on the road, and when they finished work on *Rockin' in the Rockies,* they were scheduled to head out on a tour that would ping-pong the trio around the country until they returned to Columbia studios in March to film their next short. Two days after Christmas, San Francisco was their first stop, where they would spend two weeks working into the new year at the Golden Gate Theatre, an old vaudeville palace turned movie house, poking and slapping between showings of *Belle of the Yukon,* a musical starring Randolph Scott, Gypsy Rose Lee, and Dinah Shore. The Three Stooges topped a "gala holiday stage show" that featured juggler Roy Royce, the Hartnells dancing team, impressionist Ollie O'Toole, and "extra added attraction," singer and actress Marion Hutton ("sister of Bombshell Betty"). *The Billboard* reported that the Golden Gate broke records on New Year's Eve and New Year's Day. From there, the Stooges would make their way to New Orleans before moving on to cities including Cleveland, Boston, and Chicago. That would be a lot of miles and a lot of work—and then, on the way to New Orleans, Curly broke down. The slaps, the exertion, and the travel were too much. He was ill. He probably suffered another stroke. Moe was beside himself with concern—concern about the tour. In his mind, canceling the appearances was not an option. Neither was an appearance by "the Two Stooges," especially not those two second bananas. Curly was the star.

Moe did come up with a solution. It was revealed in the *New Orleans Times-Picayune* on January 18, 1945:

> Moe and Shemp Howard and Larry Fine, who were the originals in the Three Stooges act, compose the trio to appear here. Curley Howard, who took Shemp's place after the act had been organized some years and whose appearance is familiar to movie audiences, is not on the current tour because of illness.

The newspaper story, touting the Stooges' appearance at the St. Charles Theatre (between showings of *Bowery Champs*, starring Huntz Hall and the East Side Kids), was accompanied by a publicity photo of the Three Stooges—Moe, Larry, and Curly, with Shemp's head pasted over Curly's. This would not be the last time that cover-up was attempted.

Somehow, Moe had convinced Shemp to leave Toluca Lake and meet him and Larry in New Orleans. The show went on, but without Curly, what was the point? You can bet the kids were disappointed, and without Curly—at least his *presence*—the Three Stooges weren't the Three Stooges, were they? Word spread along the circuit. *Variety* reported that "stands in Cleveland, Boston, and Chicago had to be called off."

The tour was canceled after all, leaving two big questions: Given Curly's obvious infirmities, should the tour have gone on at all? And how did Moe get his older brother to rejoin the old act and take the slaps and hits—loud enough to be heard in the back of the theaters—at a time that Shemp was hoping to take his solo career to a new level? Surely, Shemp wasn't tempted by the offer of money. Perhaps he saw what was already in the cards. A couple of weeks before he boarded the train for the show in New Orleans, Shemp had worked with Jules White on *A Hit with a Miss*—in which he played a role that Curly had immortalized in 1934 in *Punch Drunks*. When he returned to Hollywood, he would be back at Monogram studios to film *Trouble Chasers*, working with Billy Gilbert and Maxie Rosenbloom one last time—for the first time as an actual team of "three stooges." Shemp had to wonder—or at least somebody had to question—whether his hiring by Columbia Pictures wasn't connected to Curly's decline. He was being thrown a few appearances in features, but he was being tied to comedy shorts, produced and directed by the team that was grinding out Three Stooges comedies.

No, most likely, Moe did the convincing. Since childhood, he had set himself up as the boss. He was Jennie; he was Ted Healy. He knew that if he used the family card, he could "guilt" Shemp into stepping in—just this once, of course. Besides, this wasn't the first time Moe was prepared for the loss of the most important member of his comedy team.

And once again, he just happened to have a brother waiting in the wings.

Curly Howard was checked into the Santa Barbara Cottage Hospital, a community facility about ninety miles up the coast from the Hollywood gossip columnists, on January 23, 1945. Doctors tended to him and ran many tests, which led to some very concerning diagnoses. Curly was found to be suffering from high blood pressure, malignant hypertension, obesity, a retinal hemorrhage, and, most concerning, myocardial damage. Curly had not only suffered strokes but also, apparently, more than one heart attack.

Curly left the hospital on February 9, 1945. After a brief respite in Palm Springs, he made his way back to the Columbia lot a month later to film the latest Stooges short. *If a Body Meets a Body* was a remake of *The Laurel-Hardy Murder Case*, a Laurel and Hardy short from 1930. Jules White made the connection a bit more obvious by casting Fred Kelsey, who played the police chief in the original, as a detective and giving him the same lines he had recited fifteen years earlier. This short, perhaps most of all, reveals Curly's decline. He's very low-key, sometimes appears lost, and slurs his words. Much of his dialogue would have to be dubbed in postproduction. It's believed that he had suffered a stroke, his second or third, sometime between leaving the hospital and arriving at the studio. Moe later claimed that he tried to delay production to give Curly more time to recover but that Columbia boss Harry Cohn refused.

Edward Bernds would direct five shorts with Moe, Larry, and Curly. He got his first chance in April 1945 with *Bird in the Head*. Bernds recalled that he could never be sure which Curly would arrive on set: the ball of energy or the mumbling shell of his comic self. In this case, Curly was so slow and incoherent that Bernds was sure he was exhibiting signs of "a slight stroke." In May, when Bernds directed *The Three Troubledoers*, he said the old Curly was still not there. But somehow, in the first week of June, Curly returned in full force for *Micro-Phonies*, masquerading in drag as "Señorita Cucaracha" and lip-synching opera. Galbraith commented that the short is "generally regarded as Curly's last hurrah." Bernds said he saved his own career by convincing Columbia to switch the order of the first three Stooges shorts he directed and release *Micro-Phonies* first. He had a point. The work is so inspired that Leonard Maltin cites *Micro-Phonies* as his favorite Three Stooges short.

On July 30, 1945, Moe, Larry, and Curly were moonlighting at Monogram Studios to make another feature film, *Swing Parade of 1946*. Starring with Gale Storm and Phil Regan, they reworked some of their old routines into the script, including bits they had done with Ted Healy at MGM (perhaps a little posthumous revenge for his threats when they struck out on their own after *Soup to Nuts*). *Swing Parade* wrapped on August 25. Three days later, Moe, Larry, and Curly were back at Columbia for work on their final short for the year. Jules White directed *Uncivil War Birds*, a remake of *Mooching through Georgia*, a Buster Keaton short that White had directed in 1939 (he would also mooch some stock footage from the original). After the last scene was lensed on August 28, the Stooges could take a much-needed break. Curly would have a full five months to recharge and recuperate before returning on January 30, 1946, to film *Monkey Businessmen* with Hugh McCollum and Edward Bernds.

Somebody forgot to remind Moe. In September, Moe led—and in Curly's case probably dragged—his fellow Stooges east for more stage work. On Friday, September 21, the trio opened a week's run at the Earle Theatre in Philadelphia, leading the stage show that accompanied screenings of the Jack Oakie film *On Stage Everybody*. Margaret Kaye wrote in the *Philadelphia Inquirer* that "the Three Stooges received a hearty welcome on their appearance and kept the audience in a hilarious mood with their zany doings." (The Earle was closed on Sundays, so the Stooges squeezed in a show that day at the Stanley Theatre, across the Delaware River in Camden, New Jersey). Then it was on to four weeks in New York City: seven days a week and multiple shows per day at the Strand Theatre at the corner of Broadway and 47th Street in Times Square. This wasn't a Broadway show like the *George White Scandals* they were part of in 1939. Like their show at the Earle, which featured on the bill "Oriental Beatrice Fung Oye" and "Eddie (Strawberry) Russell, Negro monologist and dancer (getting a remarkable amount of tone and fun from his cigar box violin)," this was a stand left over from the vaudeville days, the Stooges doing their act between showings of *Mildred Pierce*, the movie starring Joan Crawford.

The *New York Daily News* gave the show a brief mention:

> Russ Morgan and his orchestra head the new Strand stage show, with Marjorie Lee as the featured vocalist. The Three Stooges furnish the comedy, Tommy Dix contributes a number of popular song numbers and the Graysons provide the dance routines.

Moe had to be able to see that his younger brother, the star of the act, was fading and that his timing was off, but the slaps and physical comedy continued. Moe did not curtail the engagement. Despite his reported shock earlier in the year, when the doctors at the Cottage Hospital reeled off Curly's ailments, his daughter Joan Howard Mauer wrote that "Moe was convinced that many of Curly's problems stemmed from his loneliness." *Loneliness.* So Moe did what any concerned relative would do. He set up Curly on a date with a relative of the theater owner. Marion Marvin Buxbaum was an attractive blonde secretary with a ten-year-old son from a previous marriage. She and Curly must have hit it off because on October 17, 1945, two weeks after they met, they were married.

The Stooges closed at the Strand on October 25. The next day, they were in Providence, Rhode Island, for three days of performances between showings of *Tiger Woman* at the Metropolitan Theatre. This was the last stop on their East Coast swing but not the end of their tour. They headed back to California and on November 7 opened a week at the Golden Gate Theatre in San Francisco.

Curly brought his new bride to California, where they settled into a new house at 4635 Ledge Street in Toluca Lake. The marriage did not last. The couple separated on January 14, 1946, and Curly filed for divorce. The split made national news. The Howard camp painted Marion as a gold digger, but her countercharges of abuse and other bad behavior reflected very poorly on Curly. When the divorce was granted in June, the judge ruled in Marion's favor.

Meanwhile, Curly's health was not improving. Moe had no choice but to give him a rest, so no live dates were scheduled in the first half of 1946. Well, no live dates out of town. In February, reasoning that it didn't require any travel, he agreed to a week's booking alongside the Judy Canova musical comedy film *Hit the Hay* at the Orpheum Theatre in downtown Los Angeles. Curly made it through, but the Orpheum gig would be his last time onstage and his last personal appearance of any kind with the Three Stooges.

Shemp filmed his last solo feature appearance for Columbia Pictures in March and April 1946. *Blondie Knows Best* was the eighteenth of twenty-eight Columbia comedies based on *Blondie,* Chic Young's long-running comic strip about the pretty blonde housewife and her dimwitted, sandwich-loving husband, Dagwood Bumstead. Edward Bernds cowrote the feature, which starred Penny Singleton and Arthur Lake, and the plot was similar to the story Bernds had cooked up for *When the Pest Begins*: Dagwood accidentally wrecks his neighbor's car and garage. This time, the neighbor files a lawsuit. Shemp plays the process server trying to hand Dagwood a subpoena that Dagwood is ducking. Shemp's character Jim Gray is at a serious disadvantage. He is nearsighted. He plays the gag through the picture, and his asides and slapstick bits add an additional comic element to the family comedy.

While Shemp was filming *Blondie Knows Best*, Edward Bernds was directing the Three Stooges in *Three Little Pirates*. Once again, Curly seemed to be getting back to an approximation of health. "He was almost his old self in that," Bernds said, "but then a week or ten days later, he was making a picture with Jules White, and that's where he passed out and they finally realized it was a stroke."

Curly actually suffered that serious stroke eighteen days after *Three Little Pirates* had been completed. And in the time between *Pirates* and that last picture, White had wedged in another Three Stooges short. *Rhythm and Weep* was an offbeat comedy in which the Stooges meet up with a trio of female dancers on a rooftop where they've all arrived to commit suicide. Galbraith remarked that *Rhythm and Weep* features Curly with much longer hair and "probably his last-ever first class 'Woo-woo-woo!'"

On May 6, 1946, twenty days after production wrapped on *Blondie Knows Best*, Moe Howard, Curly Howard, and Larry Fine were in a soundstage on the Columbia lot, waiting to film the final scene on the final day of a four-day shoot for *Half-Wits Holiday*. Curly had been in bad shape throughout the production of the two-reeler, and in many cases, director Jules White had to work around him. On this Monday afternoon, Curly was resting in the director's chair when the assistant director called the cast onto the stage to film a pie-throwing fight. Everyone responded—everyone except Curly. Moe was the first to notice his brother slumped in the chair, chin on his chest, mouth distorted, and tears running down his face. Curly tried to speak, but words would not come. He had suffered a massive stroke. This was serious, life-and-death stuff, and Moe knew it. He remembered that he, too, was crying when he clasped his brother's hand, embraced him, and kissed his cheek and forehead. Then?

> I had the studio car take him home while I finished the scene.

Jules White went over the script for that final scene—the pie fight—and divided Curly's remaining lines between Moe and Larry. Emil Sitka was waiting on set in his first of many appearances as a supporting actor on Stooges films. He noticed Curly's absence, but "I thought it was just a change in the script. It was only after the picture had been completed that I found out he took ill." Curly, meanwhile, was taken to a hospital. Moe said that he later arranged for Curly to receive care and therapy at the Motion Picture Country House in Woodland Hills.

Curly's film career was, for the most part, over. Who could ever replace him?

Twenty-Two

Return of the Stooge

"I had the feeling that this would be the end of the Three Stooges. Who could take Curly's place? He was a genius in his field."

Moe Howard remembered well the moment when he realized that Curly's stroke was so serious that he would not be able to make any more short comedies, let alone travel to make personal appearances in cities and towns around the country. "Larry and I wondered if it was possible to revive the Three Stooges," Moe wrote in his autobiography. "Many performers were presented to me by agents, but they didn't have a tenth of what was needed to fill the bill. Finally it hit me: Why not Shemp?"

Why *not* Shemp?

"He had been one of the Stooges before Curly," Moe reasoned, so why not? Moe leaves out details that make it less than likely that Shemp was not thought of immediately and in fact had been considered or was even kept in place for the role long before his youngest brother was immobilized. After a golden era of characterizations at Universal and other studios, Shemp had been hired back at Columbia Pictures, home to the Three Stooges, at the same time that Curly, the star of the Stooges' short comedies, was clearly on a downward spiral. When Shemp made his own short comedies, he worked with the Three Stooges' writers, producers, directors, and supporting actors—and sometimes versions of their scripts. He visited the Stooges when they were in production (his presence on the set of *Three Little Pirates* was captured on film that surfaced in 2007).

Moe also forgot to remember (or at least neglected to mention) that he had Shemp in his pocket all along, having convinced his older brother in January 1945 to drop everything and join him and Larry Fine on the road after Curly broke down on tour. Larry's biographers Steve Cox and Jim Terry put it very bluntly: "Moe knew changes were in store and began grooming his brother Shemp for a return."

Moe claimed that he stood firm when the Columbia "front office" rejected his suggestion of Shemp as a replacement because he looked too similar to Moe. "I told them it's Shemp or you don't have the Stooges anymore at Columbia. They quickly changed their minds."

"In the end, I think it was at Moe's insistence that Shemp take Curly's place," Edward Bernds told Michael Fleming years later. But while Bernds agreed that "some of the people in the front office did think that Shemp looked too much like Moe," he recalled another reason for hesitation: Shemp's own series of shorts. "His series would probably do very well by itself," Bernds said. "They would have to sacrifice it."

Jules White's limited budgets and Shemp's position as a contract player made the move almost a fait accompli. "Really, Shemp was the obvious choice," Jeff Abraham says. "The budgets were really tight at Columbia and they weren't going to go after someone from another studio who may cost them money. The simplest solution was to hire someone they already had under contract. And it was repeated years later when Joe Besser replaced Shemp. Besser was also under contract to Columbia."

Shemp supposedly agreed to step in under some duress—and only after insisting that Moe ensure that his role as a Stooge would only be temporary. The contract signed by Moe, Larry, Curly, and Shemp that was dated September 31 (they must have used a Stooges calendar; September 30 is followed by October 1) reflects that, stating that "presently Jerry Howard is incapacitated and that Shemp Howard shall render his services in place instead of Jerry Howard." When Jerry Howard was "physically able to render his services," Shemp's employment as a Stooge would be terminated. An amendment to the contract, signed by all four on October 21, stipulated that Shemp could pursue roles in feature motion pictures when he wasn't filming with the Three Stooges but that his salary "shall be reduced to one thousand two hundred and fifty dollars a week."

That salary cap on loan-out work would seem to indicate that Shemp sacrificed income by joining the Three Stooges. Brent Seguine discovered that that was not necessarily the case. In an article for *The Three Stooges Newsletter* in 2015, he wrote that an examination of Shemp's income tax returns and earning statements from 1943 to 1947 showed that the move was financially lucrative.

A bigger question was whether Shemp, at fifty-one, was sacrificing a lucrative future and possible cinematic greatness if he did indeed remain with Moe and Larry.

"Possibly," says Leonard Maltin, the film critic and longtime Three Stooges fan. "His most rewarding period was the forties. He got good parts in good movies and prominent roles, working with other comics in films. And now he's just going to be part of a trio. So I think it was a something of a sacrifice."

"A sacrifice? Shemp may have felt that way," Billy West, the voice actor and prominent Stooges fan and impressionist, says. "But I think Shemp was a journeyman. 'Where am I going today? Abbott and Costello? Okay. Cool. Where am I going today? I'm gonna be in some film.' Probably all he wanted to do was work. I could see all of them with that immigrant mentality, because my uncles were like that. They're up in heaven, looking down at me, going, 'You had a chance to work eighteen hours a day and you didn't do it? You putz.' That turns you into a journeyman. If it's work, it's good. I can see them doggedly chasing down work, and Shemp, I think he just had ants in his pants. He just wanted to go and see where it would take him personally."

Critic Stuart Galbraith IV also takes time to consider the question. "Was it a good career move or a bad career move to go back to the Stooges? It seems to me that the market for two-reel comedies really plummeted dramatically in the late forties. And by 1950, the Stooges were still going and they were still doing these Andy Clyde two-reel comedies at Columbia, but there wasn't much else being done. I think most of the other studios gave up on two-reel comedies by then." Galbraith adds,

> And at the same time, I think the types of comedies that Shemp was doing with Abbott and Costello and W. C. Fields, as well as the sort of Damon Runyon-type comedies that were really suited to his talents and the *Arabian Nights*-type things that he occasionally pops in, those kind of genres were also going away. So I think possibly Shemp thought, 'Well, if I want to keep working steadily, I better go back to the Stooges,' because then at least he's under this contract to do so many short subjects per year. Even if they only had a one-year contract, it was a guarantee of work for so many weeks to do so many shorts.

"There's two answers to that," Nick Santa Maria says in response to the "sacrifice" question. "The first answer is yes, he did. I think he sacrificed a career in features and he could have grown from Universal, which was sort of an A-minus studio. I do think he gave up that opportunity. But the other answer is 'no,' because what's he remembered for? It's the question of immortality or him having a more satisfying career—and maybe living longer."

Curly's stroke and the decisions regarding his successor were not about to interrupt business on Harry Cohn's movie lot or Jules White's calendar. Four days after Curly's collapse on the set of *Half-Wits Holiday*, the Three Stooges were scheduled to work with Edward Bernds on what would have been their ninety-eighth Columbia short. *Pardon My Terror* was Bernds's rewrite of *To Heir Is Human*, a 1944 Columbia short starring Harry Langdon (which was a remake of *You're Next!*, a Walter

Catlett two-reeler from 1940). Moe, Larry, and Curly would play a trio of detectives investigating a possible murder. With the Stooges sidelined, Bernds pulled in another of Jules White's comedy teams, Gus Schilling and Richard Lane, to take over. There wasn't much time to rewrite the script, so Bernds handed Curly's lines to Schilling, while Lane got Moe's. Larry's lines were divided between them. Three detectives were now two. Supporting players and Stooges regulars Emil Sitka, Dudley Anderson, and Christine McIntyre remained in place. The short was knocked out in four days, as usual. (In the end, Bernds wouldn't miss out on having the Stooges perform his script. He would remake *Pardon My Terror* with Moe, Larry, and Shemp in December 1947 as *Who Done It?*.)

Bernds was set to direct another Three Stooges short beginning on June 5. Once again, a beat was not to be skipped by Jules White's short subject department. By this time, there again were three. Shemp Howard was on board for *Fright Night*. With his hair greased to the max and parted in the middle, he looked different enough from Moe—and he walked right into a role that had been written for Curly and fit right in to the team (although he is noticeably taller than the other two). Shemp's work with

Shemp replaced Curly in the Three Stooges in 1946 in time for Fright Night *and took his first slap from Moe about seven and half minutes in.*

Billy Gilbert and Maxie Rosenbloom, his familiarity with the Columbia shorts team, and his past and more current work with Moe and Larry onstage all came into play. So did his professionalism and experience as a solo performer. With his ad-libs, bits of business, and that bag of tricks, he had more to offer than the other two and, in some ways, more to offer than Curly.

In *Fright Night*, Shemp, Moe, and Larry portray trainers for boxer Chopper Kane, who is about to face Gorilla Watson for the heavyweight title. After some back-and-forth battering of the three by a boxing dummy, Shemp is recruited to be Chopper's sparring partner—"No, no! Not me, fellas. I never had a glove on in my life. Besides, I bruise easy!" He follows with a comic balletic set piece: blinded when the headgear slips over his eyes ("Wait a minute, where did everybody go?") and stumbling into a ring post, almost strangled trying to climb through the ropes into the ring ("Now I know how a gopher feels!"), taking a pummeling while fighting with one glove tied to the ropes, and trying to dance away from another beating.

Shemp gets his first slap from Moe about seven and half minutes into the eighteen-minute short, and when gangsters Moose and Chuck show up to demand that Chopper take a dive, Shemp's original boxing series—you remember, the one that Moe claimed was the reason Shemp had quit the act back in 1932—gets a reference:

> MOOSE: All right, now get this straight. That palooka of yours, he ain't winnin' his fight with Gorilla Watson.
> MOE: Why not?
> MOOSE: Because Big Mike says so.
> MOE: But listen—
> MOOSE: No buts. Just see that that palooka of yours gets himself knocked out. C'mon, Chuck.
> *The gangsters exit.*
> SHEMP: They can't do this to us. I'll call the police! I'll call the fire department. I'll, I'll call the Marines! I'll—
> MOE: Shut up!
> SHEMP: That's what I mean. I'll shut up.

In the final scene, after the Stooges are chased by the gangsters through a maze of crates in a warehouse, a stray bullet causes a can of red paint to splash onto Shemp. "Blood!" he cries. "I'm dyin'! Everything is gettin' dark . . . Moe! Larry!" Shemp follows with the first utterance of a sound that would become something of a catchphrase, one that writer Mitchell Shannon called his "tactful counterpoint to Curly's 'Woob-woob-woob'":

Hee-bee-bee!

"*Fright Night* turned out to be a pretty good picture," Bernds said, "and it was apparent that Shemp would get by very nicely." Shemp's replacement of Curly would have gone even smoother, perhaps even unnoticed, if not for *Fright Night*'s opening titles, which reflected the interchangeability of actors in Jules White's department and the haste with which the change was made. The title card announcing the Three Stooges featured cut-out headshots of Curly, Larry, and Moe. In this case, a photo of Shemp's head, a little too large, is pasted clumsily over Curly's.

Edward Bernds was back in the director's chair, and Shemp was the central character in the next Three Stooges short, a western parody that began filming on July 8. In *Out West*, Shemp is sent "out west" to recuperate from an enlarged vein in his right leg that his doctor, played by Vernon Dent, sketches for him.

"I ain't gonna lose my leg, am I, Doc?" Shemp asks. "I've had it ever since I was a little kid." "Oh, of course not," the doctor replies. "Just go out west. Couple of months and you'll be just as good as new." We next see the three, in cowboy duds and chaps, in the Red Dog Saloon, where bad guy Doc Barker (Norman Willis) overhears Shemp bragging about "the biggest vein you ever saw." Barker assumes he's talking about gold:

> DOC BARKER (*viewing the sketch*): I could do things with a vein like that.
> SHEMP: You mean operate?
> DOC BARKER: That's right, pardner. We'll really go to work on it. No small-time stuff, either. If it's near the surface, we'll use twenty men with pick and shovels . . . and if the vein is any deeper, we'll use dynamite.
> SHEMP: Oh, no! Not on my vein!
> DOC BARKER: There are tinhorns around who say Doc Barker ain't a big operator. Well, they won't have a leg left to stand on.
> SHEMP: Neither will I!

The Stooges learn that Doc Barker has kidnapped and locked up the good guy, The Arizona Kid (Jock Mahoney, billed as Jacques O'Mahoney, his real name), with plans to wed his gal, Nell (played by Christine McIntyre). They spring the Kid from jail and defeat the bad guys while the cavalry is still on the way.

The Three Stooges had a break after *Out West*. The first two shorts with Shemp had worked out well. How the public would respond was another story. There truly was no replacing Curly, but his work over the past three years had been noticeably lacking. Shemp would be seen as either a second-rate stand-in, a rumpled greasy mug in place of the lighter-than-air man-child, or an invigorating boost to a tired team.

The break should have given the new Three Stooges time to take a breath and reassess. Instead, Moe took them out on the road. "They were on the road a lot," Jules White told David Bruskin. "The pictures, of course, made them more popular. Between Chicago and Boston, they'd have a lot of bookings. Then they'd change the act a little bit and return to play again. That's where their big money came in. They never stopped."

The first stop of the Three Stooges' Shemp era was in Chicago on August 28, 1946: two weeks at Colosimo's restaurant and nightclub at 2126 South Wabash Avenue. The joint was a popular destination for locals and tourists alike, a swank nitery with a nice stage, dance floor, line of chorus girls—and a colorful past. Mob boss "Big Jim" Colosimo had opened the place in 1910 and was ambushed and shot dead at the front door ten years later (possibly plugged by Al Capone, who had been hired as bartender at a whorehouse that Colosimo operated up the street). The Stooges did better than Big Jim at Colosimo's but not by much. Will Davidson of the *Chicago Tribune* led the attack: "The ice show that opened the new Colosimo's restaurant some months ago was a high point in that famous café's history. The current show starring the Three Stooges is a new low." Davidson added,

> I found the Stooges amusing in the movies and in vaudeville years ago but the present group is my current nomination for the nadir in nonsense. You can anticipate nearly every gag line, and those you can't usually are disgusting.

The Stooges were booked for three weeks at Colosimo's. They left town after two.

Then it was on to Louisville, Kentucky; Washington, D.C.; and Columbus, Cleveland, Cincinnati, and Dayton, Ohio. The Stooges' final stop was in Boston on November 7: a week at the RKO Boston Theatre, headlining a stage show that accompanied screenings of the film noir *The Killers*. *Boston Globe* reviewer John W. Riley called the show a "whizzer"—that is, "if you aren't biased against the antics of the Three Stooges . . . the same old gags and horseplay they have been using within this reporter's memory."

Back in Hollywood, the filming schedule resumed on the Columbia lot, where before the end of the year, they would film two more shorts with Edward Bernds. *Squareheads of the Round Table* went into four days of production on December 9. The short comedy was shot on sets left over from *The Bandit of Sherwood Forest*, a swashbuckler starring Cornel Wilde as Robin Hood's son. The working title, *The Three Stooges in King Arthur's Court*, gives an idea of the plot. On December 16, it was on to *The Hot Scots*. Three graduates of detective correspondence school get hired to work at Scotland Yard—well, actually *in* the yard, picking up trash and pruning hedges, before they get the chance to solve a mystery in a Scottish castle (while Bernds gets more use from the old castle sets). According to Stuart Galbraith IV, "This one cashes in on renewed American interest in Scotland following the success of *Brigadoon* on Broadway." As McMoe, McLarry, and McShemp, the Stooges wear kilts and speak with Scottish accents. Both films would be held back from release until 1948. (Jules White would get his shot at directing the Three Stooges on the castle sets in May 1947 with *Fiddlers Three*.)

That was quite a way for Shemp Howard to top off a busy year. In many ways, it must have seemed like old times, with all the good and bad that entailed. After all the years he had spent working toward a reputation as a respected and versatile character actor, here he was, back onstage and on film, getting slapped and poked, mouthing hoary gags, and engaging in pants-dropping buffoonery.

But 1946 wasn't over just yet. Filming of *The Hot Scots* was completed on December 19. Christmas was around the corner, and Moe Howard was not about to let the opportunity to make a little more green slip by. At least they didn't have to travel far. On Christmas Day, the Three Stooges headlined a holiday stage show that ran through New Year's Eve at the Million Dollar Theater in downtown Los Angeles (*The Missing Lady*, starring Kane Richmond as The Shadow, was the featured film). "There is no way to account for the antics of these comedians," Marie Mesmer wrote in the *Los Angeles Daily News*. "Anything can happen in their slapstick routine—and usually does." She added,

> From the moment these versatile, charming gentlemen appear on the stage, they sprawl, fall, and slap each other around in a way that the clunk of heads knocking together may be heard in the last row of the theater.

As they had done since opening at Colosimo's, the new old Stooges trotted out routines they had been running through since the early days in vaudeville, including "(I Have a Girl Named) Nellie," the singing and slapping number they had performed with Ted Healy in *Soup to Nuts*. Shemp took most of the hits and slaps in "Nellie," as he did through most of the show. The audiences weren't looking for something new from the old Stooges, and without Curly, Shemp as recipient of slaps, pokes, and punches would do just fine.

On January 28, 1947, it was back to work at Columbia. *Hold That Lion!* was the fifth film Shemp made with Moe Howard and Larry Fine as the Three Stooges and the third to be released. Produced and directed by Jules White, its arrival in theaters on July 17, 1947, made it the one-hundredth comedy in Columbia's Three Stooges series.

In *Hold That Lion!*, the Stooges come into a large inheritance that is stolen by a sleazy attorney whom they chase onto a train, accidentally letting loose a caged lion in the process. This leads to a touching moment in Three Stooges history and a nagging moment in Shemp Howard's legacy.

There is undeniable poignancy in the scene in which Moe, Larry, and Shemp walk through a train car, looking for the thieving shyster, Icabod Slipp. They come on a passenger who is sleeping with a derby hat covering his face. Larry lifts the hat, revealing a man with a full head of hair and a clothespin clipped to his nose. Moe removes the clothespin, and the man lets out a snore, a "Woo woo woo!," and a bark: "Ruff! Ruff!"

A stroke-hobbled Curly needed only to feign sleep for a cameo appearance in Hold That Lion! *(1947)—the only time the three Howard brothers shared the screen.*

Looking at the sputtering, sleeping figure, Shemp asks, "What is that? A cocker spaniel?" "No," Moe replies. "I think it's just a spaniel." The passenger is Curly Howard. It is the first and only time the three Howard brothers shared a scene on film.

According to Jules White, the historic scene was a spur-of-the-moment idea that struck him when Curly happened to be visiting the set. "Apparently he came in on his own, since I didn't see a nurse with him," he said. "He was sitting around, reading a newspaper. As I walked in, the newspaper he had in front of his face came down and he waved hello to me. I thought it would be funny to have him do a bit in the picture and he was happy to do it."

The scene was filmed on a closed set on the last day of production after the rest of *Hold That Lion*! had been completed. Moe said he had hoped it would give Curly the impetus to get back to work.

A scene in *Hold That Lion!* in which Larry, Moe, and Shemp are hiding in a wooden crate that holds a live lion has been presented as further evidence of Shemp Howard's disabling "phobias." The lion, Emil Sitka said, "was so sickly he would fall asleep in the middle of a take," yet "when Shemp heard that there was a lion on the set, he was really panicked. I thought he was kidding, but he wasn't. When he finally shot the scene, the technicians had to put a glass between the lion and Shemp . . . he was that scared." The fact that a pane of glass was installed to protect the stars of the film from any possible mishap became a point of ridicule for Shemp. It wasn't the first and would not be the last.

In *Brideless Groom*, Shemp's Uncle Caleb has died, leaving Shemp a substantial inheritance that he can collect only if he finds and marries a woman within forty-eight hours of the reading of the will. Filmed from March 11 through 14 and directed by Edward Bernds, the seventeen-minute short is one the highlights of Shemp's Three Stooges oeuvre. It is full of laughs, beginning in the opening scene. "Professor Shemp Howard, Teacher of Voice" is accompanied by pianist Larry Fine as he works with a tall, amorous—and apparently tone-deaf—student, Miss Fanny Dinkelmeyer (played by Dee Green). Shemp waves his conductor's baton as she works her way through Johann Strauss's "Voices of Spring":

> MISS DINKELMEYER (*singing*): The birds return to skies of blue! Ah ah ah! Ah ah ah! Ah ah ah ahhhh! Ah ah! (*screams*) *Ah ahhhhhh!*

Shemp recoils. Larry stops playing the piano.

SHEMP (*to Miss Dinkelmeyer*): No, no. You are too fortissimo, too allegro, too Cointreau.

MISS DINKELMEYER: Oh, is that bad?

SHEMP: It ain't good. You're supposed to be singin' about the voices of spring, not the eruption of a volcano. Give with the throat, not with the bellows.

MISS DINKELMEYER: Oh! Oh, professor, you want it more like a bird!

SHEMP: That's it. That's it. Give me the bird!

Larry, who has fallen asleep, begins to snore. Shemp hits his arm, and the piano lid slams on Larry's hand with the sound of a dissonant piano chord.

LARRY: Oh! (*pulls his hand out of the piano*) Oh! Look!

Larry shows Shemp his crooked fingers. Shemp grabs and straightens them.

SHEMP: Play!

They try again. Miss Dinkelmeyer again sings off-key and starts screaming.

SHEMP: Enough. Enough! That's enough! That's enough! We've done enough for today. You might hurt your voice. You know, bend it, crack it, or break it or something.

MISS DINKELMEYER: Oh professor, you're so considerate. Hahaha! I'm just crazy about you!

She reaches for Shemp and grabs his tie, but Shemp pushes her away.

SHEMP: Don't forget, we've got another lesson Tuesday.

Shemp walks her to the door.

SHEMP: Gargle with old razor blades.

DINKELMEYER: All right, professor. I know you wouldn't want anything to happen to my throat.

She pats Shemp's face and exits. Shemp closes the door and turns to Larry.

SHEMP: Except to have somebody cut it.

While the scene was an obvious inspiration for Jerry Lewis's singing lesson with Hans Conried as Professor Mulerr in the 1964 film *The Patsy*, *Brideless Groom* is also remembered for the segment in which Shemp and Moe are trapped in a telephone booth, tangled in cords and chains. When Shemp's face is pressed against the glass, the resulting image is frightening enough to scare off a potential bride and, unapologetically and definitively, offers Shemp as a front-runner for the title of "The Ugliest Man in Hollywood."

Even squashed in a phone booth in Brideless Groom *(1947), Shemp wasn't quite the Ugliest Man in Hollywood.*

Director Bernds recalled another scene whose importance may have escaped viewers' attention but that proved to him that no matter what qualms Shemp may have had about his new role as a Stooge, he was willing to go above and beyond in the call of comedy. Here, Christine McIntyre mistakes Shemp for her cousin Basil and greets him with hugs and kisses. When the real cousin Basil phones, the script calls for McIntyre to give Shemp a good slap. In the early takes, she apparently was too gentle, too timid. After a few more tries, Shemp got serious. "Honey," he said, "if you want to do me a favor, cut loose and do it right. A lot of half-hearted slaps hurts more than the good one. Give it to me, Chris, and let's get it over with."

Bernds said that on the next take, McIntyre "let Shemp have it. It wound up as a whole series of slaps. The timing was beautiful. They rang out like pistol shots. . . . Then Chris delivered a haymaker—a right that knocked Shemp through the door."

After the punch connects and Shemp is launched back, in the split second before the camera cuts, a freeze of the footage shows Shemp's greasy hair fly back and his face register the pain. That punch broke Shemp's nose. McIntyre burst into tears and apologized profusely.

"It's all right, honey," Shemp told her. "I said you should cut loose and you did. You sure as hell did!"

And so Shemp's career with the Three Stooges got off to a rollicking start. The schedule, with most downtime filled by tours and stage work, would continue over the next two years. In May 1947, when there was a break in the filming schedule, Moe, Larry, and Shemp traveled to San Francisco to play a week at the Golden Gate Theatre. They spent a week in Seattle in June and on September 25 were in Baltimore, Maryland, the first stop on a twenty-week road trip that took them to Massachusetts, Virginia, North Carolina, South Carolina, Tennessee, and Georgia before veering back north to Connecticut, Pennsylvania, Massachusetts, and New Jersey. In 1948, it was a week in Chicago at the end of January, then another tour that kept them on the road through May, followed by more roadwork in July and October. On October 19, they were in New York City and had a spot on Milton Berle's *Texaco Star Theater*, their first time performing on television. (Almost exactly a year later, on October 12, 1949, the Stooges filmed their first television pilot, *Jerks of All Trades*, for the ABC network. The idea was that each week, they would try a new occupation. Chaos would follow. In the first episode, filmed before a live audience, they were interior decorators. The pilot never aired, and Columbia blocked the series, claiming it would compete with their two-reelers.)

The grind of personal appearances, stage work, radio spots, trains, automobiles, hotels, military bases, and children's hospitals could be brutal, especially for men who were past or hovering near the edge of fifty years old and taking literal beatings onstage at every show. When syndicated columnist Erskine Johnson corralled the Three Stooges in the summer of 1947, he focused on the slapstick violence.

"I got a broken nose once," Shemp volunteered.

"Yeah," Moe said. "But he won't tell you how he got it, so I will. Larry was taking a bow on the stage of a theater and his elbow came up and hit Shemp's nose. Even when it started to bleed, we didn't believe it—we thought it was a gag that the blood was only chocolate. So Larry took another bow, and let his elbow come up and hit Shemp again. Shemp started yelling and then we knew it was on the level—that his nose really was broken." Johnson reported,

> Another time Moe was beating Shemp over the head when they were playing at the Casa Mañana nightclub in New York. For some reason it wasn't getting the usual laughs, so Shemp whispered, "Hit me harder. They can't hear it above the dishes." So Moe hit harder and the people laughed. "Now

Shemp, Moe, and Larry run a restaurant called The Casbahbah in Malice in the Palace *(1949); Curly was cast as an angry cook but wasn't well enough to complete the role. © 2024 C3 Entertainment, Inc. All Rights Reserved.*

> we ask the waiters to keep those dishes quiet when we're on," Shemp said. "It's a lot easier on my head."

Johnson almost got the story right. The Three Stooges did perform at the Casa Mañana, impresario Billy Rose's nightclub in the old Earl Carroll Theatre space on Seventh Avenue and 50th Street in 1938 and 1939—but with Curly, not Shemp. The sentiment, however, was accurate enough. Shemp was back in the ring with the Stooges in more ways than one.

His work with the team paid off in 1948, when Columbia Pictures offered the Stooges a two-year contract for more two-reelers and even a feature film. It seemed obvious to some that the "temporary" tag attached to Shemp's tenure was, well, temporary.

Despite signs of hope, Curly was never able to retake his place in the lineup. In July 1947, he was well enough to marry a restaurant hostess named Valerie Newman. She was his fourth wife and in 1948 gave birth to a daughter named Jane. The family lived in a rented house at 12555 Riverside Drive in Toluca Lake, where Valerie cared for the baby and increasingly for Curly.

In June 1948, Jules White offered Curly another cameo role in a Three Stooges short. In *Malice in the Palace,* Moe, Larry, and Shemp own a small restaurant. Curly was cast as an angry cook, but he wasn't up to completing the work. His scene wasn't used, but a production still showed up on a lobby card. The photograph shows Curly, very thin and with a large mustache, wielding a meat cleaver and grasping Larry by the hair while Moe and Shemp look on.

In December 1948, Shemp reunited with Abbott and Costello, joining the production of their latest comedy, *Africa Screams.* Abbott and Costello had stepped away from Universal Pictures to make an independent film at Nassour Studios at Sunset and Wilton Place, about half a mile east of Columbia's studios. As Nick Santa Maria points out, this was one of the few films in which the duo had a say in casting, and they brought on friends like Joe Besser and Shemp. In *Africa Screams,* Costello, as mild-mannered Stanley Stevenson, and Abbott, as his pal Buzz Johnson, join a safari to the jungles of Africa, where a tribe of cannibals chases them toward their cooking cauldron before the pair is rescued by a gorilla.

Shemp has the role of Gunner, a big-game hunter and sharpshooter who just happens to be practically blind. With his thick eyeglasses dusted off from his bag of tricks, Shemp stands out in the role. He is able to flex some acting chops he hadn't used since joining the Three Stooges. It's a part that should have burnished his reputation, maybe even led to more solo roles. Instead, *Africa Screams* would provide ammunition for generations of Three Stooges biographers, more evidence that Shemp was not only "the fourth Stooge" but also the frightened Stooge, the scaredy-cat with all the phobias.

Twenty-Three

Shempophobia

December 4, 1948, was a very cold day in Los Angeles. The city awoke to find that a strong and frigid northwest flow of air from the ocean had left a thin layer of ice across the region. Car windshields, lawns, and streets were white with frost, and puddles from the previous day's rain had frozen over. But on this Saturday in Los Angeles, the city's coldest December 4 since 1909, life, work, and holiday preparations went on.

At Nassour Studios on Sunset Boulevard in Hollywood, director Charles Barton was on the Stage 4 soundstage, directing a scene for *Africa Screams*. While other soundstage sets had been designed to represent a lush, tropical jungle, the cavernous, expansive Stage 4 had been filled with 200,000 gallons of water (mixed with milk for the proper look on camera) to re-create the Ubangi River. The milky water's depth, according to various sources, was somewhere between three and four feet.

The scene was a simple transition in which supporting players Joe Besser and Shemp Howard float on a raft past the camera. Besser was a "nance" vaudeville comedian who took his whining, "sissy" act into films (and would perhaps become best known for his television role as "Stinky Davis," the oversized brat in the Little Lord Fauntleroy outfit, on *The Abbott and Costello Show* in 1952 and 1953). He was an old friend of Shemp's and would eventually take Shemp's place in the Three Stooges. On this day, the script called for the two comic actors to sit back-to-back atop a four-foot-high stack of trunks, cargo, and other supplies balanced on the raft. Two extras stood bow and stern, paddling, while the raft was pulled by a boat. The river's depth didn't seem to pose any danger to the actors but for some reason was causing great distress to Shemp Howard.

"Shemp was beside himself with fear and refused to get on the raft, even though the water wasn't up to his knees," Barton said. "I had to literally carry him on to the raft."

"He was afraid he was going to drown," Besser wrote in his autobiography. Besser did his best to calm the actor while the director attempted to get the shot, but Shemp could not settle into his place atop the stack.

Besser suggested that Shemp hold on to him. "Shemp took a grip around my shirt and he gripped it so hard that he almost tore it off. He was that scared!" When Shemp announced that he was feeling seasick, Barton had to be satisfied with what he had already filmed and shut down production for the day.

Besser hopped down from the raft as "everybody abandoned ship" and left the soundstage—everybody but Shemp Howard. Neither Shemp's colleagues nor the crew helped him down from the stack of props. "They left poor Shemp up there by himself," Besser wrote. "He wanted to come down, but nobody would help him."

"They left him sitting on the raft as a gag," Barton said.

Shemp screamed, "Will someone get me down from here?! Hurry up, fellas. I'm getting sick!"

Recalled Joe Besser, "Everybody laughed uproariously."

At around a quarter to five that afternoon, Besser and Shemp were back in the dressing room they shared in an underground bunker at Nassour Studios. Shemp was leaning over the sink, washing his face and wiping away any remaining specks of vomit that may have remained from his dash to the bathroom after Besser finally got someone to rescue him from the raft in Stage 4.

"The dressing rooms were below street level, and the only way of getting above ground was by way of a stairway that led up to the street," Besser recalled. "As he began washing off his makeup over the sink, a terrific earthquake shook the building."

According to the California Institute of Technology (Caltech), the first shock hit at 4:43:42 p.m. A second, more severe shock was registered nineteen seconds later. This second temblor shook the city and Southern California for more than a minute. The seismograph at Caltech recorded the shock waves at six and three-quarters in intensity ("very strong") on a scale that recorded a maximum of eight and a half. In Los Angeles, buildings swayed, plaster fell from ceilings, windows broke, and cracks appeared on the sides of apartment houses.

In the subterranean chamber of Nassour Studios, water sloshed in the sink, an overhead light fixture swung, the walls shook, and both men struggled to maintain their balance. Besser remembered that Shemp "had his pants halfway down so he kept tripping over his costume as he made a run for it."

According to Besser, Shemp screamed, "Every man for himself! Goodbye, Joe! This is it!" He recalled telling Shemp to "shut up" and that he

Seated atop the raft on a water-filled soundstage, Shemp had a panic attack while filming a scene for Africa Screams. *When the shoot wrapped, the crew left him stranded there. United Artists/Photofest © United Artists*

"laughed a lot watching Shemp trip over himself." But as the violent shaking continued, Besser admitted, "I was scared, too.

"Finally, we climbed up the stairs near the dressing room and the stairs shook so bad that I had to drag a frightened Shemp up to safety."

As Besser told it, that wasn't the end of Shemp's traumas. While it's possible that he or his coauthors combined incidents from the sixteen-day *Africa Screams* shoot into a single day, Besser claimed that Shemp revealed "another fear" when Besser offered to drive him home after the quake. Shemp refused. "The brakes will probably go out," he said, "and we'll be killed." Besser wrote that he did convince Shemp to get into the car. Ironically, "Shemp's premonition proved true: my brakes *did* go out!"

Besser used the hand brake, and Shemp made it home safely, never the wiser. The point was made, and it was a point that went along with the popular perception of Shemp that followed him into the afterlife: he had "phobias." In this case, Besser had documented fear of heights, water, earthquakes, and automobiles. Add that to the tales of the phobic, frightened man who feared dogs, flying—and lions.

But in this case, Joe Besser contradicted some of those theories. As the earthquake rumbled and the room kept shaking, he stopped laughing at Shemp and admitted that inside he was afraid as well, hoping against hope that they would make it out of the cellar before the ceiling collapsed on them, entombing them beneath the Nassour lot. Phobias are defined as "irrational fears." Is it irrational to be afraid during an earthquake? Is it irrational to fear getting into a car with Besser, who mentioned that "I had been driving less than a year at the time" and whose car brakes did, indeed, fail on the ride? How irrational is it to be afraid of a snarling dog or a lion, as "old" or "drugged" the beast may have seemed in hindsight (the lion looked spry enough on-screen).

A sidebar to Joe Besser's *Africa Screams* story is an outtake from *Africa Screams* that features Shemp, as nearsighted Gunner, walking through the jungle, thinking he's following Lou Costello's character while he's actually preceded by a chimpanzee, leaping and spinning in front of him. "He's got his glasses on, he can't see, and he's walking around. He thinks he has Lou, but it's a chimpanzee and he can't tell," Nick Santa Maria says. "And he's walking along with the monkey, and the monkey walks offstage and Shemp just says out loud, 'Whatsa matter? You been eatin' olives, ay?'" The crew breaks into laughter.

It's notable that Shemp did not request that a pane of glass be placed between him and the chimpanzee during the takes. There have been many harrowing news reports in recent years of chimps attacking humans: tearing off faces, fingers, and genitals with superhuman strength and fury. Similar stories were in the news around the time that *Africa Screams* was filmed in October 1948. Shemp surely was aware of the lawsuit filed by Charlotta Thompson. The actress was attacked, clawed, and bitten by a chimpanzee on the Columbia lot in 1943, when she was working as a stand-in for Evelyn Keyes on *Dangerous Blondes*. (The *New York Daily News* reported that the rampaging primate "frightened the electricians, who scampered up the ladders and took refuge on the catwalks.") Shemp appeared in *Strange Affair*, the "unofficial sequel" to *Dangerous Blondes*.

Shemp, it is clear, was a sensitive artist who suffered from anxiety and may in fact have experienced panic attacks. Friends and acquaintances would agree with the description offered in *The Three Stooges Scrapbook* by Irma Leveton, a friend of Moe's wife: "It's hard to imagine that a man with a face like that—he looked like a killer—was really a gentle man."

Leveton volunteered that Shemp was afraid of dogs—although he had a collie named Wags. "He used to walk down the street with a stick in his hand to protect himself. If a dog ever came near him, he would have fainted."

Edward Bernds described Shemp as "sensitive and kind-hearted." Bernds told Edward Watz a story about Shemp and director Jules White, who also lived in the Toluca Lake neighborhood. Watz wrote,

> One day, Shemp arrived at the studio, frazzled and shaking with rage. [Bernds said,] "Shemp told me that he saw Jules in his backyard with a rifle, shooting at birds in the trees. He said, 'How d'ya like that guy, shootin' at the poor little boidies!'" It was about an hour before Shemp calmed down sufficiently so that the Stooges could get to work.

Moe's son-in-law Norman Maurer remembered that Shemp "couldn't step on an ant," yet, in 2012, in a *Los Angeles Times* article recalling her idyllic days growing up in Toluca Lake, Sandie Howard-Isaac wrote of her grandparents' victory garden at 4604 Placidia Avenue. "My grandfather owned a gun—only to use on pesty gophers that would steal all the carrots."

An intriguing cataloging of Shemp's supposed phobias was offered by members of Shemp's family. Geraldyn Howard Greenbaum, Shemp's daughter-in-law, and her two daughters—Shemp's granddaughters Jill Howard Marcus (born May 2, 1953) and Sandie (born on October 5, 1956, ten months after Shemp's death)—host the *Shemp Howard Goils Group* on Facebook, a page that celebrates the man they call "Papa Shemp." In the aforementioned livestream session in November 2019, the women responded to viewers' questions about Shemp and his "phobias":

> SANDIE: A lot of people have asked over the years. . . . I'm not one hundred percent sure. Was Shemp afraid of dogs?
> JILL: No.
> GERI: Never! They had a dog, Wags. They always had dogs. But he was afraid of a lot of things.
> JILL: And they had Fifi and Lady, which were miniature poodles.
> GERI: And Wags.
> SANDI: Wags was like a little terrier.
> JILL: He loved anim— He loved dogs.
> GERI: Oh, he loved dogs.
> JILL: The only time that he was really ever afraid was in [*Hold That Lion!*], because they did have him behind a glass panel when the lion appeared. He was a little intimidated by the lion.
> SANDIE: Who wouldn't be?
> JILL: Yes. That was the only problem. He did have phobias, but that was not one of them.
> GERI: He had a lot of phobias.
> SANDIE: Like?

Shemp, supposedly deathly afraid of dogs, with his costar in Jiggers, My Wife! *(1946).*

GERI: Well, he didn't want to fly so, whenever they would go on personal appearances they had to take trains. And they had to take trains all the time. He would never fly. He was afraid. And after that accident with the car [supposedly with his son Mort, not in 1913, as Moe had written], he never drove. He went on a train.
SANDIE: So he did travel by trains. How about boats?
GERI. Uhh . . . no—
JILL: He did like to fish.
GERI: Fishing, but—
SANDIE: Off a pier!
GERI: Yeah. . . . But he wasn't crazy about boats.
SANDIE: We all knew that Gramma Babe, Shemp's wife, she wouldn't go on elevator. She always took the escalator wherever we went, and she didn't even really want to do that.
GERI: She had phobias, also.
SANDIE: When it was in their heyday and he didn't drive, when did Gramma Babe stop driving?
GERI: She never did. Never drove.
JILL: Yeah, they didn't really need a car when they lived in New York before they came out to California, and when they did come out to California, Dad was a teenager by then, and I believe Dad got his license and he took them wherever they needed to go, besides taxis . . .
SANDIE: Even though Dad said, "I will never drive with you again—"
JILL: Well, that was before this all happened. They really were very comfortable with taxis.
GERI: Or friends. They had a lot of friends who would pick them up.
SANDIE: And this was in Toluca Lake?
GERI: Toluca Lake, and Beverly Hills.

As their question-and-answer session continued, Shemp's relatives contradicted many of the long-held beliefs about Shemp's "phobias." Shemp was afraid to drive a car but owned a Ford before smashing into a barbershop window while driving with Mort (a carbon copy of a story Moe told about Shemp as a teenager). He was afraid of riding in cars yet was comfortable sitting in taxicabs driven by strangers. He was "afraid" to fly but traveled by train (as most touring acts at the time still did). Moe told of the time that Shemp insisted he was getting seasick—"just standing on a dock, fishing." Yet Shemp was among the regulars who fished from the Santa Monica Pier, which jutted far into Santa Monica Bay. And in July

1951, while the Three Stooges were in Pensacola, Florida, to perform for servicemen at the Naval Air Station, Vice Admiral John Dale Price took Moe, Larry, Shemp, and co-headliner Morton Downey on a fishing trip in the Atlantic Ocean. Moe wrote that Price ordered navy helicopters to fly overhead, scouting schools of fish for their boat. Photos of Shemp on the dock, showing off their catch after the trip, reveal no signs of wear, tear, anxiety, or fear.

Shemp was never formally diagnosed by a medical professional or doctor as "phobic." The label was imposed on him by friends and acquaintances more than seventy years ago, and the label remained unchanged through decades of Stooges books and articles. It was an easy caricature to keep in place because the most popular Three Stooges—Moe, Larry, and Curly—are caricatures or cartoons. In their act, Moe was the perpetually angry, bullying "boss" in the bowl haircut; Larry the dim, bald "everyman" with the porcupine hair springing out everywhere on his head but on top; and Curly the round, boyish clown, the uncoiled ball of energy and comedy. In life, they were just as easy to characterize: Moe the serious businessman, charting the course and doing everyone's taxes; Larry the sideman and gambler; and Curly the libertine and lothario, arbuckling himself toward a debilitating stroke.

The Three Stooges—Moe, Larry, and Curly—are easy to turn into cartoons and simple to merchandise. Perhaps the "phobic" label was, in part, a projection of Shemp's Stooges screen persona onto his life off-screen. The constantly frightened character was really a new persona Shemp had pulled from his "bag of tricks" when he rejoined Moe and Larry. Despite the varied characters he had portrayed in his earlier work, the popularity of the Three Stooges shorts would almost guarantee that this would be the one most people would be familiar with.

"Sometimes a story is too good to let go of—Shemp being the ultimate scaredy-cat," says Jeff Abraham. "I think some people might be mixing up what Shemp was like in the Stooges films with Shemp in real life."

"He sure could act scared," Billy West comments. "He'd be totally horrified that something would happen. And he poured it on, that's for sure. He made the scared thing way bigger than life, and he made a high art out of it. Lou Costello had the scared thing and Curly absolutely had a beautiful aesthetic about being scared, but I think [Shemp] did that better than anyone else."

West says he had also heard that Shemp was "scared in real life. . . . I think he was scared of shellfish, like lobsters really gave him the willies."

"I believe his fears were well-grounded," says Nick Santa Maria, "but as with anything, especially in Hollywood, things are exaggerated. Somebody may have palled around with Shemp for two weeks and saw him do something and then all of a sudden, 'Yeah, I saw him walk away from a dog; he must have had this horrible fear of dogs.' Most things you hear come from somewhere, and the truth is usually somewhere in the middle. I believe he was just a neurotic person. I don't think he was an unhappy person, I think it was the opposite. I think he was a very happy person, but I think he was very neurotic."

Stuart Galbraith IV observes that it's hard to imagine Moe, Larry, or Curly "as being anything other than Stooges." Shemp, he says, "was different." Shemp was a Stooge by contract, but he appeared to be a real person who brought a humanity to the group on-screen and onstage and was a sensitive yet complicated artist in "real life."

It can be agreed that Shemp was an anxious man. He may indeed have suffered panic disorder. A study cited by the National Library of Medicine concluded that "up to 33.7 percent of the population are affected by anxiety disorder in their lifetime." Anxiety is common today and, more important, is recognized and treated.

Joe Besser, in his recollection of the earthquake on the set of *Africa Screams*, may have accidentally hit on the root of Shemp's condition, one that covers almost too neatly every one of the aspects that have been grouped as individual "phobias" as well as the childhood trauma that Moe recalled in books and interviews. Besser said he witnessed "another dimension of Shemp's anxiety: his fear of death."

There's another aspect of Shemp's personality that doesn't quite fit with the image of a man who is frightened by his own shadow. Yes, Shemp took a lot of punches and slaps onstage and on-screen, and he didn't like it. He was a gentle man, but his favorite sport was boxing—not as a participant but as a fan. Shemp often took in the fights at Hollywood Legion Stadium, the 6,000-seat fight venue on El Centro Avenue just south of Hollywood Boulevard. And he didn't cower in the last row as the boxers battled. He was the Jack Nicholson or Spike Lee of the sport, a celebrity regular at ringside. "I used to go with Babe and Shemp and my husband Mort to the Hollywood Legion Stadium," Geri Howard Greenbaum remembered. "And we would go on Friday nights and we always would bring a newspaper, and I'd say, 'Why do we need the newspaper?' Well, I found out." Greenbaum explained,

> We sat in the second row and the blood from the boxers would be flying and we would have to take the newspapers and hold them up over our faces so we wouldn't get covered with the blood. But the funniest thing was that when we did finally put our newspapers down, every punch that the fighters would take, Shemp would take the punch and he would jump back. And then when they would throw their fists to hit, Shemp would be fighting. And

> he would take every punch and he would throw every punch . . . and he'd get all caught up in the fight, shadowboxing from his seat. He'd be as much a part of the show as the boxers themselves. And when they'd ring the bell . . . between rounds, the ring attendants would come down and towel Shemp off and give him a drink, which always got a big hand from the crowd, and that pleased Shemp because he loved his fans so.

"And he was the second attraction, because it was the boxers on the stage in the arena, and it was Shemp sitting in his seat. He was like the third boxer in the ring."

Twenty-Four

Stage and Screen . . . and Stage

Days after wrapping his work on *Africa Screams,* Shemp was back on the Columbia lot with Moe and Larry to film *Three Hams on Rye* with Jules White. The three-day shoot began on December 14. After a brief break, they returned to the road. On December 23, 1948, the Stooges were back at the Hippodrome in Baltimore for six days of shows followed by a week at the Adams Theatre in Newark, New Jersey, where they co-headlined a vaudeville bill with drummer and bandleader Buddy Rich. Midway through the Newark stand, the Stooges hightailed it across the Hudson River to Manhattan to make their second television appearance. They were the big-name guests on *New Year's Eve Party,* a two-hour CBS television special cohosted by Shemp's pal Morey Amsterdam and pop singer Barry Wood. The show kicked off at 11:00 p.m. on December 31 and included cut-ins from the celebration in Times Square.

After the Newark stand, with three shows per day, ended on January 5, 1949, the Stooges trained it back west. They would return to the East Coast at the end of April for a week (now four shows per day) at the Earle Theatre in Philadelphia (with a show in Camden, New Jersey, on Sunday, when the Earle went dark). There were also appearances in Brooklyn and in and around Chicago in April and May, but the roadwork actually slacked off in 1949. Many movie theater chains were no longer showing short subjects, the Three Stooges were getting less exposure, and there was a decline in demand to see these middle-aged men and their age-old routines in the flesh.

That was unfortunate because the old routines were as sturdy as ever. The *Variety* reviewer who had a seat in the Hippodrome the day after Christmas wrote that the Stooges trotted out "their familiar comedies to top returns, timing their knockabout skillfully and making their hoke song and dance dramatic sketch stand up to the hilt. Could have stayed on . . . but wisely left them hollering for more."

The roadwork would pick up with a couple of long tours in 1950, and live appearances would continue to be of great importance to the Three

Stooges and their bank accounts into the 1960s. Proof of their durability and the extent of their work and travel, from the vaudeville days of the 1920s and their time with Ted Healy through July 18, 1969, is documented, exhaustively and meticulously, in *A Tour de Farce: The Complete History of the Three Stooges on the Road,* an astonishingly detailed volume that was assembled, written, and published by Gary Lassin, the Three Stooges authority, fan club president, founder and curator of the Stoogeum, and husband of Larry Fine's grandniece.

Moe, Larry, and Shemp didn't have much time to rest or regroup when they disembarked in Los Angeles in January 1949. There was work waiting for them at the Columbia Pictures studios—lots of it. Jules White's short subject department was waiting with a stack of scripts and a tight schedule. Over the next thirteen weeks, the Stooges would complete a year's worth of shorts. Eight two-reelers were split between the two units: four produced by Hugh McCollum and directed by Edward Bernds and the other half directed and produced by Jules White:

January 11–14: *Dopey Dicks,* directed by Edward Bernds
January 25–28: *Vagabond Loafers,* directed by Edward Bernds
February 7–10: *Punchy Cowpunchers,* directed by Edward Bernds
February 15–17: *Hugs and Mugs,* directed by Jules White
February 22–25: *Studio Stoops,* directed by Edward Bernds
March 14–17: *Self Made Maids,* directed by Jules White
March 29–April 1: *Dunked in the Deep,* directed by Jules White
April 1–14: *Slaphappy Sleuths,* directed by Jules White

The critics would agree that the Edward Bernds shorts were superior to White's, but there were highlights among the work of both directors. *Vagabond Loafers* would be a historic work but not in a way that could be favorable to Shemp. It was the second time he was handed a remake of the Three Stooges' 1940 classic *A Plumbing We Will Go*—he was paired with El Brendel in *Pick a Peck of Plumbers* in 1944—but the first time he would be compared to Curly, Stooge to Stooge. Shemp was in Curly's role, at times reworking it gag for gag, including the classic scene that became known as Curly's "maze of pipes." It was, like that maze, a no-win situation.

"Shemp is the one who gets caught in that maze of pipes in the bathtub and he's very good, his reactions are great," Leonard Maltin says. "Is he funnier doing that routine than Curly? No. But he's funny."

Stuart Galbraith gave high marks to the B-western spoof *Punchy Cowpunchers,* which "deviates from the usual Stooge two-reeler, all in service to the comedy. Rare among the Stooges' Columbia two-reelers, it's got a musical score and it plays more like an ensemble comedy." *Studio Stoops* contains a memorable segment in which Shemp is hanging outside a tenth-story window, saved from splattering only by a telephone's expanding scissor extender. *Self Made Maids,* directed by Jules White, presents the Three Stooges in multiple roles. They play artists who fall in love with three women whose portraits they paint. In drag, they play the women: Moella, Larraine, and Shempetta. At the end, Moe, Larry, and Shemp are their infant children. Moe also plays the women's father. Through use of split screen, there are six Stooges in some shots, and with the use of a double, Moe chases himself. But although the short opens with a card announcing that "all parts in this picture are played by the Three Stooges," critic Galbraith has long been vexed by an odd anomaly: "For no good reason, one shot in a hotel lobby features an unidentified extra seated and reading a newspaper. Why this one person was added to the otherwise all-Stooge cast is a mystery."

("Man in Lobby" is credited in the IMDb as Ted Mangean, who had more than fifty uncredited roles in films dating back to Mack Sennett comedies. In *Self Made Maids,* he was also Larry's stand-in and stunt double.)

Shemp also starred with the Stooges in *Gold Raiders,* a United Artists feature film in which they play Wild West peddlers hired by an insurance man (played by long-in-the-tooth and wide-in-the-waist former cowboy star George O'Brien) to protect gold shipments from bad guys. Edward Bernds directed the movie in December 1950. *Variety* called it "a mediocre low-budgeter . . . grooved for the Saturday matinee market . . . slapstick stuff . . . purely for the elementary school set." *Boxoffice* agreed that "kids will enjoy the face-slapping antics of the Three Stooges. . . . Saturday morning is a good time if you generally draw the patronage of youngsters." The words were not particularly complimentary but were prescient. The youngsters—the "elementary school set"—of the 1960s would be the key to the Stooges' popularity that extended well into the twenty-first century.

The Stooges had a couple of shorts scheduled for production in February 1951, which would turn out to be a busy month. *Pest Man Wins,* which was filmed from February 12 through 15, was a remake of *Ants in the Pantry* from 1936. *Pest* pilfers pie-fight footage from both of 1941's *In the Sweet Pie and Pie* and *Half-Wits Holiday*, the last short starring Moe, Larry, and Curly. Jules White directed *Pest Man Wins* (as well as the two shorts he filched from). Next, it was on to *The Tooth Will Out* with McCollum and Bernds—after a stop on the Sunset Strip in West Hollywood.

Ciro's, the nightclub known for its celebrity clientele, was the site of a wedding on Sunday, February 18, 1951. In a joyous family celebration, Morton Howard, the twenty-three-year-old son of Shemp and Babe, tied the knot with twenty-year-old Geraldyn Mankoff. The young couple had met in 1948 after her graduation from Fairfax High School. According to the bride, their first date was over cheesecake at the Sportsmen's Lodge restaurant on Ventura Boulevard in Studio City.

Shemp was close to and very proud of his son, who had served in the U.S. Coast Guard and was embarking on a successful business career as an owner of the Ce-How self-service filling station on Alameda Boulevard in Burbank. Mort and his partner Ben Ceson would go on to own eighteen Ce-How locations in and around Los Angeles. (Three Stooges lore has it that Mort's self-serve stations were the first in the nation; gasoline historians give the honor to Frank Ulrich, who opened self-service pumps at the corner of Jillson Street and South Atlantic Boulevard in Commerce, California, in 1947.)

The next day, it was back to work. The Stooges spent a mere two days shooting *The Tooth Will Out* and by the end of the week were packed up to go on the road again. Moe, Shemp, and Larry were heading out to meet their public, only this time they wouldn't be settling in for weeklong residencies at once-grand vaudeville theaters and plush hotels. Remember, the times—and demand—had changed. The Three Stooges had to make their way to Minnesota by February 26—and not Minneapolis–St. Paul but the town of Winona. On that Monday, they would top an eight-act vaudeville bill in the auditorium of the Winona State Teachers College. The *Winona Republican-Herald* noted that this was the first time "the pleasantly insane Three Stooges" had made a stop in the small city of Winona. "Residents of this area have laughed at the antics of the Three Stooges for many years on screen but few, perhaps, have ever watched the boys perform in person." The writer added,

> The Three Stooges in real life are Moe Howard, Shemp Howard, and Larry Fine. Shemp's name is derived from a childhood mispronunciation of Sam, his real name. Larry is identified to moviegoers by his fuzzy locks, while Moe wears bangs.

There was a children's matinee at 4:30 p.m. and two evening shows before the troupe jumped into cars for the drive through the cold and windy badlands of South Dakota. On the road ahead were gigs in armories and auditoriums; a detour to Winnipeg, Canada; and a ride back into Minnesota on March 10. As soon as the trio got home, they were off again for a comparatively quick run to San Bernardino, California, for two shows at the National Orange Show. In the evening show, they got to share the stage with Bob Hope.

When there was space in the schedule, Moe tried to fill it. He arranged for the Stooges to be back on the road in May for another tour of Canada, and in July, they set off for six weeks of free shows at military bases and installations as part of another package that included Morton Downey, the popular American-born Irish tenor.

There were also more shorts to shoot before the end of the year, including *Gents in a Jam,* the last Three Stooges short produced by Hugh McCollum and directed (and written) by Edward Bernds. For years, McCollum seemed to be in constant battles with Jules White, and no one was surprised that White would give him the heave-ho. The chance came in 1952, when Columbia's short subject division was downsized and White convinced the front office that two units were no longer needed. After McCollum was fired, Edward Bernds quit in solidarity. He and McCollum went off to produce and direct Bowery Boys movies.

The remainder of Shemp's career offered fewer opportunities to shine. Budgets got tighter. More and more stock footage was crammed into the two-reelers. Shoots got shorter.

"When Curly started going downhill because of his strokes, some of those shorts are really painful to watch because he's just so completely out of it, and a lot of the shorts are not very good," Stuart Galbraith IV says. "When Shemp came along, suddenly there was this burst of energy. Part of it was Shemp rejoining the team and what he was bringing to it, and I think a big part of it also was the Hugh McCollum–Edward Bernds sort of 'second team' that was running at Columbia parallel to Jules White and his gang. It's really clear that the Hugh McCollum–Edward Bernds shorts with Shemp are far superior overall to the Jules White–directed ones, because those guys were young and hungry and trying harder. And they're really funny, partly because they're putting more effort into them. They're also doing something a little different from the standard Jules White slapstick, but it's also because of Shemp being really hilarious at times, and the energy that he brought to it.

"But McCollum and Bernds leave, and so now the Stooges are stuck pretty much only with Jules White. And also they start really slashing the budgets. After about 1952, it's stock footage craziness where there's no chance to do anything good."

On the first day of 1952, the Three Stooges were in Manhattan for an appearance on the *Frank Sinatra Show*, a variety series filmed at CBS Studio 50 (renamed the Ed Sullivan Theater in 1967). In this episode, Sinatra has hired Moe, Larry, and Shemp as servants for his annual New Year's Eve party. Pandemonium and hilarity ensue. The episode also featured Louis Armstrong, Yvonne De Carlo, Alan Young, and Vernon Dent. That would be the Stooges' last road trip for the year.

Meanwhile, there were new worries about Curly Howard. The youngest brother's condition never really improved since his last attempt at work in *Malice in the Palace*. A series of strokes in 1949 left him partially paralyzed, and he had been in and out of hospitals and nursing homes ever since. His condition, physical and mental, had only worsened in 1951. After another stroke in March, he'd been transferred to the North Hollywood Hospital and Sanitarium.

On January 7, 1952, as the Three Stooges began three days of filming on the short *He Cooked His Goose*, Moe received a call from the sanitarium. Curly's condition had deteriorated to the point where he had to be moved to another facility. As they continued production, he and Shemp realized that their kid brother was on his deathbed.

On January 18, Curly died at the Baldy View Sanitarium in San Gabriel, California. He was forty-eight.

On January 19, his death was reported in newspapers across the country:

> One of the famed Three Stooges died yesterday. . . . The Three Stooges specialized in "muscular humor"—roughhouse slapstick of the broadest sort. Curly Howard, who had his wavy brown hair and waxed mustache cut "to the bone" when he joined the act, had to take many of the whacks during the routine. (Associated Press)

On January 20, Curly's funeral got under way at 2:00 p.m. at the Malinow and Simons Mortuary on Venice Boulevard in the Venice section of Los Angeles. His body was transported across the city for burial at the Home of Peace Memorial Park, a Jewish cemetery in East Los Angeles.

On January 21, hours after leaving the cemetery, the Stooges were back at Columbia with Jules White to film *Up in Daisy's Penthouse*. The short was a remake of *3 Dumb Clucks* from 1937. Shemp had the part that Curly had played, a dual role as himself and his father.

As difficult as the return to work might have been, the three-day shoot was not without laughs behind the scenes. Erwin Dumbrille, who would go on to a long career as a film editor at Warner Bros., was a student at the

University of Southern California when White invited his film class to the set of *Daisy's Penthouse*. "We came on the day that only the Stooges were needed," he said. "For all the low comedy antics he created, Jules liked to be perceived as being a wise man." He remembered,

> It was just after lunch. As Jules patiently explained to the students what he as director hoped to achieve, Shemp broke wind—loudly! Jules stopped in mid-sentence, paused for a moment, then continued his lecture. Shemp did this several more times until the entire class finally collapsed in laughter. Shemp then hollered out something like, "Hey, Jules, now tell 'em how we manufacture our own sound effects!"

The old vaudeville circuits had dried up. The demand in the sticks wasn't there. So in 1953, the Three Stooges "went Vegas." At a time that the entertainment scene in Las Vegas was really starting to diversify and comedy was at the top of everyone's list, the trio was booked at the Sahara Hotel and Casino for two weeks, two shows per night, beginning on February 10. They pulled out on February 4. *Variety* reported the reason was that Shemp had suffered an injury to his leg. It was later reported that he had been in an automobile accident. There was no word on whether he was driving. (There has also been no confirmation on whether the accident report was a cover-up for something potentially more serious. A story has circulated and lived through the Internet that at some date during this period, in the weeks after completing a two-day shoot on *Goof on the Roof* on November 19, 1952, Shemp experienced a "minor stroke." His wife Babe was supposedly the source of the story. No medical records have surfaced to confirm the reports, and Shemp's survivors say it's not true.)

On April 27, Moe, Larry, and a seemingly fit Shemp completed a single day's shoot for *Musty Musketeers*, a remake of their own *Fiddlers Three* from 1948. The next day, it was fast work on *Pals and Gals*, a remake of *Out West*, the short in which Shemp had that large vein on his leg. Stuart Galbraith IV called *Pals and Gals* "Jules White's idea of revenge" since he was credited as director even though a great majority of the short is comprised of stock footage from McCollum and Bernds's short.

Shemp had some original material on his hands on May 2, 1953, when Mort and Geraldyn gave him and Babe a granddaughter, Jill. Shemp was, family members say, a doting grandfather, "Papa Shemp."

He was probably still passing out cigars to his pals and coworkers when he returned to the Columbia lot to film another Three Stooges short on May 11. This production was not a one-day session he could walk through with his eyes closed (the better to be poked that way) but a full five-day epic. The Three Stooges were about to go 3-D.

Versions of 3-D films had been around for decades, but the medium saw a real resurgence since November 1952 with the release of *Bwana Devil,* a B-movie that was the first full-length color feature with scenes that appeared to be in three dimensions ("A lion in your lap . . . a lover in your arms!") when viewed through disposable cardboard eyeglasses with filtered lenses. The gimmick was seen as a weapon against the competition of television and a way to get people back into movie theaters. Other studios followed.

"Our sales manager, Abe Schneider, called me and said, 'I've got two 3-D features but I have no short subjects and I need enough to fill out a show,'" Jules White recalled. "'How quickly can you get me a 3-D comedy?' 'For you, exactly the day before yesterday.' They didn't have great senses of humor. They were businessmen. With me, everything was a gag. I sat down and started to think what was the best Three Stooges idea I had made which I could improve and remake in 3-D. I came up with *Spooks!*. Felix Adler wrote the script. So I made the first 3-D short with the Stooges."

Spooks!, which cast the Stooges as detectives caught in a house with a mad scientist, was acknowledged at the time as the first 3-D movie short. The 3-D effects begin with the title card as the disembodied heads of Shemp, Larry, and Moe float toward the camera (Larry bumps it) before falling into place, as usual, under the opening Three Stooges credit. The effect isn't perfect; the lighting reveals their shoulders cloaked in black, but for audience members wearing the special glasses, much fun followed.

"I've never heard greater screams of laughter nor seen a more riotous reaction in all my life," Jules White said. "Any object traveling toward the camera made it look like you would be hit with it. We spaced gags so we didn't just keep throwing things. We had a gorilla in one of these pictures, lumbering right into the lens."

Spooks! offers another all-time Stooges highlight in a scene in which a bat flies into the room, squeaking away as it heads toward the camera and Larry, Shemp, and Moe, who can't seem to believe what they're seeing. In a close-up, the audience sees why. The bat has Shemp's face. It chirps, "Heebeebeebeebeebee! Ruff! Ruff! Ruff!"

Shemp looks on in horror and exclaims, "What a hideous, monstrous face!"

Spooks! was rush-released on June 15 to play along with Columbia's 3-D western *Fort Ti,* directed by the future movie gimmick king William Castle. *Boxoffice* rated the short as "Good":

> The Three Stooges in their first 3-D feature are not actually "Three Times as Funny in 3-D" as the ads proclaim, but the novelty angle of having dishes and custard pies apparently flying toward the audience will amuse and

When this bat menaced the Stooges in the 3D short Spooks! *(1953), Shemp exclaimed, "What a hideous, monstrous face!" Columbia/Photofest © Columbia*

entertain patrons far more than their ordinary flat comedies. The boys still bop each other on the head and gouge each other's eyes in the early scenes, but the finale is a typical "custard pie comedy" finish.

Jules White had the Stooges back on the lot on June 30 for an additional 3-D project. *Pardon My Backfire,* with the trio portraying auto mechanics out to capture some escaped convicts, was another unusually long shoot, also taking five days to complete. The short was in theaters by August 15, accompanying Columbia's 3-D western *The Stranger Wore a Gun*, starring Randolph Scott, Ernest Borgnine, and Lee Marvin. *Boxoffice* called *Backfire* an improvement over *Spooks!*, "mainly because a large amount of objects are seemingly thrown directly at the audience. Knives, buckets of water, and other things coming toward the patrons are bound to make them duck. Whether they will laugh depends entirely on whether they enjoy the crude slapstick antics of the Stooges."

3-D was a kick in the pants and a boon for the Three Stooges and movies in general—but not for long. "All of a sudden, however, 3-D fell out from under us," said White. "It didn't last long at all. Suddenly we found ourselves with thousands of little eye shades. As for the shorts . . . we were able to release them flat—non-3-D."

On July 31, 1953, the Three Stooges were back in Nevada and playing a casino for the first time. It wasn't Las Vegas but Stateline, on the southeastern shore of Lake Tahoe. Sahati's State Line Country Club and

Casino, on Route 60, billed itself as "The Monte Carlo of Lake Tahoe." The Stooges' two weeks of shows at Sahati's may have helped them secure another attempt to conquer Las Vegas. They were booked at the Fabulous Flamingo Hotel and Casino on October 1. The Flamingo was known for its lavish stage shows, and the Three Stooges show included several teams of dancers. The contract called for a two-week engagement. The Stooges lasted one show. They were gone after opening night. One report said it was because of "illness." Another claimed they were fired because they "didn't suit management."

There were no trips in 1954. The Three Stooges made seven new shorts, although there wasn't all that much filming to do. "Practically all the remaining Stooge shorts were remakes, where they were eighty to ninety-five percent stock footage, and they were only doing one or two days of new footage for each short," says Stuart Galbraith IV. "They would do a

In Heavenly Daze *(1948), Shemp's arousal at the sight of the angelic Miss Jones is signified by his rising wings, followed by his trademark* "Heebeebeebeebee!" *© 2024 C3 Entertainment, Inc. All Rights Reserved.*

completely original short maybe one out of every six or seven, but they were mostly remakes."

Billy West cites one of these remixes as among his favorites. It's one in which Shemp dies—and for the second time.

Bedlam in Paradise was an enhanced version of *Heavenly Daze* from 1948: Shemp is denied entrance to heaven unless he returns to Earth and "reforms" Moe and Larry. The additional material, filmed on July 19, 1954, includes Shemp's deathbed scene (with Moe and Larry wailing in grief as his spirit rises toward the ceiling) and a dance number added to the original opening scene at the gates of heaven. "He's up there and there's rain clouds, those cheesy, vaudeville rain clouds that you could see the strings on them and everything—that would always make me laugh," West says. "But Shemp has wings and he sees this devil girl." The "devil girl," played by actress and dancer Sylvia Lewis, arrives in a blast of smoke, fire, and temptation. She wears a skintight catsuit and sequined devil horns. Her hips sway as she approaches Shemp, waving a scarf in front of him:

> HELEN: Hello, big boy. My name is Helen.
> SHEMP: Helen what?
> HELEN: Blazes!
> SHEMP (*bowing*): Oh, charmed to know you!
> HELEN: Why don't you come down and see us sometime? We have some really hot dances. Dance?
> SHEMP (*nods*): "Uh-hmm!!"

Beginning with a kick higher than Shemp's head, Helen goes into a sultry dance while Shemp follows in a fast, skipping shuffle—his dance as comedic as her moves are sexy.

"And his wings start to perk up and they're flapping and it suggests an erection!" West says, likening the gag to the double entendres in Warner Bros. cartoons where "Bugs Bunny would become stiff as a board right after some girl kissed him."

"It just reduces me to helpless laughter every time I see it. I go, 'Why do I love this?' And I don't care how many times I see it, I'll be counting the feathers in that costume."

It's that kind of unexpected layering that kept many kids from "outgrowing" the Stooges. The influence can be surprising as well. The Helen Blazes dance scene and setting are very similar to Jerry Lewis's avant-garde dance with "Miss Cartilage" in his 1961 film *The Ladies Man*. Miss Cartilage is also played by Sylvia Lewis.

Bedlam in Paradise was released in April 1955, seven months before Shemp's actual death.

Shemp's granddaughter Jill was about a year old when he and Babe decided they weren't seeing enough of her. So they moved out of the house on Placidia Avenue and into an apartment building about half a mile away at 10522 Riverside Drive.

"They leased the house to John Agar and they bought a fourplex on Riverside Drive," Geri Howard Greenbaum explained. "John Agar was Shirley Temple's husband, and then they had divorced and he was single and he wanted to live in Toluca Lake. So he leased the house and Grandma Babe and Papa Shemp bought this fourplex. At that time, Jill was a year old. We were living on Cahuenga [Boulevard] in an apartment house, and they wanted us to move in and be next door to them so they could be close to Jill. So we moved out of our Cahuenga apartment, moved into the four-unit apartment on Riverside Drive, and we were right next door to them. We were both downstairs, right across the hall, so they could be close to their granddaughter."

"He was very kind to me," Jill Howard Marcus said. "We had a very loving relationship. Every time I would cry, I was told that my grandfather would come over and make sure that I was okay."

On January 17, 1955, Jules White and the Three Stooges convened to shoot a few scenes in order to rework their short *Crime on Their Hands*, with an added dollop of *Hot Scots*, both from 1948, into *Hot Ice*. The following day, they shot enough new material to turn footage from 1948's *Pardon My Clutch* into a new short titled *Wham-Bam-Slam!*

But not everything was a quick, demeaning, fill-in-the-holes job. On January 24, White launched another unusually extensive Stooges shoot—an entire three days for a comedy that would not be jammed with stock footage and that wasn't even a remake. *Blunder Boys* was a contemporary spoof, a parody of *Dragnet*, the police procedural television series starring Jack Webb as Detective Joe Friday. Paced throughout the short, the Stooges stop to identify themselves, Jack Webb style and flashing badges. Moe: "My name's Halliday." Larry, all seriousness: "I'm Taraday." And Shemp? He has a different name for each spot: "I'm Saint Patrick's Day! . . . Groundhog Day . . . New Year's Day . . . Christmas Day . . . Independence Day . . . Labor Day!"

Another hallmark of the *Dragnet* series was the production company credit at the end of each episode: a hand hammers a stamp onto a metal sheet that reveals the roman numeral VII: "A Mark VII Production." In the final moments of *Blunder Boys*, Moe imitates the image by hammering a stamp onto Larry's forehead: "VII 1/2 THE END."

Blunder Boys would screen in theaters on November 3, the last Three Stooges short released in Shemp's lifetime.

On March 11, 1955, Shemp Howard celebrated his sixtieth birthday.

On April 29, Moe, Shemp, and Larry filmed an episode of the *Eddie Cantor Comedy Theater* in Hollywood. The syndicated television series starring the popular eye-rolling entertainer featured sketches and some musical acts. The trio was featured as three crooks who think they're breaking into a bank, which was actually the U.S. Mint. The episode aired on July 18 and was Shemp's last television appearance.

Shemp's last day of filming before his death was July 1, 1955, when he, Larry, and Moe filmed only enough footage to turn 1949's Hokus Pokus *into* Flagpole Jitters. *© 2024 C3 Entertainment, Inc. All Rights Reserved.*

On June 30, The Stooges spent a day filming some scenes for *For Crimin' Our Loud*. As detectives for the Miracle Detective Agency (the sign on the door reads, "If we solve your crime it's a miracle"), they run through a scene of violent comedy antics in their office before responding to a telephone call, together, in song: "Hello . . . hello . . . hello-o-o." Larry adds, "The harmony's bad. We didn't have time to rehearse." (Galbraith comments, "That may not have been a joke.") Most of the rest of the sixteen minutes is taken from *Who Done It?*, the Stooges short released in 1949.

The following day, Friday, July 1, 1955, they filmed enough scenes to turn *Hokus Pokus* from 1949 into *Flagpole Jitters*.

Then the Three Stooges had some time off.

On November 22, Shemp went to the fights.

TWENTY-FIVE

The Death of Shemp

The fights at Hollywood Legion Stadium on Tuesday, November 22, 1955, got under way at 8:30 p.m. with a trio of four-round preliminary bouts. Welterweights Eddie Asti and Forrest Davis fought to a draw, middleweight Dave Cochran prevailed over Joey Brooks with a technical knockout (TKO) in the second round, and lightweight Jesse Resendez scored a fourth-round TKO over Joe Smyer.

When undercard headliner Vince Delgado stepped into the ring against Cleo Lane for a scheduled eight rounds of middleweight boxing, some in the crowd of 5,000 were still getting to their seats. Delgado got his TKO in the fifth round. The judges had him winning every round until then.

It was the main event that fight fans had come out to see: a ten-round battle between two Angelenos, lightweights in division only. Cisco "Automatic" Andrade was a colorful pug, known nationally because many of his exciting brawls had been televised. He was ranked fourth among challengers for the championship and a fight away from a title shot if he made it past Kenny Davis. Davis was a scrappy former international Golden Gloves champion with a killer attack, but Cisco had the edge. He was a three-to-one favorite.

This bout would not be glowing from television screens in living rooms across the country. The only witnesses to this historic fight would be the ones inside the enclosed stadium. General admission was $2.50; reserved seats went for $4, $6, and $8. There were Hollywood celebrities in the house, not the least of whom was one of boxing's most entertaining spectators. Shemp Howard was ringside with his pals Al Winston and Bobby Silverberg. Shemp, described by his daughter-in-law as "the third boxer in the ring," who in his seat often acted out the fights in front of him, was in a fine mood. One could say he lived for the fights. This would be his final bout.

The two fighters met in the center of the ring, where referee Mushy Callahan barked out a few instructions, made them touch gloves, and sent them to their corners for the first round. The crowd cheered. The bell clanged. The fighters charged toward each other, and Kenny Davis came on strong, matching Cisco, jab for jab, unrelenting. Round 1 was his. So was round 2. A lot of spectators who had placed their bets on the favorite were balling their own hands into fists of frustration as they watched Davis unleash left hooks. Cisco's eyes were puffy, his face bruised. Rounds 3 and 4: Cisco was taking the worst walloping of his career. By the end of round 5, he had a scrape on his cheek, and all three judges had Kenny Davis ahead by at least two points.

An upset was in the making. No one was looking to see what Shemp was doing in his seat as the bell rang for round 6. The crowd roared, and Cisco Andrade suddenly came to life. From whatever reserve he had been holding, the fighter began smashing Davis. *Bam! Bam!* He tore a gash over Davis's left eye. *Smack!* He ripped open the side of Davis's mouth. *Crunch!* Cisco bashed Davis in the nose, and blood spurted. This was when Shemp would have been handing out sections of a newspaper for his friends to shield themselves from the red rain. But for now, he and everyone else around the ring were on their feet. Most incredibly, so was Kenny Davis! Cisco continued to pound away until the bell tolled three times. Davis staggered back to his corner. He had not fallen to the canvas. He was surely defeated, but his fight had been heroic beyond expectations. No one expected him to answer the bell for round 7—but he did, and now Cisco went in for the kill. Davis staggered and bounced among the ropes, always bouncing back for more. By now, his face was covered in blood that dripped onto his chest. He was hardly fighting back at all. Many in the crowd were shouting for Mushy Callahan to stop the fight. Stop the slaughter! But Davis refused to drop to the canvas. He survived until the three bells ended the seventh round and was ready to go for the eighth, but his manager threw in the towel. What a fight. What a fighter. What a night.

Shemp and his friends had lots to talk about as they stepped outside onto the sidewalk of El Centro Avenue, made their way through the crowd, and got into a waiting taxicab. It was a lighthearted ride. The three men told jokes and traded stories. Shemp was about halfway home to Toluca Lake when he pulled out a fine Havana cigar and lit it. The taxi was coming over the rise at Barham Boulevard, heading into the San Fernando Valley, and Shemp may have told a joke and smiled when he slumped over onto Al Winston. Winston thought Shemp was joking when he noticed the ashes from Shemp's cigar on his trouser leg.

"Hey Shemp, you're burnin' my suit."

It was a gag, right? Shemp seemed to have a smile on his face—except he didn't respond. Something was wrong. He wasn't breathing. Bobby Silverberg shouted for the driver to make a detour to a hospital. The closest was St. Joseph Hospital in Burbank. Shemp was already dead by the time they unloaded his body from the back of the taxi and rushed him inside.

Comic Shemp Howard of 3 Stooges Dies
Veteran Actor, 60, Stricken by Heart Attack in Auto

> Shemp Howard, 60, veteran stage and screen comedian and one of "The Three Stooges," died Tuesday of a heart attack. Mr. Howard and a friend, Robert Silverberg, had attended the fights at Olympic Auditorium and were enroute home when the comedian was stricken. Silverberg sped to Saint Joseph's Hospital in Burbank but Mr. Howard died before they reached the hospital. . . .
>
> The trio of comedians recently celebrated their 40th year in show business. They had just signed a new contract with Columbia studios—the 23rd annual contract—for production of eight short subjects.

The story on page 21 of the *Los Angeles Times* was wedged into the left corner of what was otherwise a full-page ad for the Bullocks department store's Thanksgiving sale and was not accompanied by a photograph. The writer got some of the details, including the boxing venue, wrong, but the most important information was in the headline: Shemp Howard was dead.

The death certificate placed Shemp's death at 11:00 p.m. in Burbank, en route to St. Joseph Hospital. The cause of death was listed as "acute coronary thrombosis due to hypertensive heart disease." There was no autopsy, however, and in the years since, Shemp's daughter-in-law and her family have insisted that death was actually the result of a cerebral hemorrhage, a "brain bleed."

"Shemp did not have a heart attack or a stroke," Geri Howard Greenbaum insisted, "at least not that I ever heard of, and I was there with Mort and his mother the entire time. It was my understanding that Shemp had a massive cerebral hemorrhage."

The *Los Angeles Times* story was correct on one point. The Three Stooges had indeed recently inked a contract with Columbia for eight new comedy shorts. When Shemp died, they had completed only four of them. The *New York Times* article announcing Shemp's death made mention of the team's new contract and added, "Moe Howard and Mr. Fine will probably complete the schedule without a third partner."

Moe and Larry would complete the schedule, but they would have a third partner: their dead brother, Shemp.

Moe wrote in his autobiography that Shemp's last hours on Earth began as "an ordinary day" (although in an unfortunately typical fashion, Moe mistakenly remembered the day as November 23). According to Moe, before his evening at the fights, Shemp had spent the afternoon at the racetrack. There's no record Shemp's attendance, but there was harness racing on November 22, 1955, at Hollywood Park, the thoroughbred horse racecourse in Inglewood, about ten miles south of Hollywood. The track was muddy that day because of a rainstorm on Monday.

"When I heard the news that night," Moe wrote, "I was dumbfounded."

"I'll always remember how we found out," Moe's son Paul said in his documentary series. "We had just finished dinner and the phone rang. When dad put down the receiver, his famous face of stone couldn't hide his anguish or his pain. All he said was, 'Shemp's gone,' and went into another room to be alone with his grief. But mom wouldn't let that happen. She joined him to share the tragedy."

Larry Fine's recollection of events, combined with the time of Shemp's passing, makes that memory somewhat unreliable. In *One Fine Stooge,* Larry said that on November 22, he received a phone call from Dallas, Texas, offering the Three Stooges "a lot of money" for a series of annual stage appearances. "I said, 'Well, I have to call Columbia to find out our schedule, if it will permit us to go away for that length of time.' I told him I'd call him back tomorrow. I immediately got on the phone and called Shemp's house and his wife got on the phone and I said, 'Let me talk to Shemp.' And she says, 'He just left for the fights.' There was a championship fight that night. So I said to her, 'Have him call me the minute he comes home. It's very important'":

> It got to be about eleven o'clock and I knew he should be home, so I got on the phone attempting to bawl him out. Moe's wife got on the phone and I said, "What are you doing there?" She said, "I just came over. Shemp's dead." I was shocked. I asked, "What happened?" And she told me that Moe was at St. Joseph's Hospital right now. When Shemp died in the back of a car, they drove him right over to the hospital.

As it did with Curly, the Malinow and Simons Mortuary handled the funeral arrangements. There was a service at 1:00 p.m. on Friday, November 25, at the Home of Peace Mausoleum Chapel at the Home of Peace

Memorial Park. Shemp's family, friends, and colleagues attended. Emil Sitka never forgot the arrival of Vernon Dent, the actor who had appeared in more Three Stooges shorts than any other supporting player. Dent, long a diabetic, had gradually been losing his eyesight. Now, at age sixty, he was blind.

"Vernon came into the parlor wearing a yarmulke like everyone else since this was a Jewish ceremony," Sitka recalled. "He was led in by his arm and brought up to Shemp's casket. The man accompanying Vernon told him, 'This is Shemp.' Vernon was staring straight ahead at the wall—it was then that I realized he was blind. Vernon felt Shemp's hand, then his face very gently. Everyone else had been filing past the casket quickly, but Vernon took his time, giving a last goodbye to his friend. It was one of the most moving things I ever saw."

Shemp was entombed in a crypt in the indoor Corridor of Eternal Life mausoleum. Curly, older brother Jack, and parents Solomon and Jennie are also in the Home of Peace Jewish cemetery. (Shemp's son Morton, who succumbed to cancer in 1972, and Shemp's wife, Gertrude "Babe" Frank, who died ten years later, are interred at Mount Sinai Memorial Park in the Hollywood Hills.)

Shemp had made seventy-four short comedies with the Three Stooges. He still had four to go.

Moe wrote that it took weeks "to gather my thoughts, to make plans for the future, to try once more to put the act together again." It took forty days for him, Larry Fine, and Jules White to get back to work, knocking off the four short comedies remaining in the most recent Columbia contract. They did it by pretending that Shemp had never died. Joe Palma, one of the regular supporting actors in Three Stooges shorts, was recruited to stand in for Shemp because he had the right body type. It was quite fitting that before he began his acting career, Palma had worked as a mortician in his family's funeral home in Manhattan.

The four short subjects that came to be known as the "Fake Shemp" comedies are not as abhorrent as history would have them. Each film is in the sixteen-minute range and basically a reworking of a past Three Stooges comedy from 1949. Each short is full of stock footage, with the addition of a few new scenes shot in a single day in January 1956. Palma shows up in a scene or two, shot from behind, with his hair combed down on the sides in an approximation of Shemp's center-parted grease mop, and often hunched over. He is used only briefly to fill in continuity gaps. He is not running through entire comedies doing a Shemp imitation. That said, the brief moments in which he does appear are obvious and laughable for the wrong reasons. When he attempts to ape Shemp, it can be painful to watch.

On January 10, 1956, Moe and Larry and "Fake Shemp" shot scenes for *Rumpus in the Harem,* a retooling of *Malice in the Palace.* Joe Palma has his back to the camera in a couple of Stooge huddles (in one scene, Palma's face can be seen for a split second when the image is frozen in video or digital formats). In a chase scene in which the Three Stooges are dressed, inexplicably, in Santa Claus outfits, Palma doubles for Shemp. Shemp's actual voice is dubbed in, crying, "Wha-Moe! Moe, Larry! *Heebeebeebeebee!* Moe! Help! *Heebeebeebeebee!* Moe! Help!" as Palma runs by.

The following day, January 11, Palma must have been feeling his oats. In *Hot Stuff,* a remake of *Fuelin' Around,* he actually attempts to imitate Shemp's voice. As undercover agents disguised with fake beards, the trio are in an office hallway. In the opening moments, Palma actually looks toward the camera, so the deception is obvious before he turns his back to the camera, bending over to peep through a keyhole. "Boys," Moe says, "we gotta be careful to make sure nobody followed us." Palma barks, "Right!" A woman passes through. "Shemp," says Moe, "that dame looks suspicious, you better follow her." "Right!" Palma repeats and exits, back to camera, with an exaggerated Groucho lope. Later in the short, again with his back to camera, Palma flaps his elbows and emits a "Heebeebeebee!" before making a crab-walking exit that is almost deliberately *not* Shemp.

When the production team got back to work the following Monday, January 16, there may have been some discussion about Palma's emoting. *Scheming Schemers* was a rejigging of *Vagabond Loafers* (a remake of 1940's *A Plumbing We Will Go*). There is a brief scene in which Palma's face is shielded by a collection of pipes and a tool bag he's carrying, while Shemp's voice is again dubbed: "Hold yer horses, will ya?" But *Scheming Schemers* is less offensive for Palma's role than the closing line recited by Moe Howard.

As Moe and Larry Fine stand covered in custard from a (stock footage) pie fight, he says, "Hey, where is that puddin' head Shemp?" Moe and Larry then tilt their heads and look heavenward. Cut to Shemp, trapped in his maze in the bathtub, a metaphor if there ever was one.

By the following day, when scenes were filmed for *Commotion on the Ocean*, someone may have put his foot down. The remix of *Dunked in the Deep* (with some additional footage from the 1948 short *Crime on Their Hands*) shows Palma's back passing behind Larry and Moe during part of a conversation that's mixed into stock footage. Somewhat fittingly, the working title for this short was *Salt Water Daffy*, which was also the name of Shemp's Vitaphone film from 1933, his solo screen debut.

The filming of those shorts was not the first time a double had been used to stand in for a deceased or otherwise unavailable actor, but the term "Fake Shemp" became industry slang for the practice thanks to Sam Raimi, the director, producer, and Three Stooges fan. The pioneering horror filmmaker came up with the term in his early days, making Super 8 movies in the 1970s, and popularized "fake Shemps" after long production delays on his 1981 horror film *The Evil Dead* forced him, actor Bruce Campbell, and others in the crew to stand in for performers who were no longer on location. Raimi made it a tradition. The credit roll for his 1992 film *Army of Darkness* lists sixteen "Fake Shemps" among the cast.

The Stooges would carry on. Joe Besser, who was already signed to Columbia, was recruited to fill in as the third Stooge. He would make sixteen shorts as one of the Three Stooges. One that might be of note to Shemp fans is *Rusty Romeos*, a reworking of the Moe, Larry, and Shemp short *Corny Casanovas*, in which the Three Stooges are unaware they're all engaged to the same Mabel. In an additional scene shot on February 13, 1957, Mabel places a framed photograph of Besser on a table in her parlor. But when Moe and Larry later fight in the parlor, Shemp's photograph has taken its place. That's because the fight was lifted from *Corny Casanovas*; Jules White counted on no one noticing.

Besser remained with the team until Columbia shut down the short subject department and canceled the Three Stooges' contract in December 1957. The following year, Moe and Larry brought Joe DeRita on board. DeRita was round like Curly. He looked a little like the original, with much less comedic talent. Nevertheless, they called him "Curly Joe."

In 1958, Screen Gems, a Columbia Pictures subsidiary, found a way to cash in on the 190 Three Stooges shorts in their vault. The company began selling packages of Three Stooges comedies to television stations and syndicators. Adults who had grown up with the Stooges now saw their own children in front of the television sets, intrigued by this slapstick—and violent—comedy trio. Most of these featured the team of Moe, Larry, and Curly—and the kids loved Curly.

Curly and Shemp were not there to reap the rewards that this new life on television brought the Three Stooges. Moe, Larry, and Curly Joe made movies. In 1963, they were seen in cameo roles in the all-star comedy film *It's a Mad, Mad, Mad, Mad World* and *4 for Texas*, the comedy western starring Frank Sinatra and Dean Martin. They appeared on television shows and filmed a new series that included animation and through the 1960s were among the most successful and highly paid live acts in the country.

But Moe was carrying around some sense of guilt, no?

Twenty-Six

Who Killed Shemp?

The assertion by his family that Shemp died from a cerebral hemorrhage, not a heart attack as the death certificate states, places him in the same general category as Curly, who succumbed from a cerebral hemorrhage in 1952 after a series of strokes, and even Larry Fine, who suffered several strokes before his death from a cerebral thrombosis in 1975. A cerebral hemorrhage, also known as a "brain bleed," is a type of stroke in which an artery in the brain bursts. A cerebral thrombosis occurs when a blood clot forms in the brain, leading to swelling and bleeding, or hemorrhaging, in the brain.

"They kept getting whacked in the head," Billy West says of his beloved Stooges. "That was coming up the hard way. That was the school of hard knocks. I'm sure accidents happen. Think about how accidents happen on the football field, and then a few years later you find out that some guy you remember being a young buck is suddenly forty and develops a cerebral hemorrhage, blood clots to the brain, or just brain damage."

In the case of the Three Stooges, "accidents" may have built up over decades. Larry Fine was known to have callouses and rough skin on the left side of his face, which he claimed was a result of the slaps and hits he took from Moe (although some attributed the scarring on his chin to a lifetime of playing the violin). Larry was partially paralyzed by a stroke in 1970. He wound up at the Motion Picture Country House in Woodland Hills, California, where he suffered several more strokes before his death at age seventy-two on January 24, 1975. During that time, he and a collaborator managed to complete and publish an autobiography called *Stroke of Luck*. Moe Howard was still banging away at his version of events when he died on May 4 of that year at the Cedars-Sinai Medical Center in Los Angeles. He was seventy-seven. Moe died of cancer, the only one of the original four Stooges to avoid death by bleeding brain.

Nick Santa Maria expresses a theory. "I think Moe helped to kill two of his brothers with his work-obsessed ethic. He wouldn't quit. He wouldn't slow down and he wouldn't let them slow down. Twenty years, or however many years, of constant abuse—and they were really getting hit, they were getting slapped—it was rough. But he has two brothers, very healthy when they come into the act—and I'm just speculating. This is pure speculation on my part, just a theory—but I really think that the beatings and the constant work schedule helped kill his brothers and his partner." Santa Maria adds,

> Of the group, I think Moe was the most mercenary. I think he would have done anything for money. The other thing to remember is that when Shemp was making those shorts in the fifties—the awful ones that that were just pieced together—regardless, he's doing stunts, he's dancing around, he's doing his boxing schtick, he's falling down, he's having things fall on his head, his brother's slapping him every two seconds. He was sixty! I'm sorry, I really think Moe's love of money helped to kill his partners—facilitated it, let's put it that way.

Medical experts agree that head trauma can increase the chances of a stroke by weakening the blood vessels or disrupting the blood-clotting function in the brain. Cerebral hemorrhages can be caused by head trauma. And while there are other health factors that lead to both, an overlooked detail in Curly Howard's first hospitalization seems to buttress the theory.

After his failing health reached the point that he was forced to drop out of a Three Stooges stage tour in January 1945 (to be replaced by Shemp), Curly was hospitalized in Santa Barbara. The medical staff's list of Curly's ailments included high blood pressure, malignant hypertension, obesity, and myocardial damage—and also a retinal hemorrhage. The blood pressure issues, hypertension, obesity, and even heart damage could be attributed to his sybaritic lifestyle, including his intake of alcohol and greasy food. The retinal hemorrhage? That could be the result of his combined illnesses, but experts agree that a most common cause is a blow to the head.

Santa Maria recalls being very impressed when his father told him he had seen Moe, Larry, and Curly in live performance. "He and his friends in the late thirties went to see the Three Stooges in Brooklyn, appearing with a movie, and they did their act, the same act that they did for seventy years. He said, 'We thought they were terrible. They weren't funny. There were no sound effects, so every time they hit, we winced!'"

Corroborating testimony came from Moe's daughter. Joan Howard Maurer wrote in the biography *Curly* about the cumulative damage resulting from "the multitude of bangs and bops that Curly received on hundreds of theater stages across America." Perhaps to take some of the heat off her father, Maurer attributed some of the permanent injury to violence inflicted by "drunks and children" who encountered Curly

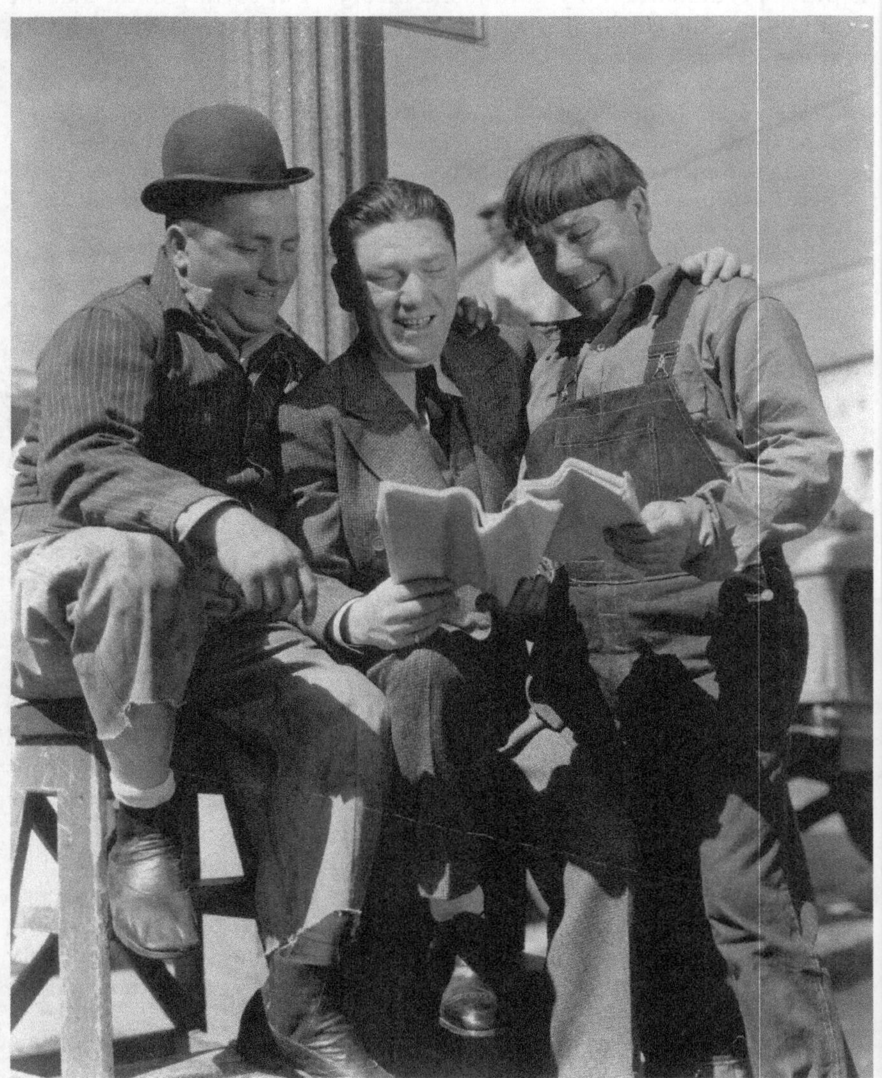

The brothers Howard comparing scripts in 1934, when everyone was healthy and Shemp had a solo career.

in real-life situations. Believing that Curly was as impervious to violent strikes as he was on stage and screen, they would punch or otherwise "smack him hard on his famous, indestructible bald head."

Maurer wrote of an ambush on the Atlantic City boardwalk in 1935, when an eight-year-old boy carrying a small cane ran up behind Curly and "took a tremendous swing and conked him over the head with the cane," causing Curly's eyes to glaze and his legs to buckle.

The incident could have happened, or the anecdote could be a twist on the possibly deadly encounter that Harry Houdini—Maurer's first cousin once removed—experienced in a dressing room in 1926, when a fan sucker-punched the escape artist in the stomach. She also may have been repeating family lore set down by her father. In 1947, when Moe was working with Larry Fine and Shemp, he told syndicated columnist Erskine Johnson that "the three of them were walking on the Atlantic City boardwalk when a kid about nine spotted them, walked up, and cracked them over the head with a heavy cane."

"If that kid had been an inch taller," Moe told Johnson, "I would have kicked his teeth right down his throat."

Whether or not the boardwalk incident occurred, attacks by civilians were infrequent. Stooges performances were not. Moe's daughter also recalled watching up close from the wings as they did their act onstage:

> When Moe belted him with a flat of his palm, the slap resounded throughout the theater. Saliva flew out of Curly's mouth and I winced while the audience roared with infectious laughter. . . . Then Moe, as a topper, would give him a resounding slap in the face or his traditional two-finger poke in the eyes.

She noted that similar abuse was common in the short comedies the Stooges made for Columbia:

> Most of the films were violent and the bruises which Curly endured were many. It's amazing he survived the battering in which his bald dome took the brunt of the punishment.

The reminiscences from Moe's daughter brings two interviews to mind.

One is from 1951, when the Stooges spoke over the phone to Brent Gunts of WBAL radio in Baltimore.

"You didn't hit Moe while you were talking to me, did you?" Gunts asked Larry.

"He does the hitting," Larry replied. "Much to my discomfort . . . I'm the 'he who gets' . . . You only have to look at my face to see it."

Speaking to Shemp, Gunts commented, "I bet you're gonna be knocking them around on the stage, aren't you?"

"Not I," said Shemp. "but Moe is gonna do the knockin'."

"It's not an act, then, huh?"

"Oh no, no, no," Shemp said. "If you saw the lumps and bumps on our eyes, you'd know it."

The other interview took place on television when Moe was a guest on the *Mike Douglas Show* in 1973.

"I was smart," Moe said. "I took Healy's place."

Twenty-Seven

Shemp Lives!

"Screen Gems didn't release all of the shorts at once." Leonard Maltin is talking about the deal that sold the Three Stooges comedies to television stations in the late 1950s and early 1960s. "They did an initial package of seventy-five or eighty shorts, and then when they were so successful, they did a second and then a third package. And so I didn't see Shemp for quite a while, and by the time he was revealed to me, he seemed a poor substitute for Curly—because Curly was just so funny. And he was no Curly. But then, who is? Who could be? Curly was one of a kind. But I couldn't see past that at first.

"As a kid, I was impatient and demanding. I wanted more Curly! I've really only come to appreciate Shemp in later years, as the talented comedian he is."

Maltin, the film critic and historian, has described himself as someone who "grew up watching the Stooges . . . and didn't discard them as an adult." His recollections of experiencing the trio when they began appearing on television were shared by millions and explains why Shemp Howard might be seen as nothing more than a pretender in comparison to his younger brother Curly.

It wasn't just that the Three Stooges were introduced to the television generation as "Moe, Larry, and Curly"; it was that Curly was unlike anything kids had seen before. He was a once-in-a-generation comedy phenomenon, dropped in from a *past* generation like some arrival from outer space. He looked like a big baby. He acted like a kid. He made funny noises. He barked like a dog. He spun in circles on the floor—and boy, could his head take a beating! When Shemp suddenly entered the picture, there was no way that this . . . adult . . . funny as he was, would inspire the wonder of a Curly. And Shemp's work, well, a lot of it seemed pretty familiar.

Maltin says the fact that many Stooges shorts featuring Shemp were patched-up remakes of Curly originals is only one reason any comparison requires "a big qualifier." The shorts were being made more cheaply; Del

Lord, their best director, left the scene; and the films themselves were just not as strong and not as funny. So Curly might have found himself in the same circumstance, had he lived."

Maltin says that Curly was not necessarily a "better" Stooge than Shemp. "Not better. Different. Because [Shemp] didn't have a single persona. He had different schtick that he relied on successfully, but he didn't have a strong screen personality that was his alone. Did that make him a lesser Stooge? No, not at all. It made him a very capable Stooge, but the gags had to change, the material had to be rethought. So, it's not fair to compare one to the other."

Shemp, Maltin has determined, is "a near great. It's not bad to be a near great. I mean, a lot of people never get that far."

The cult of Curly was born in front of those television sets in the 1960s, a childhood influence that carried on through generations of fans who appreciated good old-fashioned dumb comedy. One needn't be an intellectual to appreciate the gags, and no matter which way mainstream pop culture turned or is turning, Moe, Larry, and Curly have a place. Adds Maltin, "It does say something that the Marx Brothers are no longer in vogue, but the Stooges prevail."

The appreciation of Shemp developed after the kids grew up, forming a more sophisticated and cynical cult of young people and outsiders who had moved on to *MAD* magazine and *National Lampoon* and lived through Watergate, disco, and punk in the 1970s. Billy West, for example, was fascinated by the Three Stooges as a child in Detroit and credits them for "the rewards of a misspent youth: I was learning comic timing, I was learning how to act, I was learning one of the pillars of comedy."

In the early 1980s, West was in Boston, making a name for himself doing voices and characters on Charles Laquidara's radio show, cracking up listeners with spot-on imitations of the Stooges and creating situations and spinning wild Shemp scenarios. He had not yet met the artist and illustrator Drew Friedman, who was in New York City, sitting in his apartment sketching portraits of Shemp, who had become something of a muse. West was friends with comedy writer and producer Eddie Gorodetsky. Friedman was pals with comedian Gilbert Gottfried. After West arrived in New York and became a regular on Howard Stern's radio show in the late 1980s, they all got together. "All we had to do, wherever we were, was to start throwing out random Shemp lines like, 'Moe! There's a gorilla in there!,'" West recalls:

All the kids loved Curly. Shemp has attracted an older, darker, and more sophisticated cult of knuckleheads.

> And nobody else in the world could know what we were talking about. "*He-e-e-re I am, Moe!*" It was like grist for our mill. That and a million other peripheral things that only writers and comics cared about. It's like constantly building on this storage bin of richness.

From those early influencers, the image of Shemp—that personality, that face—came to represent something in popular culture, just as the face of pro wrestler Andre the Giant meant something when it appeared on the "Obey Giant" stickers that were showing up everywhere around the same time.

Shepard Fairey, the artist behind the Obey Giant project, wrote in its *Manifesto*, "The sticker has no meaning but exists only to cause people to react, to contemplate and search for meaning in the sticker. . . . The various reactions and interpretations of those who view it reflect their personality and the nature of their sensibilities."

GQ writer Mike Flaherty landed on a connection between the two images when he pointed out that Shemp "gave up his flourishing movie career in order to keep the Stooges (and brother Moe's career) alive. . . . In the world of professional wrestling, agreeing to lose a match for the greater dramatic good is called 'doing the job' and considered the most honorable of gestures. Thus (and with an eye toward the broad, brutal violence that wrestling and the Stooges share), Shemp is the original jobber."

"A wise person of discriminating taste once remarked, 'Shemp Howard is the George Harrison of Stooges. Underrated, underappreciated—but the truly discerning recognized his brilliance.' I didn't say those words of wisdom, but I agree with the sentiment wholeheartedly," Edward Watz wrote in *Comique*. "The shorts Shemp made in Brooklyn for Vitaphone in the 1930s are frequently wild and hilarious; they're also available on DVD and a bargain at any price. Plus, Shemp had bits and pieces in films that are barely worth watching except for bits and pieces." The work is also easy to find online: shorts like *Salt Water Daffy*, *My Mummy's Arms*, *Mr. Noisy*, and *Bride and Gloom* and films including *Convention Girl*, *Hollywood Round-Up*, *The Bank Dick*, *Murder Over New York*, *San Antonio Rose*, *Cracked Nuts*, *Hellzapoppin'*, and *Private Buckaroo*. Everybody has seen the Curly shorts. You see one, you get the idea of Curly. Shemp, though?

"He wasn't always 'Shemp,' the defined Shemp, the undiluted Shemp that we see in the Stooges shorts," Billy West says. "He did variations of himself. In the Shemp shorts, which I think are funny as hell, he's not as hapless as he is in the Stooges. He's his own man. And he was the most instinctive actor of the three of them, I believe."

Stuart Galbraith IV viewed dozens of Three Stooges shorts and wrote insightful reviews of all of them. Does he have a favorite Shemp moment? "One thing that I always think of when you mention something like this, is a scene in *Sing a Song of Six Pants*. All it is, is Shemp reading the comic pages in the Sunday newspaper. He's in a chair and he's reading it, and he's enjoying it so much that he starts laughing hysterically at these comic strips. And it's just him laughing, but it's really, really funny because his reactions are so unfiltered. He's just having a blast and his laughter is contagious. He was able to make something out of nothing.

"He was part of the Stooges near the beginning and he was part of the Stooges in the late middle period, and he was just this freelance comic actor the rest of the time, so I guess he doesn't fit in the same category as a star comedian or part of a star comedy team for a big chunk of his career. But he was hilarious and he was really great and added to a lot of films.

"And it's really a shame, I was thinking about all the other things he could have fit in. For instance, it's very easy to imagine him as being part of the Preston Sturges stock company. He would have fit in in those pictures very easily. And I could see him having funny parts in Billy Wilder comedies. Not huge, major roles but one or two really funny scenes, definitely. And any kind of Damon Runyon material, he would have been great."

"I think Shemp is a great second banana," Nick Santa Maria says. "I don't think he's a great starring comedian. I don't think he's a great wit. I think he's got a great sense of silliness. You very seldom hear a witty line out of him. They're mostly non sequiturs . . . non sequitur silliness. And that was what Shemp was best at. He was very pliable. His face kind of said it all. It was very doughy and expressive. And he could fit in anywhere, unless you're doing Noel Coward drama or sophisticated comedy.

"And I think Shemp could have continued a career in features. Not as a star, but as a supporting player. Had he lived, he would've had a fine career as the neighbor in So-and-so's sitcom. I could definitely see that, more so than Moe or Larry, who needed each other. And to me, Curly was a cartoon character with no depth. Just a lot of silly fun. I think Shemp would have had a long career. Even on stage. *Guys and Dolls*. And he was the perfect type also for Nat Hiken, who was the king of television in the 1950s and early sixties, who loved character people. He loved faces like Shemp's."

"We know he's a genius," Billy West says. "He stood the test of time. The Shemps are one in a million. If there's a Mount Rushmore of comedy, Shemp would be on it. Because he was a comedic superlative."

Too much? Billy West puts it another way: "Riding over Barham Boulevard—in a car—and telling jokes, and suddenly the guy next to him, his leg is burning! That's such a Stooge way to die!"

Shemp Howard Filmography

SHEMP WITH TED HEALY, MOE "HARRY" HOWARD, AND LARRY FINE

Soup to Nuts (Fox Film Corporation) Released September 28, 1930

SHEMP SOLO

Salt Water Daffy (short) (Warner Bros./Vitaphone) Released September 16, 1933
Close Relations (short) (Warner Bros./Vitaphone) Released September 30, 1933
Paul Revere, Jr. (short) (Warner Bros./Vitaphone) Released October 7, 1933
Gobs of Fun (short) (Warner Bros./Vitaphone) Released October 21, 1933
In the Dough (short) (Warner Bros./Vitaphone) Released November 25, 1933
Here Comes Flossie! (short) (Warner Bros./Vitaphone) Released December 9, 1933

Howd' Ya Like That? (short) (Warner Bros./Vitaphone) Released January 13, 1934
Henry the Ache (short) (Van Beuren Productions) Released January 26, 1934
The Wrong, Wrong Trail (short) (Warner Bros./Vitaphone) Released February 10, 1934
Mushrooms (short) (Warner Bros./Vitaphone) Released February 14, 1934
The Knife of the Party (short) (Van Beuren Productions) Released February 16, 1934
Everybody Likes Music (short) (Van Beuren Productions) Released March 9, 1934
Pugs and Kisses (short) (Warner Bros./Vitaphone) Released March 10, 1934
Very Close Veins (short) (Warner Bros./Vitaphone) Released April 14, 1934
Pure Feud (short) (Warner Bros./Vitaphone) Released April 21, 1934
Corn on the Cop (short) (Warner Bros./Vitaphone) Released April 28, 1934
I Scream (short) (Warner Bros./Vitaphone) Released May 19, 1934
Rambling 'Round Radio Row #9 (short) (Warner Bros./Vitaphone) Released May 19, 1934
Art Trouble (short) (Warner Bros./Vitaphone) Released June 23, 1934
My Mummy's Arms (short) (Warner Bros./Vitaphone) Released July 28, 1934
Daredevil O'Dare (short) (Warner Bros./Vitaphone) Released August 11, 1934
Smoked Hams (short) (Warner Bros./Vitaphone) Released October 20, 1934

So You Won't T-T-T-Talk (short) (Warner Bros./Vitaphone) Released November 3, 1934
Dizzy & Daffy (short) (Warner Bros./Vitaphone) Released December 15, 1934
A Peach of a Pair (short) (Warner Bros./Vitaphone) Released December 29, 1934

His First Flame (short) (Warner Bros./Vitaphone) Released March 9, 1935
Convention Girl (Falcon Pictures) Released May 1, 1935
Why Pay Rent? (short) (Warner Bros./Vitaphone) Released, May 4, 1935
Serves You Right (short) (Warner Bros./Vitaphone) Released June 15, 1935
On the Wagon (short) (Warner Bros./Vitaphone) Released August 24, 1935
The Officer's Mess (short) (Warner Bros./Vitaphone) Released November 9, 1935

While the Cat's Away (short) (Warner Bros./Vitaphone) Released January 4, 1936
For the Love of Pete (short) (Warner Bros./Vitaphone) Released March 14, 1936
Absorbing Junior (short) (Warner Bros./Vitaphone) Released May 9, 1936
Here's Howe (short) (Warner Bros./Vitaphone) Released June 6, 1936
Punch and Beauty (short) (Warner Bros./Vitaphone) Released August 15, 1936
The Choke's on You (short) (Warner Bros./Vitaphone) Released September 12, 1936
The Blonde Bomber (short) (Warner Bros./Vitaphone) Released November 28, 1936

Kick Me Again (short) (Warner Bros./Vitaphone) Released February 6, 1937
Taking the Count (short) (Warner Bros./Vitaphone) Released April 24, 1937
Hollywood Round-Up (Columbia Pictures) Released November 16, 1937
Headin' East (Columbia Pictures) Released December 23, 1937

Not Guilty Enough (short) (Columbia Pictures) Released September 30, 1938
Home on the Rage (short) (Columbia Pictures) Released December 9, 1938

Behind Prison Gates (Columbia Pictures) Released July 28, 1939
Another Thin Man (MGM) Released November 17, 1939
Glove Slingers (short) (Columbia Pictures) Released November 24, 1939

Money Squawks (short) (Columbia Pictures) Released April 5, 1940
The Lone Wolf Meets a Lady (Columbia Pictures) Released May 30, 1940
Boobs in the Woods (short) (Columbia Pictures) Released May 31, 1940
Millionaires in Prison (RKO Radio Pictures) Released July 26, 1940
Pleased to Mitt You (short) (Columbia) Released September 6, 1940
The Leather Pushers (Universal Pictures) Released September 13, 1940
Give Us Wings (Universal Pictures) Released November 21, 1940
The Bank Dick (Universal Pictures) Released November 29, 1940
Murder Over New York (20th Century Fox) Released December 13, 1940
The Invisible Woman (Universal Pictures) Released December 27, 1940

Lucky Devils (Universal Pictures) Released January 3, 1941
Six Lessons from Madame La Zonga (Universal Pictures) Released January 17, 1941
Buck Privates (Universal Pictures) Released January 31, 1941

Meet the Chump (Universal Pictures) Released February 14, 1941
Road Show (Hal Roach Studios) Released February 18, 1941
Mr. Dynamite (Universal Pictures) Released March 7, 1941
The Flame of New Orleans (Universal Pictures) Released April 24, 1941
News of the Day Vol. 12 272 (Abbott and Costello public service announcement for U.S. War Bonds) Released May 21, 1941
Too Many Blondes (Universal Pictures) Released May 23, 1941
In the Navy (Universal Pictures) Released May 30, 1941
Tight Shoes (Universal Pictures) Released June 13, 1941
San Antonio Rose (Universal Pictures) Released June 20, 1941
Hit the Road (Universal Pictures) Released June 27, 1941
Cracked Nuts (Universal Pictures) Released July 31, 1941
Hold That Ghost (Universal Pictures) Released August 7, 1941
Appointment for Love (Universal Pictures) Released October 31, 1941
Hoosier Boy Makes Good (short about the Indiana Society of Chicago's thirtieth annual banquet and tribute to movie censor Will H. Hays) (Universal Pictures) Released December 13, 1941
Hellzapoppin' (Universal Pictures) Released December 26, 1941

Butch Minds the Baby (Universal Pictures) Released March 20, 1942
Mississippi Gambler (Universal Pictures) Released April 17, 1942
The Strange Case of Dr. Rx (Universal Pictures) Released April 17, 1942
Private Buckaroo (Universal Pictures) Released June 12, 1942
Strictly in the Groove (Universal Pictures) Released November 20, 1942
Pittsburgh (Universal Pictures) Released December 11, 1942
Arabian Nights (Universal Pictures) Released December 25, 1942

How's About It? (Universal Pictures) Released February 5, 1943
It Ain't Hay (Universal Pictures) March 19, 1943
Keep 'Em Slugging (Universal Pictures) Released April 2, 1943
Crazy House (Universal Pictures) Released October 8, 1943

3 of a Kind (Monogram) Released July 22, 1944
Pick a Peck of Plumbers (short) (Columbia Pictures) Released July 23, 1944
Moonlight and Cactus (Universal Pictures) Released September 8, 1944
Strange Affair (Columbia Pictures) Released October 5, 1944
Open Season for Saps (short) (Columbia Pictures) Released October 27, 1944
Crazy Knights (Sam Katzman Productions for Monogram) Released December 8, 1944

Off Again, On Again (short) (Columbia Pictures) Released February 16, 1945
Trouble Chasers (Sam Katzman Productions for Monogram Pictures) Released June 2, 1945
Where the Pest Begins (short) (Columbia Pictures) Released October 4, 1945
A Hit with a Miss (short) (Columbia Pictures) Released December 13, 1945

The Gentleman Misbehaves (Columbia Pictures) Released February 28, 1946
Mr. Noisy (short) (Columbia Pictures) Released March 22, 1946
One Exciting Week (Republic Pictures) Released June 8, 1946
Dangerous Business (Columbia Pictures) Released June 20, 1946
Society Mugs (short) (Columbia Pictures) Released September 16, 1946

Blondie Knows Best (Columbia Pictures) Released October 17, 1946

Bride and Gloom (short) (Columbia Pictures) Released March 27, 1947

Africa Screams (Nasbro Pictures) Released May 27, 1949

SHEMP WITH MOE HOWARD AND LARRY FINE AS THE THREE STOOGES

Fright Night (short) (Columbia Pictures) Released March 6, 1947
Out West (short) (Columbia Pictures) Released April 24, 1947
Hold That Lion! (short) (Columbia Pictures) Released July 17, 1947
Brideless Groom (short) (Columbia Pictures) Released September 11, 1947
Sing a Song of Six Pants (short) (Columbia Pictures) Released October 30, 1947
All Gummed Up (short) (Columbia Pictures) Released December 18, 1947

Shivering Sherlocks (short) (Columbia Pictures) Released January 8, 1948
Pardon My Clutch (short) (Columbia Pictures) Released February 26, 1948
Squareheads of the Round Table (short) (Columbia Pictures) Released March 4, 1948
Fiddlers Three (short) (Columbia Pictures) Released May 6, 1948
The Hot Scots (short) (Columbia Pictures) Released July 8, 1948
Heavenly Daze (short) (Columbia Pictures) Released September 2, 1948
I'm a Monkey's Uncle (short) (Columbia Pictures) Released October 7, 1948
Mummy's Dummies (short) (Columbia Pictures) Released November 4, 1948
Crime on Their Hands (short) (Columbia Pictures) Released December 9, 1948

The Ghost Talks (short) (Columbia Pictures) Released February 3, 1949
Who Done It? (short) (Columbia Pictures) Released March 3, 1949
Hokus Pokus (short) (Columbia Pictures) Released May 5, 1949
Fuelin' Around (short) (Columbia Pictures) Released July 7, 1949
Malice in the Palace (short) (Columbia Pictures) Released September 1, 1949
Vagabond Loafers (short) (Columbia Pictures) Released October 6, 1949
Jerks of All Trades (unsold TV pilot) (short) (Columbia Pictures) October 12, 1949
Dunked in the Deep (short) (Columbia Pictures) Released November 3, 1949

Punchy Cowpunchers (short) (Columbia Pictures) Released January 5, 1950
Hugs and Mugs (short) (Columbia Pictures) Released February 2, 1950
Dopey Dicks (short) (Columbia Pictures) Released Thursday, March 2, 1950
Love at First Bite (short) (Columbia Pictures) Released May 4, 1950

Self Made Maids (short) (Columbia Pictures) Released July 6, 1950
Three Hams on Rye (short) (Columbia Pictures) Released September 7, 1950
Studio Stoops (short) (Columbia Pictures) Released October 5, 1950
Slaphappy Sleuths (short) (Columbia Pictures) Released November 9, 1950
A Snitch in Time (short) (Columbia Pictures) Released December 7, 1950

Three Arabian Nuts (short) (Columbia Pictures) Released January 4, 1951
Baby Sitters Jitters (short) (Columbia Pictures) Released February 1, 1951
Don't Throw That Knife (short) (Columbia Pictures) Released May 3, 1951
Scrambled Brains (short) (Columbia Pictures) Released July 7, 1951
Merry Mavericks (short) (Columbia Pictures) Released September 6, 1951
Gold Raiders (United Artists) Released September 14, 1951
The Tooth Will Out (short) (Columbia Pictures) Released October 4, 1951
Hula-La-La (short) (Columbia Pictures) Released November 1, 1951
Pest Man Wins (short) (Columbia Pictures) Released December 6, 1951

A Missed Fortune (short) (Columbia Pictures) Released January 3, 1952
Listen, Judge (short) (Columbia Pictures) Released March 6, 1952
Corny Casanovas (short) (Columbia Pictures) Released May 1, 1952
He Cooked His Goose (short) (Columbia Pictures) Released July 3, 1952
Gents in a Jam (short) (Columbia Pictures) Released September 4, 1952
Three Dark Horses (short) (Columbia Pictures) Released October 16, 1952
Cuckoo on a Choo Choo (short) (Columbia Pictures) Released December 4, 1952

Up in Daisy's Penthouse (short) (Columbia Pictures) Released February 5, 1953
Booty and the Beast (short) (Columbia Pictures) Released March 5, 1953
Loose Loot (short) (Columbia Pictures) Released April 2, 1953
Tricky Dicks (short) (Columbia Pictures) Released May 7, 1953
Spooks! (short) (Columbia Pictures) Released June 15, 1953
Pardon My Backfire (short) (Columbia Pictures) Released August 15, 1953
Rip, Sew, and Stitch (short) (Columbia Pictures) Released September 3, 1953
Bubble Trouble (short) (Columbia Pictures) Released October 8, 1953
Goof on the Roof (short) (Columbia Pictures) Released December 3, 1953

Income Tax Sappy (short) (Columbia Pictures) Released February 4, 1954
Musty Musketeers (short) (Columbia Pictures) Released May 13, 1954
Pals and Gals (short) (Columbia Pictures) Released June 3, 1954
Knutzy Knights (short) (Columbia Pictures) Released September 2, 1954
Shot in the Frontier (short) (Columbia Pictures) Released October 7, 1954
Scotched in Scotland (short) (Columbia Pictures) Released November 4, 1954

Fling in the Ring (short) (Columbia Pictures) Released January 6, 1955
Of Cash and Hash (short) (Columbia Pictures) Released February 3, 1955
Gypped in the Penthouse (short) (Columbia Pictures) Released March 10, 1955
Bedlam in Paradise (short) (Columbia Pictures) Released Thursday, April 14, 1955
Stone Age Romeos (short) (Columbia Pictures) Released June 2, 1955

Wham-Bam-Slam! (short) (Columbia Pictures) Released September 1, 1955
Hot Ice (short) (Columbia Pictures) Released October 6, 1955
Blunder Boys (short) (Columbia Pictures) Released November 3, 1955

Laff Hour (feature-length shorts compilation) (short) (Columbia Pictures) Released January 1, 1956
Husbands Beware (short) (Columbia Pictures) Released January 5, 1956
Creeps (short) (Columbia Pictures) Released February 2, 1956
Flagpole Jitters (short) (Columbia Pictures) Released April 5, 1956
For Crimin' Out Loud (short) (Columbia Pictures) Released May 3, 1956

THE "FAKE SHEMP" SHORTS

Rumpus in the Harem (short) (Columbia Pictures) Released June 21, 1956
Hot Stuff (short) (Columbia Pictures) Released September 6, 1956
Scheming Schemers (short) (Columbia Pictures) Released October 4, 1956
Commotion on the Ocean (short) (Columbia Pictures) Released November 8, 1956

Selected Bibliography

BOOKS AND MAGAZINES

Abraham, Jeff, and Burt Kearns. *The Show Won't Go On: The Most Shocking, Bizarre, and Historic Deaths of Performers Onstage*. Chicago Review Press, 2019.

Applegate, Debbie. *Madame: The Biography of Polly Adler, Icon of the Jazz Age*. Anchor Books, 2022.

Bawden, James, and Ron Miller. *You Ain't Heard Nothin' Yet: Interviews with Stars from Hollywood's Golden Era*. University Press of Kentucky, 2017.

Bernds, Edward. *Mr. Bernds Goes to Hollywood*. Scarecrow Press, 1999.

Besser, Joe, Jeff Lenburg, and Greg Lenburg. *Not Just a Stooge*. Excelsior Books, 1984.

Braund, Simon. "The Tragic and Twisted Tale of the Three Stooges." *Empire*, July 2012.

Bruskin, David N. *Behind the Three Stooges: The White Brothers*. Directors Guild of America, 1993.

Cassara, Bill. *Ted Healy: Nobody's Stooge*. BearManor Media, 2015.

Coniam, Matthew, and Nick Santa Maria. *The Annotated Abbott and Costello*. McFarland & Company, 2023.

Costello, Chris. *Lou's On First*. St. Martin's Griffin, 1982.

Cox, Steve, and Jim Terry. *One Fine Stooge: Larry Fine's Frizzy Life in Pictures*. Cumberland House, 2006.

Cullen, Frank, with Florence Hackman and Donald McNeilly. *Vaudeville Old & New*. Vols. 1–2. Routledge, 2006.

Davis, Lon, and Debra Davis, eds. *Stooges among Us*. BearManor Media, 2008.

Del Valle, Cezar. *The Brooklyn Theater Index. Volume II: Manhattan Avenue to York Street*. Theatre Talks, LLC, 2010.

Dick, Bernard F. *The Merchant Prince of Poverty Row: Harry Cohn of Columbia Pictures*. University Press of Kentucky, 1993.

Egan, Kate. *The Evil Dead*. Columbia University Press, 2011.

Erickson, Hal. *A Van Beuren Production*. McFarland & Company, 2020.

Erish, Andrew A. *Vitagraph: America's First Great Motion Picture Studio*. University Press of Kentucky, 2021.

Fleming, Michael. *The Three Stooges: An Illustrated History from Amalgamated Morons to American Icons*. Doubleday, 1999.

Furmanek, Bob, and Ron Palumbo. *Abbott and Costello in Hollywood*. Perigee Books, 1991.

Garner, Paul "Mousie," and Sharon F. Kissane. *Mousie Garner: Autobiography of a Vaudeville Stooge*. McFarland & Company, 1999.

Gordon, Roger L. *Supporting Actors in Motion Pictures*. Dorrance Publishing, 2018.

Hittner, Arthur D. *Honus Wagner: The Life of Baseball's "Flying Dutchman."* McFarland & Company, 1996.

Hogan, David J. *Three Stooges FAQ*. Applause Theatre & Cinema Books, 2001.

Howard, Moe. *Moe Howard & the 3 Stooges*. Citadel Press, 1977.

Howard, Moe. *I Stooged to Conquer*. Chicago Review Press, 2013.

Johnston, Jim. *Essays, The Art of Description*. Vol. 1. Fulton Books, 2017.

Lassin, Gary. *A Tour de Farce: The Complete History of the Three Stooges on the Road*. The Stoogeum, 2023.

Lenburg, Jeff, Joan Howard Maurer, and Greg Lenburg. *The Three Stooges Scrapbook*. Updated ed. Chicago Review Press, 2012.

Liebman, Roy. *Vitaphone Films: A Catalogue of the Features and Shorts*. McFarland & Company, 2003.

Maltin, Leonard. *Leonard Maltin's 2009 Movie Guide*. Plume, 2008.

Manago, Jim. *Behind Sach: The Huntz Hall Story*. BearManor Media, 2015.

Matus, Irvin Leigh. *Urbanography: Where the Dream Was Made*. The Composing Stack, 2000.

Maurer, Joan Howard. *Curly: An Illustrated Biography of the Superstooge*. Citadel Press, 1985.

Mueller, Jim. "Shemp's Last Cigar." *Cigar Aficionado*, Winter 1996–1997.

Munn, Michael. *Jimmy Stewart: The Truth behind the Legend*. Skyhorse Publishing, 2006.

Nachman, Gerald. *Seriously Funny: The Rebel Comedians of the 1950s and 1960s*. Pantheon, 2003.

Neibaur, James L. *The Andy Clyde Columbia Comedies*. McFarland & Company, 2018.

Oderman, Stuart. *Roscoe "Fatty" Arbuckle: A Biography of the Silent Film Comedian*. McFarland & Company, 1994.

Okuda, Ted, with Edward Watz. *The Columbia Comedy Shorts*. McFarland & Company, 1986.

Quirk, Lawrence J. *James Stewart: Behind the Scenes of a Wonderful Life*. Applause Books, 1997.

Seely, Peter, and Gail W. Pieper, eds. *Stoogeology: Essays on the Three Stooges*. McFarland & Company, 2007.

Seguine, Brent. "Stooge Myth Busters: They Must Be Income Tax." *The Three Stooges Journal*, no. 156, Winter 2015.

Smith, Don G. *Lon Chaney, Jr., Horror Film Star (1906–1973)*. McFarland & Company, 1996.

Solomon, Jon. *The Complete Three Stooges*. Comedy III Production, Inc., 2001.

Perich, Terry, and Kathleen Perich. *Postcard History Series: Jeannette*. Arcadia, 2006.

Thomas, Bob. *King Cohn*. G. F. Putnam's Sons, 1967.

Watz, Edward. "Shemp Sightings." *Comique—The Classic Comedy Magazine*, Autumn 2020.

White, Jules. *Jules White Papers*. Academy of Motion Picture Arts and Sciences, Margaret Herrick Library.

Wijdiks, Eelco F. M. *Cinema, M.D.: A History of Medicine on Screen*. Oxford University Press, 2021.

ONLINE MATERIAL

Adams, Les. *Hollywood Round-Up, Crazy House* plot summaries. IMDb.com.

AFI Catalog of Feature Films. *The Jazz Singer* (1927).

Balducci, Anthony. *Critics Sing Praises of Moss and Frye*. Anthony Balducci's Journal, 2015.

Bandelow, Borwin. *Epidemiology of anxiety disorders in the 21st century*. National Library of Medicine, 2015.

Cress, Robby. *The Toluca Lake Homes of Shemp Howard*. Dear Old Hollywood, 2014.

Digital Research Library of Illinois History Journal. *The Rainbo Building's History*, 2016.

Dobbs, G. Michael. *Enjoy the Shemp for What He's Worth*. The Reminder, 2009.

Emergency Hospital Systems. *Can a Head Injury Cause a Stroke*? EmergencyHospitals.care, 2023.

Fairey, Shepard. *Manifesto*. ObeyGiant.com, 1990.

Farrell, Steven G. *Essay: Make Us Laugh Again, Funnymen*. BattleRoyaleWithCheese.com, 2018.

Flaherty, Mike. *Why I'm Boycotting "The Three Stooges."* GQ.com, 2012.

Galbraith, Stuart IV. *Three Stooges: The Ultimate Collection*. DVD Talk, 2012.

———. *Vitaphone Comedy Collection, Volume Two: Shemp Howard (1933–1937)*. DVD Talk, 2014.

History.com editors. *Stock Market Crash of 1929*. History.com, 2010.

Johns Hopkins Medicine. *Phobias*. HopkinsMedicine.org, 2023.

Leith, Sam. *I Wish More People Would Read . . . Damon Runyon's Stories*. The Guardian UK, 2020.

Los Angeles City Planning. *Jewish History, Theme 5: Entertainment Industry, 1908–1980*. LACity.org, 2016.

Mayo Clinic Staff. *Chronic Traumatic Encephalopathy*. MayoClinic.org, 2023.

Mensah, Ebenezer. *Revolutionizing the Pump: The Birth of Self-Service Gas Stations and Cheaper Fuel in Los Angeles*. Breaking News, 2023.

Ness, Caro. *Pittsburgh (1942) Film Review*. Eye for Film, 2006.

Nesteroff, Kliph. *Outrageous and Courageous: The Myth and Legend of Shecky Greene*. WFMU's Beware of the Blog, 2011.

Pullen, Sidney. *Burlesque: The "Other" Side of Vaudeville*. American Vaudeville, University of Arizona, vaudeville.sites.arizona.edu, 2023.

Retina Associates, LLC. *Causes of Retinal Hemorrhage*. KCRetina.com, 2023.

Shannon, Mitchell. *Shemp Is the Thinking Man's Curly: Why the New Beatles Is Dumb-and-Dumber Than the New Stooges*. MitchellShannon.com, 2012.

Stecher, Raquel. *Guest Reviewer "Frank" on The Vitaphone Comedy Collection: Volume 2: Shemp Howard (1933–1937)*. Out of the Past blog, 2014.

Thorn, John. *Lost (and Found) Baseball, Part 2*. Our Game, Blog of Official MLB Historian John Thorn, 2012.
ThreeStooges.net editors. *The Filmography*. ThreeStooges.net, 2023.
Trav S.D. *Willie and Eugene Howard: Comes the Revolution*! Travalanche, 2009.
Whitney, Dave. *Schilling and Lane: Forgotten Comedy Heroes*. Pete Kelly's Blog, 2008.

AUDIO AND VIDEO

Gale, Bob. Moe Howard interview. WTAF-TV, Philadelphia, April 27, 1973.
Hello Baltimore, Brent Gunts interviews Moe Howard, Larry Fine, and Shemp Howard. WBAL Radio, April 6, 1950.
Hey Moe, Hey Dad! The Three Stooges 100 Year Journey Told by Moe's Son. Video series, Frank Basile, producer; Paul Howard, producer emeritus. C3 Entertainment, 2015.
Internet Archive. The Three Stooges Films and Books. Archive.org, 2023.
Lamparski, Richard. Moe Howard interview, WBAI Radio, New York, 1970.
Stooge-O-Rama: The Men behind the Mayhem and Even More Mayhem! Blu-ray collection, Kit Parker Films, 2023.
The Mike Douglas Show. Guest Moe Howard. Episodes 12.02, 13.69, 1973.
Tubi. Three Stooges shorts and documentaries. TubiTV.com.
YouTube. Three Stooges comedy shorts. YouTube.com.

Acknowledgments

In selecting a compelling biographical subject from the many under-recognized talents in the history of entertainment, it takes a special intellect, personality, and, some might say—I will say—*genius* to come up with the name of Shemp Howard. Lee Sobel is such a genius, a literary agent with a rare knack for knowing whom to unleash on what is sure to be a compelling and surprising story. A tip of the hat and many thanks to Lee, who, like Shemp, is one of a kind. And similar thanks to John Cerullo, a brilliant editor who recognized and was excited about the rich material that could be unearthed through an exploration of Shemp.

Much appreciation and admiration goes to the great artist and popular culture icon Drew Friedman, "The Vermeer of the Borscht Belt," for his contribution of words and priceless art. And no one deserves greater thanks than Alison Holloway for her love, patience, and support. Jeff Abraham, Legs McNeil, Ray Richmond, and Elli Wohlgelernter were valuable sounding boards and friends along the way.

Three cheers for the team at Applause Theatre & Cinema Books, including Barbara Claire, Chris Chappell, Emily Jeffers, Melissa McClellan, Meaghan Menzel, and Bruce Owens, for their care and expertise that improved on this project; for Ani Khachoian and Roberto Merkell at C3 Entertainment; and for Derek Davidson of Photofest, who went above and beyond in the quest for memorable pictures.

And thanks and hats off to those who contributed to this project. For their time and insights: Billy West, Bill Cassara, Stuart Galbraith IV, Leonard Maltin, Nick Santa Maria, Edward Watz, and Bradley Server. For their work and words: Mark Arnold, Les Adams, David N. Bruskin, Steve Cox and Jim Terry, Hal Erickson, Shepard Fairey, Mike Flaherty, Shecky Greene, Geri Howard Greenbaum, Jill Howard Marcus, Sandie Howard-Isaac, Chandler Isaac, Paul Howard, Jeff and Greg Lenburg, Joan Howard Maurer, Steve Lally, Kliph Nesteroff, Trent Reeve, Brent Seguine, Michael Shannon, and John Thorn.

And thanks to Alexis Arakelian, Alan Bisbort, Joe Bolton, Michael Braverman, Peter Brennan, Doug Bruckner, Mike Catalano, Jon Crowley, Donato Di Camillo, Dana Gould, Frank Grimes, Tom Hearn, Sally Jade Holloway Kearns, Sam Kearns, Matt Lubich, Alex Rosas, Frank Santopadre, Alfie, Billy, and the never-forgotten Brian and Clarence.

A special mention goes to Gary Lassin of the Stoogeum and Three Stooges Fan Club, with praise for his *A Tour de Farce*, a book that is as difficult to put down as it is to pick up (because it's so heavy!).

Oh, and thanks, Shemp.

Index

Abbott, Bud, 138, 195
Abbott and Costello, 95, 105, 137–40, *140*, 142, 183; Gilbert-Shemp team and, 167; number of movies with Shemp and, 141; in Runyon movie, 152–53; Santa Maria book on, 106; Shemp reunited with, 195
Abbott and Costello Meet Frankenstein, 144
The Abbott and Costello Show, 196
Absorbing Junior, 115
Ackerman, Elaine (second wife of Curly), 161–62
acromegaly, 152
Actors' Equity Association, 92
Africa Screams, 195, 196–99, *198*
Allan K. Foster Girls, 34, 36, *39*, 61
Alper, Murray, *124*
alternative comedy, 158
Amsterdam, Morey, 157, 206
Andrade, Cisco "Automatic" (boxer), 220, 221
Andrenni, Lawrence, 53
Andrews Sisters, 102, 139, 141, 145, *145*, 146, 164; Merry Macs and, 142
Animal Crackers, 78
animation, 101
The Annotated Abbott and Costello (Santa Maria, Nick), 106
Another Thin Man, 124, *124*, 125, 151
Ants in the Pantry, 209
Arabian Nights, 134, 162, 166, 183
Arbuckle, Roscoe "Fatty," 96–97, 98, 109, 161
Army of Darkness, 226
Ates, Roscoe, 108, 112
Atkinson, J. Brooks (critic), 41, 65
Atteridge, Harold, 61

Babe Egan and Her Hollywood Redheads, 59
Baker, Phil, 38, *39*, 40, 44, 51, 66; *A Night in Spain* and, 45, 50, 53
The Bandit of Sherwood Forest, 188
The Bank Dick, 130–31, *131*, 132, 133
Barrymore, John, 133
Barty, Billy, 75–76
bear (Big Boy), 62–63, 64, 66, 67, 87; on the road, 71–72
Bedlam in Paradise, 216
bedwetting, 19, 155
Behind Prison Gates, 123–24
Bensonhurst-by-the-Sea, 5
Bensonhurst Jewish Community House, 57
Bergen, Edgar, 100
Berkeley, Busby, 61, 78
Berkes, Johnny, 115
Bernds, Edward (sound editor/director), 166, 170–73, 177–79; Columbia quit by, 210; on Curly, 176; eight shorts in 1949 directed by, 207; Shemp return and, 182–84, 186–88, 190, 192; on Shemp's nature, 192, 200
Besser, Joe, ix, 90, 92, 141; Abbott and Costello request for, 195; on Shemp

phobias, 196–99; as third Stooge, 182, 226
Bible, Schmuel in, 1
"Big V Comedy" shorts, 93–96, *94*, 98–99, *103*
Billy rose's Crazy Quilt, 85–86
blackface, 15, 17–18, 20; Healy, T., and, 22, 27; Jolson and, 51
Black Monday, 71
Black Tuesday, 71
Black vaudeville stars, 18
Block and Sully, 100
The Blonde Bomber, 115
Blondie Knows Best, 178–79
Blunder Boys, 217–18
Boobs in the Woods, 126
Bowery Champs, 175
Bowman, Grace, 36, *39*
boxing, 204–5, 219; Shemp death and, 220–21
boxing comedies, 125–26
Braun, Sam "Moody," 37, 41, 50, 52
Brendel, Ed, 165–66
Breslow, Lou, 75
Bride and Gloom, 171
Brideless Groom, 190–92, *192*
Broadway, 64–65, 69–71, 168–69; Healy, T., and, 66, 85–86; 1932 Racketeers on, 87; Pete (Healy, T., dog) leap to, 30; Shemp experience on vaudeville *vs.*, 66. *See also specific shows*
Brooklyn Borough Gas Company, 69
brownface, 127
Bruce, Virginia, 151
Buck Privates, 139–41, *140*
burlesque comedy, 137–42
Busy Buddies, 164
Butch Minds the Baby, 149, 150–52, *151*, 162
Buxbaum, Marion Marvin, 178

Cagney, James, 94
California Institute of Technology (Caltech), 197
Calling All Kids, 115
Cantor, Eddie, 35, 66
Casa Mañana, 194
Cash and Carry, 117
casinos, 33, 34, 212, 214–15
Cassara, Bill (Healy, T., biographer), 27, 36, 44, 77; on Healy, T., death, 119; on rejoining Healy, T., 86–87; on Sanborn, 61; on Shemp walkout, 89; on 'stooge in the box,' 82
Ce-How self-service station, 209
cerebral hemorrhages, 228–29
Chaney, Lon. Jr., *142*, 142–44
Chaplin, Charlie, 61, 160
Charlie Chan (fictional detective), 127, *128*
Chase, Charley, 169–71
Chicago: *A Night in Spain* in, 44–45, 47–50; "White" hotels in, 44
chimpanzee (Joe Mendi), 72, 199
The Choke's on You, 115
chorus girls, 30, 40, 78; in *A Night in Spain*, 34, 36, *39*, 50–51; in *A Night in Venice*, 61
Churchill, Isabelle, 27, 28, 29
Ciro's, 209
Close Relations, 93–94, 96
Clyde, Andy, 120–21, 126
Cohn, Harry, 105, 117, 121, 159, 176; Curly's stroke and, 183
coke bottle glasses, routine of, 169
Colbert, Claudette, 84
Columbia Pictures, Three Stooges at: Besser and, 182; budget cuts in 1951, 210–11; competition against Shemp, 165; Curly's health decline and, 173, 175–76; end of shorts, 159; "Fake Shemp" and, 160, 224–26; film scene shared by Howard brothers, *189*, 190; 1949 shorts directed by Bernds, 207; 1954 shorts and remakes, 215–16; number of shorts made with, 183–84; remakes, 176, 183, 209, 212, 215–16; reviewer on "mistake," 173–74; schedule, 187–88; Shemp contract to replace Curly, 182, 194; Shemp death and, 223; shorts after Curly's death, 211–12; 3-D films, 212–14,

214; Vitaphone comedy shorts compared with, 110
comic strips: Joe Palooka, 112–13, 115; from *A Night in Venice*, 69–71, *70*
Commotion on the Ocean, 226
Convention Girl, 106–7, *107*, 169
Cooley, Spade, 174
Corny Casanovas, 226
Costello, Lou, 105–6, 138, 152–53, 195; chimpanzee scene, 199. *See also* Abbott and Costello
Costello, Maurice, "Rudolph Valentino," 10
The Cowboy Star, 118
Cox, Steve, 48, 81, 88, 181
Cracked Nuts, 134, 138
Crawford, Broderick "Brod," 147–49, *148*
Crawford, Joan, 177
Crazy House, 136, 164, *165*
Crazy Knights, 167–68, *168*, 169
Crime on Their Hands, 217, 226
Crimin' Our Loud, 219
Crumb, R., ix
Cuddle Up, 27
cult of Curly, 234
Curly. *See* Howard, Jerome Lester "Babe"
Curly (Maurer), 7, 16–17, 229, 231
Curly Joe, ix, 226–27
Cut the Acts, 84

Damon Runyon's Tight Shoes, 147–48, *148*
dancers, "shimmy" invention and, 44. *See also* chorus girls
The Danger Girl, 32
Dangerous Blondes, 199
Davis, Kenny (boxer), 220, 221
Dead End, 166
the Dead End Kids, 119, 166
Dean brothers (pitchers), 107–8
death: of Curly, 211–12; of Moe, 228
death, of Shemp: "Fake Shemp" and stand-ins after, 160, 224–26; family assertions and reminiscences, 228, 231; fight match attended before, 220–21; film schedule and, 223; funeral and entombment of, 224; official *vs.* actual, 222; Shemp stand-in after, 224–26; taxicab ride and, 221–22; theories about, 228–31
Dent, Vernon (supporting player), 121, 186, 211, 224
DeRita, Joe, ix, 226
Dickens, Charles names created by, x
Dickshot, Johnny, 151
Dietrich, Marlene, 136, *137*
The Diving Belles, 12–13
Dizzy and Daffy, 107, 108, 109
Dodge, Beth, 71
dogs, 199, *201*; Healy, T., police dog (Pete), 30, 32, 38, 72
Douglas, Mike, 25, 56
draft, 139, 144, 154; Curly's rejection, 160, 162; Shemp draft and discharge, 18, 19–20, *20*
drag, roles done in, 208
Dragnet, parody of, 217–18
Dunked in the Deep, 226
Durante, Jimmy, 113, 122

earthquake, 197
East Side Kids, 166
Edison, Thomas, 8, 9
elephant, 67
Epsteins (Hockey, Morty, and Sam), 58
Everybody Likes Music, 102
The Evil Dead, 226
extra, unidentified, 208
eye pokes, 23, 85, 188, 212, 231

Facebook group, 14, 200
"Fake Shemp," 160, 224–26
farm, Horwitz family, 19
father, of Shemp. *See* Horwitz, Solomon Nathan
Fay, Frank, 166–67
Feinberg, Louis. *See* Fine, Larry
Fiddlers Three, 188
Fields, W. C., 31, 130–32, 133, 183
film-within-a-film genre, 136
Fine, Larry (Feinberg, Louis), ix–x, 4, 26, 53; callouses and scars from

hits, 228; on death of Shemp, 223; discovery of, 47–50; Healy, T., left by Shemp, Moe and, 76; "Hey Hey" routine, 51–52, 60; memoir, 88; paternity leave, 60, 61; Pinkus and, 52; Shemp return and, 181. *See also* The Three Stooges, as Howard, Fine, and Howard
fire hose gag, 110
Fisher, Ham, 112–13
Flagpole Jitters, *218*, 219
The Flame of New Orleans, 148
"The Flapper and The Philosopher," 28
Flynn, Errol, 133, 152
Fonda, Henry, 102
For the Love of Pete, 113, 115
Fox, James (Shemp stooge), 101
Fox Academy Theatre, 60
Fox Film Corporation, 74, 80
Fox Movietone, 68, 73, 101
Fox Studios, 75–76, 77, 79, 80, 86
French, Lloyd (director), 109, 111
Friedman, Drew, xi, 234
Fright Night, *184*, 184–86
Fuelin Around, 225

Galbraith, Stuart, IV (critic), 169–71, 174, 176, 179; favorite Shemp moment of, 237; on Shemp return, 183, 210; on shorts, 188, 208, 212, 215, 219, 237
The Gang's All Here, 81–82, 85
Gargan, Edward, 148
Garner, "Mousie," 81, 82
The Gentleman Misbehaves, 168–69
Gertrude Frank Girls, 30
Gertrude Hoffman Girls, 34, 40
"Get outta my way!," 107, *107*
Gilbert, Billy, 166–68, *168*, 184–85
Give Us Wings, 129, *130*, 132
Givot, George, 97, 100
Glove Slingers, 125
Gobs of Fun, 93, 97
Goldberg, Rube, 73–76, 80–81
Gold Raiders, 208
Goodwin, Ruth (tap dancer), 82, 83
granddaughter, of Shemp, 212
Grand Hooter, 169
Great Depression, 71, 73, 77, 81, 85
Greenbaum, Geri Howard (daughter-in law), 14, 200, 217
Gribbon, Harry, Shemp and, 100, 102–5, *103*
Guys and Dolls, 147, 153, 237

Haley, Jack, 94–95, 139
Half-Wits Holiday, 179, 183, 209
Hall, Huntz, 119, 129, 145, 154, 166, 175; Shemp as mentor of, 158; Shemp friendship with, 130, *130*; son of, 155
Hammerstein, Oscar, II, 81
Hans Wagner Comedies, 21
Hardy, Oliver, 32, 109, 110, 176
Harrison, George, 236
Hatton, Rondo, 96, 151, 152
Headin' East, 118–19
Healy, Betty (Brown, Betty) (born Braun) (wife of Ted), 22, 27, 37, 59, 120; divorce of, 86; as duo with Healy, T., 44; *A Night in Spain* critics and, 41, 44; vaudeville act with husband, *29*, 29–35
Healy, Betty (second wife of Healy, T.), 119
Healy, Ted (Nash, Ernest Lee, "Charles"): as abusive, 87, 88, 89, 105; alcoholism and drinking, 37–38, 44, 50, 86, 120; biographer, 27, 36, 44; Broadway and, 66, 85–86; as childhood friend of Moe, 10–11; chimpanzee routine (Joe Mendi), 72; complaining and accusations by, 79, 81; death of, 119–20; divorce of, 86; Fine discovery by, 47–50; marriage breakup, 66; marriage to Betty, 27, 59; misnamed stooges in funeral report for, 120; *A Night in Spain* success of, 42; 1931 flop of, 81–82; return of, 85; reunion with, 22–23; second wife and birth of child, 119; slaps of, 37–38, 42, 50, 52, 88; Stoogeologist correcting

story about, 26; team with wife in Chicago, 44. *See also* vaudeville, Healy, T., act on
Hebrew, 1
He Cooked His Goose, 211
Hellinger, Mark, 41–42, 55–56, *56*
Hellzapoppin', 135–36
Henry the Ache, 101, 122
Here Comes Flossie!, 93–94, 98–99
"Hey Hey" routine, 51–52, 60
His First Flame, 109, 110
Hitler, Adolf, 160
Hit the Hay, 178
Hit the Road, 129
A Hit with a Miss, 170
Hokum of 1928, 52
Hokus Pokus, 219
Hold That Ghost, 141, 142
Hold That Lion!, *189*, 189–90, 200
Hollywood, 59, 116, 118; movie studios before, 8; Poverty Row Studios, 106, 157, 166; Shemp arrival in, 117; Ted and Racketeers arrival at Fox, 74–75. *See also* Columbia Pictures, Three Stooges at; Shemp, at Columbia Pictures; Shemp, at Universal Studios; "The Ugliest Man in Hollywood"
Hollywood Hotel, 119
Hollywood Midsummer Jubilee, 74–75
Hollywood Round-Up, 118
homes, of Shemp, 120, 123; Toluca Lake and, 156–57, 164, 175, 217
Hope, Bob, 210
Horwitz, Jenne Mary, "Jennie" (mother) (nee Goldsmith), 1–2, 19, 22; death of, 159; Healy act and, 25
Horwitz, Solomon Nathan (father), 1–2, 13, 22; death of, 159
Hot Ice, 217
The Hot Scots, 188, 217
Hot Stuff, 225
Houdini, Harry, 30, 57
House, Florence, 27, 28, 29
Howard, Gertrude (nee Frank) "Babe," 30, 92, 93; as air raid warden, 157; wartime garden, 156–57
Howard, Isidore (firstborn son of Horwitzes) "Irving," 2, 3
Howard, Jacob (born Horwitz) "Jack," 3, 25
Howard, Jerome Lester "Babe" (born Horwitz) "Curly," 3, 16, 58, 90, 96, *189*; appearance after stroke, 190; arrangement for care of, 180; becoming "Curly," 30, 161; breakdown on tour, 174; Buxbaum marriage and divorce, 178; conspiracy for replacing, 175–76; Costello, L., and, 105–6; death of, 211–12; draft rejection, 160, 162; drinking of, 160–62, 172; film featuring longer hair of, 179; fourth wife of, 194; health decline of, 160, 162, 172, 173, 181; kids love of, 233; marriages of, 161–62, 194; medical staff on ailments of, 229; replacement conspiracy, 163, 175–76, 181–82; Shemp compared to, 234; slaps causing damage to head, 229; as star stooge, 161; strokes of, 176, 179, 183, 190, 211; Toluca Lake area home, 156. *See also* Shemp, Curly replaced by
Howard, Morton (only child of Shemp), 38, 116, 209, 212
Howard, Moses Harry "Moe," ix, 16; aborted skinny-dipping date, 14–15; accuracy track record, 22; acting decision as child, 8; autobiographical memory of, 13; autobiography, 5–8, 19, 47; backflip replacement request, 22; birth and nickname, 3; blackface act, 15, 17–18; as boss, 105, 161, 175; construction business of, 58; Curly replacement conspiracy and, 163, 175–76, 181–82; death of, 228; eye pokes by, 23, 85, 188, 212, 231; filmland foray of, 8; Fine discovery and, 47–48; first film appearance, 10; gap of 1925–1929, 56; growing prominence in team, 78; guilt of, 227; "Harry Howard" billing of,

25, 63, 66; in high school, 12; home in Toluca Lake area, 156; Horwitz-Howard change, 17; irony for, 67; marriage of, 30; in musical comedy, 57–58; name in census, 22; Nash, Charles Ernest Lee and (Healy, T.,), 10–11; 1928 rejoining with Healy, 58; physical appearance of, 23–24; plays performed by, 20–21; reaction to Shemp's popularity, 13, 15; in real estate, 57, 58; Shemp death according to, 223; Shemp denigrated by, 56; Shemp prominence over, 60; in singing quartet, 13; slapping by, 23, 185, 193–94, *194*; son (Paul) on night of Shemp death, 223; on *Sunflower* showboat, 16; on taking Healy's place, 232; tours demanded by, 187; trade school and, 12, 13; as Vitagraph errand boy, 9–10; walkout according to, 88; work ethic and money obsession, 228–29. *See also specific topics*

Howard, Shemp (born Horwitz, Schmuel), *6*, *235*; acting range of, 89; alleged fears of, 14, 60, 63, 69, 190, 195; with Andrews Sisters, 145, *145*, 146; appreciation of Curly *vs.*, 234, 235; Bernds on sensitivity and kindness of, 200; best work of, 137; birth name and nicknames, 1–4; birthplace confusion and records, 4, 5, *6*; brothers of, 2–3; character developed by, 236–37; as childhood comedian, 8; as comedic leader, 69; Curly compared to, 234; dance sequence and wings erection, 216; death of, 160; draft and discharge, 18, 19–20, *20*; elephant and, 67; "fake," 160, 224–26; film class appearance with White, 212; Fine discovery and, 47–50; first and last car of, 14; friendship with Dead End kid, 119; granddaughter, 212; Hall friendship, 130, *130*, 158; as having best lines in picture, 125; Healy, T., left by Moe, Larry and, 76; Healy, T., walkout of, 49, 87–89, 91; high school tried out by, 12; as Horwitz-Howard team, 17–18; insights and opinions on, 236–37; interview about slapping, 231–32; kid brother replacing, 90; Knobby Walsh character of, 88, 113–15, 125; marriage, 30; Moe on childhood personality of, 5–8; name evolution, x; 1917 vaudeville acts with brother Moe, 17–18; performing with brother as youth, 13; popularity and renderings of, ix; poster impression of, *43*; recognition and praise, 35, 38, 41, 56, 65, 72; seaside park video featuring, 68–69; shadowboxing of, 204–5, 220; short plumbing career, 12; son, 38, 116; as *Soup to Nuts* star of team, 80, *80*, 81; as star in own right, 60; Stooges joined by, 4; swimming and fearlessness of, 68–69; The Three Stooges return of, 181–83, *184*, 186–88, 190, 192, 194; "ugliest man" title, x, 96, 150–52, *151*, 191; untruths about, 60; vaudeville acts with brother, 15, 17–18, 20. *See also* Shemp, at Columbia Pictures; Shemp, at Universal Studios; Shempophobia; vaudeville, Healy, T., act on; *specific shows*; *specific topics*

Howard-Isaac, Sandie, 14, 30, 157, 200

Howd' Ya Like That?, 94

Huara, Helba, 37, 51

Human Hearts, 16

Idiots Deluxe, 173

If a Body Meets a Body, 176

IMDb. *See* Internet Movie Database

Internal Revenue Service (IRS), 49

Internet Movie Database (IMDb), 10, 20–21, 113; on *Hollywood Round-Up*, 118; "Man in Lobby" credit in, 208

In the Dough, 93–94, 98

In the Navy, 141, 148

In the Sweet Pie and Pie, 209
The Invisible Woman, 133
IRS. *See* Internal Revenue Service
I Stooged to Conquer (Howard, Moe), 47
It Ain't Hay, 152–53
It Happened in Hollywood, 118
It's a Mad, Mad, Mad, Mad World, 227
Ivan the robot dialogue, 134–35

Jagger, Mick, 56
jai alai, 47, 48
James, Harry, 144–46
The Jazz Singer, 45
Jerks of All Trades, 193
Jewish Colonization Association, 12
Jewish immigrants, in New York City, 1–2, 4–5
Jiggers, My Wife, 170, *201*
Joe Palooka, 112–13
Johnson, Chic, 135–36, 164, 166
Jolson, Al, 27, 35, 45–46, 66, 104; Fine discovery and, 47, 48, 49; impersonation, 52
Judels, Charles, 95, 100
"Just What He Asked For," 70, *70*

Kaufman, George S., 81
Keaton, Buster, 171, 177
Keeler, Ruby (wife of Jolson), 81, 82
The Knife of the Party, 101–2
Knobby Walsh (character played by Shemp), 88, 113, 115, 125

Lahr, Bert, 101, 122
Larry. *See* Fine, Larry
Lassin, Gary (Stoogeologist), 26, 207
Las Vegas, 158, 212, 214–15
Late Night with David Letterman, x
Laurel, Stan, 32, 110, 166
Laurel and Hardy, 32, 109, 110, 176
The Leather Pushers, 126–27
Leonard, Sheldon, 103, *103*
Lewis, Jerry, 38, 75, 106, 129, 216; fire hose gag borrowed by, 110
Lewis, Sylvia, 216
"liquor observation evidence," 49
Litvak Jews, 1–2
Logan's Luck. *See Human Hearts*
The Lone Wolf Meets a Lady, 126
Lucky Devils, 133
Lullaby of Broadway, 168–69

Macke, Ted, 82, 83, 84
MAD magazine, 234
Malice in the Palace, 194, *194*, 195, 211, 225
Maltin, Leonard, 89, 130–31, 151, 172, 233; favorite Stooges short of, 176; on Shemp return, 182, 207; on "ugliest man" contest, 152
"Man in Lobby," 208
Mankoff, Geraldyn (wife of Shemp's son), 209
Marcus, Jill Howard, 14, 200, 217
Marguerite Bryant Players, 20
Martin, Dean, 38, 75
Marx Brothers, 78, 81
Masquerade, 81
Maurer, Joan Howard (daughter of Moe), 7, 16–17, 21; on head bangs and violent slaps, 229, 231
Maurer, Norman, 200
McCollum, Hugh, firing of, 210
McIntyre, Christine, 192
Men in Black, 159
The Merry Macs, 142
The Merry World, 33
Micro-Phonies, 176
The Missing Lady, 188
Moe. *See* Howard, Jerome Lester "Babe"
Moe Howard and the Three Stooges (Howard, Moe), 5–8
Money Squawks, 126
Monkey Businessmen, 177
Monogram Studios, 167–68, *168*, 175; Three Stooges moonlighting at, 177
Moonlight and Cactus, 133, 164
Moran, Eddie, 81, 82
mother, of Shemp. *See* Horwitz, Jenne Mary
Motion Picture Producers and Distributors of America (MPPDA), 93

Motion Picture Production Code, 98, 106, 131
"Mouse Trap" board game, 74
movies: end of silent, 45; first movie studio, 8; synchronized sound and, 101
MPPDA. *See* Motion Picture Producers and Distributors of America
Mr. Dynamite, 134
Mr. Noisy, 170
Muggeridge, Maude Elsie Aileen. *See* Stanley, Aileen
Murder Over New York, 127–29, *128*, 134
Mushrooms, 100
Musical Novelties series, 106
Musty Musketeers, 212
My Mummy's Arms, *103*, 103–5

Nash, Ernest Lee, 10–11, 12. *See also* Healy, Ted
Nash, John Jacob (son of Healy, T.,), 119
Nassour Studios, 195, 196–97, 199
Navy Yard, 155
"nearsighted" routine, 149
Nelson, Ozzie, 162
Nertsery Rhymes, 96
Nestor Motion Picture Company, 8
New Jersey, first movie studios based in, 8
Newman, Valerie (fourth wife of Curly), 194
New Year's Eve Party (TV special), 206
New York Times, 40–41
A Night In franchise, 65
A Night in Paris, 33
A Night in Spain, 25; Fine discovered during, 47–50; grabbing and pulling described in press, 54; Healy, B., absence from, 44; Healy, T., adding new act to, 52; Jolson replacing Baker in, 45–46; lead "stooge" in, 41; in Los Angeles, 51–52; "The Photographer" routine in, 36–37, 60; reviews, 40–41; RKO version of, 59–60; road show of, 40–42, *43*, 44–45, 47–50; run of, 42; in San Francisco, 52; Shemp and Fine, L, as team in, 53; Shemp billing in, 38, *39*, 41, 42; Shemp's return to, 52; source and transformation of, 54
A Night in Venice, 50, 54, *56*; bear-wrestling scene, 62–63, 64, 66, 67; on Broadway, 64–65, 69–71; cast and staff, 61, 62; comic strips, 55–56, 69–71, *70*; dance troupes, 61; first preview of, 62; Great Depression and, 73; opening, 63–64; plot of, 65; reviews, 64–66, 67; rights to material from, 79; set-up time, 62; support role of Moe in, 58; Ted Healy's Southern Gentlemen in, 62, *63*; tour of, 71, 73; vaudeville circuit return of, 73
"A Night in Venice Day" at Luna Park, 68–69
"Nightmare Trio," 69–70
Nobody's Stooge (Cassara), 76
Not Guilty Enough, 121
The Nude Deal, 102

"Obey Giant" stickers, 236
O'Connor, Willie, 13
October Automatic Replacement Draft of 1918, 19
Off Again, On Again, 170
The Officer's Mess, 112
Olsen, Ole, 135–36, 164, *165*, 166
One Exciting Week, 169
One Fine Stooge (Cox/Terry), 48, 81
On the Wagon, 112
Open Season for Saps, 169–70
Orpheum circuit, 32
Out West, 186–87

Palma, Joe, 160, 170, 224–26
Palmer, Bee, 44
Palooka, Joe, 26
Palooka series, 112–13, 115
Pals and Gals, 212
pantomime, 127
Paramount, hit show with, 78
Pardon My Backfire, 214

Pardon My Clutch, 217
Pardon my Terror, 183, 184
parents, 1–3, 159
Parsons, Louella, 73, 75
The Passing Show, 32–34, 37, 54, 90, 91–92; 1931, 86, 88
Passions of 1926, 33
Paul Revere Jr., 97
A Peach of a Pair, 109
Pearl Harbor, attack on, 144, 155
Pest Man Wins, 208–9
"The Photographer" (from *A Night in Spain*), 36–37, 60
Pick a Peck of Plumbers, 12, 160, 165–66, 207
pie tossing, 98, 155, 179
Pinkus, Bobby, 41, 50, 52
Pittsburgh, 162
Plane Nuts, 51–52
Pleased to Mitt You, 125
Plumbing for Gold, 160
A Plumbing We Will Go, 159–60, 165, 207; remake, 225
Pope-Hartford runabout, 14
Poverty Row Studios, 106, 157, 166
Powell, William (Dick), *124*
"pre-Code era," 98–99
Price, Georgie, 34–35, *39*
Private Buckaroo, 102, 144–46, *145*
Prohibition, 44, 149
Publix circuit, 51, 81
Punchy Cowpunchers, 208
Pure Feud, 100

radio interviews, 231–32
Radio-Keith-Orpheum (RKO) circuit, on vaudeville, 18, 59–60, 73, 85, 87
Raimi, Sam, 226
Rainbo Gardens, 47, 48; IRS closure of, 49
Rhythm and Weep, 179
Rich, Buddy, 206
Richards, Keith, 56
Ride 'Em Cowboy, 142
Riley, Wilfred J. (reviewer), 65, 187
RKO circuit, on vaudeville. *See* Radio-Keith-Orpheum
RKO Radio Pictures, Shemp loaned to, 126, 138
Road Show, 133
Roaring Twenties, 71
Rockin' in the Rockies, 173–74
Rogers, Will, 157
Rolling Stones, 55–56, *56*, 66
Roosevelt, Franklin D. (president), 139, 154
Rosenbloom, "Slapsie" Maxie, 167, 185
roughhouse acts, on vaudeville, 23
routines and gags: chimpanzee, 72; coke bottle glasses, 169; fire hose, 110; first solo, 95–96; "Hey Hey," 51–52, 60; Ivan the robot dialogue, 134–35; "nearsighted," 149; "The Photographer," 36–37, 60; singing-act interruptions, 62; "Who's on First?," 138, 139
"Rubber-Faced Harry," 100
"Rube Goldberg machine," 74
Rumpus in the Harem, 225
Runyon, Damon, 147–50, *148*, 183; Abbott and Costello in movie of, 152–53; ugliest man election and, 151
Rusty Romeos, 226
Ryskind, Morrie, 81–82

Sailor McNeill, 127
Salt Water Daffy, 93–94, *94*, 122, 139, 226
San Antonio Rose, *142*, 142–44
Sanborn, Fred "Pansy," 61, 75, 136, 165, *165*; split from Healy, T., 81
Santa Maria, Nick (historian), 106, 129, 144, 153, 170, 195; on Amsterdam, 157; on chimpanzee scene, 199; on deaths of Curly and Shemp, 228–29; on Moe's money obsession, 229; on "sacrifice" question, 183; on seeing Stooges live as a child, 229; on Shemp, 139–41, 237; on Shemp fear of dogs rumor, 203–4
Scarface, 107
Scheming Schemers, 225

Schonberger, Helen (wife of Moe), 30, 57
Scott, Randolph, 136, *137*
Self Made Maids, 208
Senna, Charles (stooge for Shemp), 101
Sennett, Mack, 109, 120
Serves You Right, 111, *112*
service comedies, 141
sex scenes, 1930 "pre-Code era" and, 98–99
Seymour, Ann, 61
shadowboxing, 204–5
Shemp. *See* Howard, Shemp; Shemp, at Columbia Pictures; Shemp, at Universal Studios
Shemp, as solo performer, *230*; acting roles of 1942, 162–63; ad-libbing of, 104, 109; brief solo tour of 1928, 52; Clyde and, 120–21, 126; comedy team of Gribbon and, 100, 102–5, *103*; as fallback for Moe, 163; feature films, 106–7, *107*; first solo routine as, 95–96; first solo star billing, 111, 112, *112*; gangster screen persona of, 98; at in-laws' home, 92–93; as Knobby Walsh, 88, 113, 115, 125; last solo feature appearance, 178–79; Navy shows of, 155; nightclub owned by, 121–23; 1933 acting, 100–102; 1941 income, 154; 1945 highlights of, 170; in Olsen-Johnson comedy team, 135–36; "pre-Code era" sex scenes and, 98–99; remakes and, 134; salary, 101, 102; stooges of, 101; supporting role for dummy, 100; top billing of Pollard and, 109; trio efforts with Gilbert and Rosenbloom, 167–68; 20th-Century Fox calling for, 127–29, *128*; two-reelers and, 93, 100; Vitaphone shorts of 1934, 93–96, *94*, 98–99, 103, *103*
Shemp, at Columbia Pictures, 118–19, *124*; Brendel and, 165–66; Clyde shorts with Shemp at, 120–21, 126; competing with brothers at, 164–65; Curly decline and, 172, 175–76; dramatic roles of, 123–24, *124*; feature films in mid 1940s, *168*, 168–69; Gilbert and, 167–68; last solo with, 171, 178–79; loan to RKO, 126; MGM loan and, 124; Moe's plan to replace Curly with, 163, 175–76, 181–82; Monogram Pictures in between films with, 167–68, *168*, 175; remakes and, 121, 166, 171; repackaging and decline of Columbia, 171–72; return, 164; shorts division under White, 117, 170, 172; shorts of Vitaphone compared with, 110; solo star billing, 169; on tour with Stooges (Moe and Larry), 206–7
Shemp, at Universal Studios: Abbott and Costello troupe with, 137–42, *140*, 152–53; B-movie gems, 134; Chaney, L. Jr., and Shemp, *142*, 142–44; comedy genres and, 137–38; contract and years with, 133; Crawford's stooges and, *148*, 148–49; Dead End Kids and, 129, *130*; end of work with, 158–59; feature films and, *145*, 145–46; Fields competitiveness and, 130; home near, 156; last film, 164; Runyon world and, 147–51, *148*; "ugliest man" election at, 150–51, *151*
Shemp, Curly replaced by, 4, 90, *215*, 215–17, 233–34; broken nose of, 192, 193; conspiracy and plan leading to, 163, 175–76, 181–82; contract, 182, *184*, 194; first shorts, 186–87; Moe's version of, 181–82; number of shorts made, 224; sacrifice question, 182–83; schedule, 187–88, 193; slaps from Moe, 185; tours, 187
Shemp Howard & Co., 52
Shemp Howard Goils Group (Facebook group), 14, 200
Shempophobia: *Africa Screams* and, 196–99, *198*; boxing and, 204–5; chimpanzee scene and, 199; dogs

and, 199, *201*; fear of death and, 204; fear of flying, 202; kindness and, 200; panic attacks and, 199; phobias definition and, 199; relatives contradicting perception of, 202–3; screen persona fueling, 203–4
Sherman, Maurice, 44
shipyard workers sketch, 155
shorts, online availability of, 236
Shubert, J. J., 38, 44, 45, 61; Jolson and, 51; Shemp deal with brothers, 91
Shubert, Sam S., 61, 64–65, 91
Shurman, Charlotte, 13
Shy, Gus, 97
Siegel, Al, 44
silent movies, 32, 45, 109
"Silk Hat Harry," 100
Silvers, Phil, 122, 157
Silvers, Sid, 38, 44, 50, 51, 53
"Simple Mosquito Exterminator," 74
Sinatra, Frank, 211
Sing a Song of Six Pants, 237
Six Lessons from Madame La Zonga, 127, 133
slaps: Chaney, L. Jr., abusive, 143; Fine's scars and callouses from, 228; head injuries and traumas from, 229, 231, 232; Healy, T., 37–38, 42, 50, 52, 88; interview of Shemp on, 231–32; by Moe, 23, 185, 193–94, *194*; Moe's daughter on, 229, 231; outside of films, 231
slapstick violence, 193–94
Smoked Hams, 109
Society Mugs, 170
"Solving the Rent Problem," *70*, 71
Some Like It Hot, 152
Soup to Nuts, 28–29, 52, 61, 72; cast, 75–76; filming, 75; Fireman's Ball in, 78; Moe standing out in, 78; Parsons on, 73; quitting Healy, T., act before release of, 76; release and reviews, 79–81; rights to material from, 79; "Rube Goldberg machine" in, 74; Shemp as star of, 80, *80*, 81
"A Spanish Cafe," 41–42
Spooks!, 213, *214*
Spring Fever, 21, 73–74
Stage 1 Café, 121–23
Stander, Lionel, 95, 100
stand-up comedians, first, 166–67
Stanley, Aileen, 49
Stepping Along, 57–58
Stevens Brothers, 62–63, 64, 72
Stewart, James, 102
Still Stepping, 58
stooge, thinking man's, ix–x
"stooge," 23, 84; definition of, 82
The Stooge, 38
Stoogeologist, 26
stooges, Crawford's, 148
stooges, Healy, T., "replacement," 79, 81–82
Stooges Among Us (Howard-Isaac), 157
straight man, role of, 139–40
Strange Affair, 199
The Strange Case of Dr. Rx, 135
The Stranger Wore a Gun, 214
Strictly in the Groove, 162
Strike Up the Band, 81
Stroke of Luck (Fine), 88
Study in Black, 18
Sunflower showboat, 16
swim footage, of Shemp, 69
Swing Parade, 177
"Syncopated Toes," 27, 28, 29, *29*, 30

Taking the Count, 115
talkies, 160
Taurog, Norman, 75
technical knockout (TKO), 220
"Ted Healy and His Gang," 61; breakup of, 77–78; kids show, 69; two-man team portrayal in press, 69–71, *70*
Ted Healy and his Racketeers, 62, 72, 77; arrival at Fox, 74; contract and salary of 1932 version of, 87; Larry, Moe and Curly version of, 96; new gang and "replacement stooges," 79, 81–82; return of, 86–87
Ted Healy & Company: "hard-boiled playmates" of, 60; Moe joining, 58

Ted Healy's Southern Gentlemen, 62, *63*, 77; after breakup, 78
television, 193, 196, 227, 233, 237; CBS special on, 206; cult of Curly and 1960s, 234; last Shemp appearance on, 218
Temple, Shirley, 217
Termites of 1938, 117
Terry, Jim, 48, 181
thinking man's stooge, ix–x
The Thin Man, 124
Thirst Aid, 115
Thompson, Charlotta, 199
3-D films, 212–14, *214*
3 Dumb Clucks, 211
3 of a Kind, 167
Three Hams on Rye, 206
Three Little Pirates, 179, 181
The Three Stooges, x, *230*; accidents and, 228; acting of Shemp *vs.* other, 236–37; appearance on Sinatra show, 211; Besser as third Stooge, 182, 226; births and nicknames of, 2–3; casinos played by, 214–15; character roles of, 78; discovery of, ix; favoring different, x; film scene shared by Howard brothers, *189*, 190; first reference to "Stooges," 72; first threesome act, 62; fourth wheel of, 4; Jewish-boy reputations of, 160; last short released with Shemp, 218; Moe's work ethic and obsession, 228–29; money from tours of, 187; muddled oral history and, 24; 1930s name of, 78; number of shorts made with Shemp and, 224; as official name in 1934, 105; release and sale of shorts by, 233; Rolling Stones comic strip of, 55–56, *56*; seismic shift in roles of, 83; Shemp return to, 181–83, *184*, 186–88, 190, 192, 194, 210; shorts in 1934, 106; six actors playing, ix–x; straight man for, 82, 83, 84; support regulars, 184; as Ted Healy's Southern Gentlemen, 62, *63*, 77, 78; third Stooge after Shemp death, 224–26; Three Lost Souls, 85; as "The Three Stooges," 105; two contracts signed by, 105; on vaudeville circuit, 82–83; website, 69. *See also* Columbia Pictures, Three Stooges at; routines and gags; Shemp (Horwitz/Howard, Shemp); Shemp, Curly replaced by; vaudeville, Healy, T., act on; *specific stooges*
The Three Stooges, as Howard, Fine, and Howard: Academy Award nomination, 159; comedy highs and remakes, 159–60; competition against Shemp at Columbia, 165; Curly breakdown on tour of, 174; film appearances, 173–74; Larry, Curly, and Moe on vaudeville, 82–83; as Moe, Curly, and Larry, 62, 96; on tour instead of taking break, 177; on vaudeville, 82–83, 209–10. *See also* vaudeville; vaudeville, Healy, T., act on
The Three Stooges in King Arthur's Court, 188
The Three Stooges Newsletter, 182
The Three Stooges Scrapbook, 199
The Three Troubledoers, 176
Tillet, Maurice "The French Angel," 151–52
Tinee, Mae (reviewer), 79–80
TKO. *See* technical knockout
To Heir is Human, 183
Toluca Lake neighborhood, 156–57, 164, 175, 217
Too Many Blondes, 143, 148
The Tooth Will Out, 209
A Tour de Farce (Lassin), 207
tours, 71, 73, 177; back on vaudeville circuit, 209–10; Curly breakdown on, 174; decline in demand, 206–7; during downtime, 193, 206; Moe demanding, 187; Shemp solo, 52
Tropics, 139
Trouble Chasers, 167–68
Tuttle, Babe, 13

20th Century Fox Studios, 121, 127–29, *128*

"The Ugliest Man in Hollywood," 191; claims to, 151–52; election at Universal, 150–51, *151*; as publicity stunt, 152; Shemp and, x, 96, 150
University of Southern California, film class, 212
Up in Daisy's Penthouse, 211–12
U.S. Army, Shemp draft and discharge, 18, 19–20, *20*

Vagabond Loafers, 12, 160, 207, 225
Valentino, Rudolph. *See* Costello, Maurice
Vanities, 31
vaudeville: agents, 85; biggest star on, 45–46; blackface act on, 15, 17–18, 20; Broadway *vs.*, 66; cleanup acts, 18; The Diving Belles, 12–13; dried up circuits, 212; Horwitz-Howard brothers on (Moe and Shemp), 17–18; Howard, Fine, and Howard on (Larry, Curly, Moe), 82–83; 1951 tour on, 209–10; pioneers, 18; RKO circuit, 18, 59–60, 73, 85, 87; roughhouse acts, 23; Shemp prominence over Moe on, 60; Shemp's bride start in, 30; slowing down of, 86; two-a-day circuits on, 36
vaudeville, Healy, T., act on, 11, 27, 59–60; act with wife, *29*, 29–35; chorus girls in, 34, *39*; dog leap to Broadway from, 30; funeral report misnaming Healy's, 120; Goldberg-Healy, T., team and, 73–76, 80; Healy, T., complaints, 79; Healy betrayal, 77; Howard, Fine, and Howard leaving in 1934, 105; leaving, 105; Moe and Shemp bit parts in, 28–29; Moe's version of, 22–25, 26; mother against sons joining, 25; 1930s breakup, 77–78; on Orpheum circuit, 32; Racketeer replacements, 79, 81–82; "replacement stooges" confusion, 79, 81–82; Shemp walkout on, 49, 87–89, 91; singing-act interruptions routine, 62; Ted, Moe and Shemp in, 22–24; Ted and Pete (police dog), 30, 32, 38; "Ted Healy and His Gang," 61, 69–71, *70*, 77–78; Ted Healy's Southern Gentlemen, 62, *63*, 77, 78; whacks taken by Shemp, 37. *See also A Night in Spain*; Ted Healy and his Racketeers; *specific shows*
Vaudeville Managers Association, 79
Vernon, Wally, 121, 122
Vitagraph Studios, 9–10; shorts, 21–22; Warner Bros. buying, 93
Vitaphone, two reelers of, 93–96, *94*, 98–99, *103*, 108; call sheet, 97; closing of, 116; Columbia shorts compared with, 110; DVDs of, 236; *Palooka* series of, 113, *114*, 115; release of two-reels in 1934, 103, *103*; with Shemp as solo star, 112; timing of release, 133

Wagner, Johannes Peter "Honus," 21–22, 107
Walker, George, 18
Walsh, Jack, 84, 85
Warner Bros., 93, *94*, 96, *103*, 108–10, *112*, 112–13. *See also* Vitaphone
Waters, Arthur B. (reviewer), 63–64
Watts, Charlie, 56
Wayne, John, 136, *137*
WBAL radio, 231–32
website, Three Stooges, 69
Weisz, Erich. *See* Houdini, Harry
We Must Do Our Best, 10
West, Billy, 228, 234, 236, 238
westerns, 118–19, 214
Wham-Bam-Slam!, 217
Where the Pest Begins, 170
While the Cat's Away, 112
White, Jules, 117, 173; Bernds shorts *vs.*, 207; Curly decline and, 179–80; McCollum fired by, 210
Who Done It?, 219

"Who's on First?" routine, 138, 139
Wickes, Mary, 102
Wilder, Billy, 152, 237
William, Warren, 126
William Morris Agency, 78
Williams, Bert, 18
Wilson, Harry, 152
Wilson, Woodrow (president), 18
Wise Guys Prefer Brunettes, 32, 33
The Wizard of Oz, 95, 101, 122
Wolf, Jack, 81, 82
Woman Haters, 106
Woodcock Q. Strinker (Shemp role), 169–70
The Wrong Wrong Trail, 94
Wyman, Bill, 56

xylophone, 74

yellowface, 127
Yiddish, 1
The Yoke's on Me, 165
You Nazty Spy!, 160
Young Folks' League, 57

Ziegfeld Follies, 31